Reading
the L word

Reading Contemporary Television

Series Editors: Kim Akass and Janet McCabe

The *Reading Contemporary Television* series aims to offer a varied, intellectually groundbreaking and often polemical response to what is happening in television today. This series is distinct in that it sets out to immediately comment upon the TV zeitgeist while providing an intellectual and creative platform for thinking differently and ingeniously writing about contemporary television culture. The books in the series seek to establish a critical space where new voices are heard and fresh perspectives offered. Innovation is encouraged and intellectual curiosity demanded.

Reading the L word

Outing contemporary television

Edited by

Kim Akass and Janet McCabe

Introduction by

Sarah Warn

I.B. TAURIS

LONDON · NEW YORK

Published in 2006 by I.B.Tauris & Co Ltd
6 Salem Road, London W2 4BU
175 Fifth Avenue, New York NY 10010
www.ibtauris.com

In the United States of America and in Canada distributed by
Palgrave Macmillan, a division of St Martin's Press
175 Fifth Avenue, New York NY 10010

ISBN 1 84511 179 6
EAN 978 84511 179 3

A full CIP record for this book is available from the British Library
A full CIP record for this book is available from the Library of Congress

Library of Congress catalog card: available

Typeset in Quadraat by Steve Tribe, Andover
Printed and bound in the United States

Contents

Acknowledgements   ix

List of Contributors   xi

Regular Cast   xvii

Foreword: The Letter 'L'

Eve Kosofsky Sedgwick   xix

Preface

Janet McCabe and Kim Akass   xxv

Introduction

Sarah Warn   1

Part 1 Lesbians on TV

1   Sex and the Clittie

        Diane Anderson-Minshall   11

2   The L Word Under-whelms the UK?

        Paula Graham   15

3   Interview with Guinevere Turner (November 2004)

        Sarah Warn   27

4   New Queer Cable? The L Word, the Small Screen
        and the Bigger Picture

        Michele Aaron   33

Part 2 Looking

5   The (In)visible Lesbian: Anxieties of Representation
        in The L Word

        Susan J. Wolfe and Lee Ann Roripaugh   43

6   How Does a Lesbian Look? Stendhal's Syndrome
      and The L Word
      Dana Heller   55
7   Lipstick Leviathans: Demonologies of the Lesbian Body
      in The L Word
      Mark W. Bundy   69

Part 3 Loving
8   Heteronormativity and The L Word: From a Politics of
      Representation to a Politics of Norms
      Samuel A. Chambers   81
9   Straight-up Sex in The L Word
      Lorna Wheeler and Lara Raven Wheeler   99
10   The Chart
      Kim Ficera   111
11   'L' Is for 'Long Term': Compulsory Monogamy on The L Word
      Merri Lisa Johnson   115
12   Why is The L Word Sexy?
      Kathy Belge   139
13   What Is A Straight Girl To Do?
      Ivan's Serenade, Kit's Dilemma
      Janet McCabe and Kim Akass   143

Part 4 Labels
14   Is She Man Enough? Female Masculinities on The L Word
      Candace Moore and Kristen Schilt   159
15   Interview with Katherine Moennig (March 2003)
      Sarah Warn   173
16   The Other 'L' Word: Representing a Latina Identity
      Shauna Swartz   177
17   The Glamour Factor and the Fiji Effect
      Jennifer Vanasco   183
18   Radical Acts: Biracial Visibility and The L Word
      Sarah Warn   189
19   Hot Stuff: Music as a Language of Lesbian Culture
      Zoë Gemelli   199

20   Interview with Erin Daniels (January 2004)
      Sarah Warn   209

      The Essential L *Word* Episode Guide
      Scribe Grrrl   215
      Film and TV Guide   232
      Bibliography   235
      Index   245

Acknowledgements

The editors would first like to thank the authors – Eve Kosofsky Sedgwick, Sarah Warn, Diane Anderson-Minshall, Paula Graham, Michele Aaron, Susan Wolfe, Lee Ann Roripaugh, Dana Heller, Mark W. Bundy, Samuel A. Chambers, Lorna Wheeler, Lara Raven Wheeler, Kim Ficera, Merri Lisa Johnson, Kathy Belge, Candace Moore, Kristen Schilt, Shauna Swartz, Jennifer Vanasco, Zoë Gemelli and last, but by no means least, Scribe Grrrl – for helping to make the transition of editorship as smooth and as painless as possible. Thanks also for the wonderful, thought-provoking and pioneering work, as well as adhering to the (even for us) unusually tight deadlines with grace, humour and a real generosity of spirit (especially for those who have been through quite trying summers).

Special thanks go, as usual, to the inspirational Philippa Brewster. Her creative energy and generosity mean we can never say enough about her. Thanks also to Isabella Steer who continues to liaise so efficiently between I.B.Tauris and Palgrave/St Martin's Press, as well as all those at I.B.Tauris who have helped this project on its way to completion. Thanks also to Steve Tribe for managing the project.

We would like to acknowledge the Billy Rose Theater Collection at the New York Public library for Performing Arts. Special thanks goes to Eydie Wiggins.

Janet McCabe would like to thank the British Academy for awarding her a grant to travel and research in New York.

Thanks also to our husbands – Mike Allen and Jon Akass – for supporting us through this project and giving us the space to see it to fruition. Thanks also to Daryl and Caitlin.

Finally a huge thanks to someone who is not only a good woman but also someone we consider a good friend and colleague – Sarah Warn. The inspiration behind this book is Sarah and it was her vision which saw its inception. At every step, Sarah has given generously of her time and her wise counsel as well as contributing several pieces, including the interviews with Guinevere Turner, Katherine Moennig and Erin Daniels. It is to her that we dedicate this book, with love and in friendship.

Contributors

MICHELE AARON lectures on film studies at the University of Birmingham. She edited *The Body's Perilous Pleasures: Dangerous Desires and Contemporary Culture* (Edinburgh/Columbia University Press, 1999) and *New Queer Cinema: A Critical Reader* (Edinburgh/Rutgers University Press, 2004), and has written articles on contemporary film, queer issues, and Jewishness. Her book *Spectatorship: The Power of Looking On* will be published in 2006 by Wallflower Press.

KIM AKASS is Senior Lecturer in Film Studies at London Metropolitan University. She has co-edited (with Janet McCabe) and contributed to *Reading Sex and the City* (I.B.Tauris, 2004) and *Reading Six Feet Under: TV To Die For* (I.B.Tauris, 2005). She is currently researching representations of the mother and motherhood in American TV Drama. She is a member of the editorial board for *Critical Studies in Television: Scholarly Studies for Small Screen Fictions*, and co-series editor for *Reading Contemporary Television*.

DIANE ANDERSON-MINSHALL is the Executive Editor of *Curve* magazine as well as a founder and former editor of *Girlfriends* magazine and *Alice* magazine. She has worked in publishing since she was thirteen years old, starting her career at the *Independent Enterprise* newspaper in Payette, Idaho. Her writing has appeared in dozens of magazines including *Bust*, *Bitch*, *Venus*, *Teenage* and *Utne*, and she's enjoyed brief stints at *Details*, *Taxi*, *New York Woman* and McGraw Hill. For fifteen years, Diane's worked primarily in queer media including newspapers (*Crescent City*

Star, Vanguard, Lesbian News), magazines (*Passport, QSF*) and television (Spectrum News). Her writing has appeared in numerous anthologies including *Closer to Home, Young Wives Tales, Tough Girls, Body Outlaws,* and *50 Ways to Support LGBT Rights,* and she's the co-editor of *Becoming: Young Ideas on Gender, Identity and Sexuality.* She and her partner are launching QuirkyGirls.com and QuirkyGuys.com in 2006.

Kᴀᴛʜʏ Bᴇʟɢᴇ is a freelance writer from Portland, Oregon. Her alter-ego pens one half of the queer advice column, 'Lipstick & Dipstick' (she is Dipstick). She is also your guide to all things lesbian on lesbianlife. about.com.

Mᴀʀᴋ W. Bᴜɴᴅʏ is currently completing work on his PhD dissertation, which analyses the photography of John Dugdale and the poetry of Mark Doty, at the University of California, Riverside, where he is also a lecturer in English and held a Chancellor's Distinguished Fellowship from 2000 to 2005 (consecutively). With emphases in gay and lesbian studies, the Gothic genre, contemporary American poetry, art history and visual culture/media studies, there are, according to him, 'a million paths to explore, and *never* any dull moments!' His most recent publications are in *Reading Six Feet Under: TV to Die for* (I.B.Tauris, 2005) and *Reading Sex and the City* (I.B.Tauris, 2004); he has an article in *EntreMundos/Among Worlds: New Perspectives on Gloria Anzaldua* (Palgrave/ Macmillan, 2005) and he wrote the topic entry of 'American Gay and Lesbian Poetry', which appears in *The Greenwood Encyclopedia of American Poets and Poetry: 5 Volumes* (Greenwood, forthcoming).

Sᴀᴍᴜᴇʟ A. Cʜᴀᴍʙᴇʀs is Lecturer in Politics at University of Wales, Swansea. He writes widely in contemporary political theory, with particular interests in language, culture, and the politics of gender and sexuality, and he has published a number of articles on the queer politics of television. His first book, *Untimely Politics,* was published by Edinburgh and New York University Presses in 2003. He is currently working with Terrell Carver on two books on the political theory of Judith Butler, both to be published by Routledge in 2007.

ZOË GEMELLI is a journalist and freelance writer. She started her career writing for Canadian publications, including *NOW Magazine*, *Chart* and *Take One*. After moving to the USA, she edited the arts pages of a weekly community paper the *South End News*, and cut her teeth writing for several indie and gay and lesbian papers. She is now a regular contributor to the *Village Voice*, the *Boston Phoenix*, *Creative Loafing*, *Curve Magazine*, *Rockrgrl*, *Bay Windows*, *Philadelphia Gay News*, *GO NYC*, *Out Traveler* and other cool magazines. Her entertainingly zany story of growing up a lesbian music lover and devoted record collector is told in Brett Milano's *Vinyl Junkies* (St Martin's Griffin). Gemelli still listens to music and watches movies and television shows with the same enthusiasm as she did when she saw *Grease* (the movie) for the first time in the summer of 1978. She plans to continue her studies in creative non-fiction writing, ethnomusicology, pop culture and arts criticism. She lives in New York City with her partner and their furries. Visit www. zoegemelli.com for more information.

PAULA GRAHAM is miscellaneously indie, currently researching gendering of technology, tinkering with Linux, advocating Free/Libre software and Free Culture to women and NGOs. Online hangouts include http://www.women-cult-media.org.uk, http://live.linuxchix.org, http://eclectictechcarnival.org/drupal and http://www.socialsource.org.uk.

KIM FICERA is an award-winning columnist, author and humorist. She is author of *Sex, Lies and Stereotypes: An Unconventional Life Uncensored* (Kensington Books), a collection of essays celebrating her sexuality, and her successful column, 'From Hell to Breakfast', is now a blog. Her writing has appeared in national and regional magazines and newspapers. She is a member of the National Lesbian and Gay Journalists Association and Out Professionals.

DANA HELLER is Professor of English and Director of the Humanities Institute at Old Dominion University in Norfolk, Virginia. She is the author of *The Feminization of Quest-Romance: Radical Departures* (University of Texas, 1990) and *Family Plots: The De-Oedipalization of Popular Culture* (University of Pennsylvania Press, 1995), and is the editor of *Cross*

Purposes: Lesbians, Feminists, and the Limits of Alliance (Indiana University Press, 1997). Her most recent edited collection is *The Selling of 9/11: How a National Tragedy Became a Commodity* (Palgrave Macmillan, 2005).

MERRI LISA JOHNSON is Assistant Professor of English and Women's Studies at Coastal Carolina University. Her edited collection, *Jane Sexes It Up: True Confessions of Feminist Desire*, constructs a third-wave feminist sexual politics. She co-edited, with Katherine Frank and Danielle Egan, a book on the labour conditions of strippers called *Flesh for Fantasy: Consuming and Producing Exotic Dance*. She is currently completing an edited collection, *Third-Wave Feminism and Television Studies: Jane Puts It in a Box*, to be published by I.B.Tauris in 2006.

JANET MCCABE is Research Associate in Television Drama at Manchester Metropolitan University. She is author of *Feminist Film Studies: Writing the Woman into Cinema* (Wallflower Press, 2004), and has co-edited (with Kim Akass) and contributed to *Reading Sex and the City* (I.B.Tauris, 2004) and *Reading Six Feet Under: TV to Die for* (I.B.Tauris, 2005). She is a founding member, and co-editor, of *Critical Studies in Television: Scholarly Studies for Small Screen Fictions*, and is co-series editor for *Reading Contemporary Television*.

CANDACE MOORE is pursuing her PhD in Critical Studies in Film, Television, and Digital Media at the University of California, Los Angeles, where her dissertation focuses on queer representation on TV. She is the Film Editor of lesbian monthly *Girlfriends Magazine* and writes regularly as a media critic and entertainment journalist for various print magazines and online sites, including *Girlfriends, On Our Backs, Female FYI*, and *AfterEllen.com*. She is co-editor of the books *Resistance, Dignity, and Pride: African American Artists in Los Angeles* (CAAS Publications, 2004) and *Revolutions of the Mind: Cultural Studies in the African Diaspora Project 1996–2002* (CAAS Publications, 2003). An essay Candace authored decoding some of *The L Word*'s sex scenes will be forthcoming in the edited volume *Third-Wave Feminism and Television: Jane Puts It in a Box* (I.B.Tauris, forthcoming 2006). Candace also holds her MFA in Creative Writing from San Francisco State University and has published poetry and fiction in numerous journals, including *Fourteen Hills* and *Chinquapin*.

LEE ANN RORIPAUGH is Associate Professor of English at the University of South Dakota. Her second volume of poetry, *Year of the Snake*, was published by Southern Illinois University Press as part of the Crab Orchard Award Series in Poetry. Her first volume of poetry, *Beyond Heart Mountain* (Penguin Books, 1999), was a 1998 winner of the National Poetry Series, and was selected as a finalist for the 2000 Asian American Literary Awards. The recipient of a 2003 Archibald Bush Foundation Individual Artist Fellowship, she was also named the 2004 winner of the *Prairie Schooner* Strousse Award, the 2001 winner of the Frederick Manfred Award for Best Creative Writing awarded by the Western Literature Association, and the 1995 winner of the Randall Jarrell International Poetry Prize. Her poetry and short stories have appeared in numerous journals and anthologies.

KRISTEN SCHILT is a graduate student in sociology at the University of California, Los Angeles. Her research interests include youth culture, gender and sexuality, and the workplace. She has an article on 'zines and cultural resistance in *Youth and Society*, as well as an article on gay and lesbian media advocacy in the *Gay and Lesbian Journal of Social Services*. She is currently completing her dissertation, which examines the experiences of female-to-male transsexuals in the workplace.

SCRIBE GRRRL writes the recaps for AfterEllen.com. Currently in law school, she also writes poetry and fiction. And more recently she has become obsessed with *Bad Girls*.

SHAUNA SWARTZ is a freelance journalist who spent her first thirty-two years in Los Angeles until recently moving to Philadelphia, where her So Cal-bred appreciation for meteorological subtlety is now facing the Northeast's more garish seasonal changes. After enjoying a stint copy-editing gay men's porn (after all, there's no bigger turn-off than typos) she turned to the seedier world of technical writing. She has also written for *Bitch* magazine and is a regular contributor on AfterEllen.com.

SARAH WARN is the founder and editor of AfterEllen.com (http://www. afterellen.com), the leading entertainment site for lesbian and bisexual women. She has a BA in Women's Studies from Wellesley College and a Master's in Theological Studies from Harvard University, and worked for several years in Internet marketing before creating Erosion Media, the parent company of AfterEllen.com, its brother site AfterElton.com, and other gay and lesbian media properties.

LORNA WHEELER is a PhD candidate in English Literature at the University of Colorado, Boulder. Her teaching interests include Queer Studies and women writers/artists of the Harlem Renaissance; and LARA RAVEN WHEELER is an artist, editor, and mathematician. They live in Boulder, Colorado, with their brilliant and beautiful two-year-old daughter, Elena Ruth.

SUSAN J. WOLFE holds a joint appointment in the departments of English and of Languages, Linguistics, and Philosophy at the University of South Dakota, and has chaired both departments. Co-editor with Julia Penelope of *The Coming Out Stories* (Persephone Press, 1980), *The Original Coming Out Stories* (Persephone Press, 1989), *Lesbian Culture: An Anthology* (Persephone Press, 1993), and *Sexual Practice/Textual Theory: Lesbian Cultural Criticism* (Basil Blackwell, 1993), she has also published essays in other lesbian anthologies and articles on language and gender. A Jewish, cross-class lesbian, she lives with her life partner, Catherine Flum, two dogs, and four cats in Vermillion, South Dakota.

Regular cast

Ivan Aycock	Kelly Lynch
Dana Fairbanks	Erin Daniels
Marina Ferrer	Karina Lombard (season one)
Tim Haspel	Eric Mabius (season one)
Candace Jewell	Ion Overman
Tina Kennard	Laurel Holloman
Shane McCutcheon	Katherine Moennig
Helena Peabody	Rachel Shelley (season two)
Carmen de la Pica Morales	Sarah Shahi (season two)
Alice Pieszecki	Leisha Hailey
Bette Porter	Jennifer Beals
Kit Porter	Pam Grier
Jenny Schecter	Mia Kirshner
Mark Wayland	Eric Lively (season two)

Foreword
The letter L
Eve Kosofsky Sedgwick

Early in the pilot episode of *The L Word*, the viewer watches two young women strip and plunge into a backyard pool, romping amorously in a scene that would not be out of place in soft-core girl-on-girl pornography aimed at heterosexual men or couples. The voyeuristic framing of the scene is even accentuated: we observe it mainly from the point of view of the fascinated woman next door as she crouches behind a fence. And when she re-enters her house, we see her in turn join her boyfriend in a sexual scene that is structured by their slow, shared, relishing narrative and re-enactment of the lesbian scene she has just viewed.

This orgy of specular expropriation would seem to represent both a dream and a nightmare of *The L Word*, Showtime's long anticipated drama series, the first on television to place at front and centre the lives of a group of women most of whom are lesbian. In the demographic calculus that lay behind the decision to underwrite the series, according to Showtime executive Gary Levine, its potential appeal to non-lesbian viewers rested on the understanding that lesbian sex, girl-on-girl, is a whole cottage industry for heterosexual men. Even the 'Gay and Lesbian Alliance Against Defamation', represented by entertainment media director, Scott Seomin, sees the porn connection as a smart crossover move: if they pull them in and they get hooked on the titillation factor, that straight male is going to learn about the lives of lesbians, he told the *New York Daily News*. At the same time, less pragmatic or opportunist activists are incredulous that lesbians can be empowered by becoming, as Winnie McCroy writes in the *Washington Blade*, 'pud fodder for Joe Sixpack' (2003: 42).

Yet the actual spy in this scene is, after all, a woman, not the Neanderthal straight guy who seems to haunt the imagination of *The L Word* advance flaks and detractors alike. Jenny Schecter, a young fiction writer newly arrived to join her swimming-coach boyfriend in his West Hollywood bungalow, seems poised in these earliest episodes to offer an invitingly unformed conduit for the lesbian fixations of a variety of viewers but maybe in the first place, non-lesbian identified women. Jenny looks as foetally unformed, and eerily precocious, as that famous 1972 *New York Times Magazine* photo of Joyce Maynard, the one that accompanied her premature memoir, 'An Eighteen-Year-Old Looks Back on Life', and seems to have made J. D. Salinger fall in love with her. Jenny's imminent passion for local café owner Marina Ferrer, statuesque, enigmatic, and all shoulders and cheekbones, forms the centrepiece of the early episodes and of Showtime's publicity prose: amid denial and confusion, Jenny starts to question her sexual orientation and her love for Tim. Her attraction to Marina is powerful and ultimately irresistible.

If Jenny appears to be the non-lesbian viewer's early path of initiation into the 'L' world, the first identification of lesbians is solicited by the female couple living next door, who are (did you guess?) trying to make a baby. In their first scene the blonde thrusts a plastic stick into the hands of the brunette, who observes with wonder, 'You're ovulating.' 'Ovulating,' echoes the blonde, Tina Kennard, as reverently as if announcing the conception of baby Jesus. Our intimacy with Tina's body inseminated, peeing, ultrasounded, vomiting – continues to be near total. She turns red and sweats during sex, seldom seems comfortable in her skin, speaks (though she is tall) in a small, timbreless voice: among these women the only one without glamour, her obscurely ill-fitting point of view seems capacious enough to incorporate any viewer who would appreciate a line of sight among the lesbians.

In short, if *The L Word* is as bold and daring as claimed, its novelty does not lie in either a demographic coup or a startling use of the medium. I anticipate that its long-term audience will be not male porno hounds but the range of viewers, predominantly though not only female, who enjoy smart and well-made domestic drama, psychological and relationship-based, low on violence, criminality, and sensation. Showtime's advertising slogan, 'Same Sex. Different City', suggests that even they do not really see *The Howard Stern Show* as the main competition for their intended audience. *The L Word*'s skilfully executed narrative structure is equally conventional: the loose braid of multiple developing plots and characters that may have come to television with *Hill Street Blues* in 1981, but has a literary genealogy as old as Dickens.

And while 2003 featured plenty of hot gay headlines, *The L Word* is not ripped from them. Tina, reading the paper, remarks (with her mouth full), 'Y'know what? It makes me sick what this administration is doing to our environment,' and that marks the early episodes' high point of topicality. Edgy is not the word for the series' relation to reality or political process, any more than for its camerawork or music or the range of its tonalities. A really anarchic character like Karen Walker (Megan Mullally), the omnisexual Goddess of Misrule on NBC's *Will & Grace*, would smash to smithereens the sedate genre conventions of *The L Word*.

None of this is to say, though, that the success of *The L Word* (which I expect and hope for) won't be an important contribution to queer cultural politics. The series should make a real and unpredictable difference in the overall landscape of the media world. Palpably, the quantitative effect of a merely additive change, dramatising more than one lesbian plot at a time, makes a qualitative difference in viewers' encounter with social reality. The sense of the lesbian individual, isolated or coupled, scandalous, scrutinised, staggering under her representational burden, gives way to the vastly livelier potential of a lesbian ecology.

Even the most interesting lesbian possibilities on recent TV have been neutered by lack of context, if not the active suppression of their context. Between 1988 and 1997, for instance, ABC's sitcom *Roseanne* featured one well-publicised queer coup after another: gay and lesbian kisses, explicit fantasies, continuing characters, relationships, guest stars, coming-out scenes, even a wedding. The cumulative effect never went beyond repeated, sensational spasms of over-the-topness. Yet how rich the wasted possibilities when, for one example, the show made a big deal of implausibly outing Roseanne's mother, Bev (Estelle Parsons), in 1996, but left unexplored the entire loamy substrate of intense relations and unconventional identities among Roseanne herself, her butch sister, Jackie (Laurie Metcalf), and her smart, acidulous tomboy daughter, Darlene (Sara Gilbert).

More dispiriting and in many ways typical has been the treatment of lesbians in NBC's long-running, liberally intended hospital drama series ER. In 1997, during its third season, Jorja Fox was introduced as lesbian doctor, Maggie Doyle, but over the next three seasons her character withered for lack of attention. While she lasted she was candidly feminist, a butch clotheshorse, and good with guns. But, after one glimpse of a female ex at the shooting range, the only continuing indices to her sexuality (if they count as such) were her solidarity with an abused wife and with a heterosexual nurse infected with HIV. She offered support but could receive none in the steamy hetero hothouse of the ER. There the subject rested until 2001, when viewers saw Kerry Weaver (Laura Innes), an abrasive, reserved, unpopular, physically challenged doctor, who had been a regular on the show since its second season, astounding herself by falling passionately for a woman psychiatrist (Elizabeth Mitchell as Kim Legaspi) and subsequently for a Latina firefighter (Lisa Vidal as Sandy Lopez). Kerry Weaver is still my favourite lesbian on network TV. Astringently professional among the ER shmoozers, with her English-rose blush, pretty overbite, and ungainly limp, she is beautifully acted as a tense woman whose principles and sensuality continue to unfold and surprise. Yet even now that she is out and has had a lover and an ex, and after an affectingly executed story of conception and miscarriage, the matrix of narrative support for her is so exiguous that her lesbian plot can be dropped for a season at a time without disturbing the show's illusion of continuity.

A visible world in which lesbians exist, go on existing, exist in forms beyond the solitary and the couple, sustain and develop relations among themselves of difference and commonality: these seem, in a way, such obvious and modest representational needs that it should not be a novelty when they are met. Nor does The L Word, at least in its early episodes, meet them fully. But it's absurdly luxurious being able to explore, for instance, the portrayal of generational dynamics in this group of women, even if only between thirtysomethings and twentysomethings. Inscrutable Marina, mother-to-be Tina, and her accomplished girlfriend Bette Porter are the grown-ups, the couple showing classic symptoms of depressed libido even as the spectacle of their long-term pair-bonding magnetises the younger women.

Yet the twentysomethings, single, callow, and seemingly uneducated, do a lot of the work of articulating norms and mores for each other, the older women, and the audience. Alice Pieszecki, for instance, a journalist who reviews discos and tracks down cut-rate Botox treatments for an LA weekly, maintains 'as a kind of community service' a vast, ever-changing, n-dimensional diagram that shows who exactly has slept with whom, and how many nodes of connection mediate any two points in Sapphic space. Here, she keeps insisting, is the narrative matrix that will sustain any woman in an evolving but unbroken web of erotic relation. Alice uses fatuously knowing Valley-girl syntax; her body has the easy expressiveness of a five-year-old's; her dark eyes are deep holes in the surface of her blonde, oddly ravaged face. Her friend Shane, a fetching baby butch, is an equally unexpected mix of innocence and experience, with her bachelor insouciance, squalid history of sex work, and resonant low voice of reason and amusement. They remind me of students I've known, barely literate but tender with a willingness to care for their teachers even as they engage our pedagogic energies. At the same time Jenny, the impressionable new neighbour, emerges not as a mere ingénue cipher for lesbian panic but as someone who manipulates her visible immaturity with a Lawrentian ruthlessness. And, though a 'writer', she writes dreadfully (though it's hard to tell whether that is the impression intended).

There is a similar sense of novelistic spaciousness as a strong racial dynamic begins to unfold around the thirtysomething couple, Bette and Tina. Bette Porter, the ambitious director of a mediocre small museum, is played by Jennifer Beals, whose best-known movie work has been in racially unmarked (read: white) parts. Bette, however, like Beals, is of partly African-American descent, and the show's early episodes begin to ramify the implications of that in her relationships with Tina, with their prospective child and the choice of its sperm donor, with her partly alienated half-sister Kit, and with the inflexible father (Ossie Davis) whose approval she continues to need. It's too early to tell how revealingly these issues may reach into Bette's otherwise all-white lesbian community. What is clear already, though, is the difference made by the show's generous contextualisation of its characters' intertwined lives, where no single character, relationship, or issue need be 'the lesbian one' or the 'other-than-white one'.

The elasticity of *The L Word*'s Dickensian genre conventions allows a viewer to defer certain representational needs. In an interview with the lesbian magazine *Curve*, head writer and executive producer, Ilene Chaikin is paraphrased as saying that the show's writers represent such a diversity of lesbian experience that 'if you can't relate to chic West Coast chicks ... if the show is around long enough most lesbians will eventually see themselves' (Schenden 2004). No doubt everyone will have a wish list. I would like to order up some characters with body hair, ungleaming teeth, subcutaneous fat, or shorter-than-chin-length haircuts. Oh, and maybe with some politics. I would like to see a lot more of Pam Grier. I hope (especially in a West Coast production) that the show's sense of race will extend beyond black and white. I would like it if not every character came equipped with a handy sexual label (like bisexual Alice or the self-proclaimed male lesbian, Lisa [Devon Gummersall]). I will be relieved when the writers decide they have sufficiently interpolated straight viewers and can leave behind the lachrymose plot of Jenny's Choice. I want to see the range of ways in which gay men function in this (West Hollywood) lesbian ecology. I want the generational span to widen enough so that some of the sex can fully engage with pedagogy and maternality.

The simpler fact, though, is that I'm left eager to see more of these new friends with their bonds, families, fates and ambitions. The realist project of this show is not revolutionary but complex and space-making. If Henry James considered the nineteenth-century novel a 'large loose baggy monster', what would he have thought of serial drama on television? *The L Word* is full of promise as a 'baggy monster' an unpretentious, friendly, intelligent one, bringing new forms of companionship to the TV wasteland it optimistically haunts.

Preface

Janet McCabe and Kim Akass

'Same sex. Different city.' *The L Word* was initially marketed as a successor to HBO's soon-to-depart hit femme dramedy, *Sex and the City*. Billboards hinted that cable network Showtime's latest Sunday-night water-cooler series about a group of lesbians living and loving in LA would be just as risqué, just as sexy, just as smart, as its East Coast cousin. Like *Sex and the City*, *The L Word* is essentially an ensemble drama centring on a close-knit group of female friends who regularly enjoy gabfests. Revealing sexy secrets. Agonising over relationship protocols. Bemoaning bad dates. And ... playing the field. Like our gals from Manhattan, all the women are beautiful, all are thin, all enjoy material comfort, and all have impeccable sartorial style.

Same gender. Different sexual orientation. *The L Word* debuted at a moment when gay representation was gaining ever more currency on American television. The recent gay-TV craze exploding into primetime has been led by the Fab Five on *Queer Eye for the Straight Guy*, and gay lawyer Will Truman (Eric McCormack) and his flamboyant, Cher-loving friend, Jack MacFarland (Sean Hayes), in network sitcom, *Will & Grace*. Betsy Andrews, commenting on this current trend, notes that '[in] the mainstream eye, the new gay male stereotype has proven highly viewable. They're cute, they're smart, they're funny, they're sexy, and they've got great aesthetics' (2004: 30). Cable channels have dared to go further with unabashed portrayals of gay male relationships. From long-term couple David Fisher (Michael C. Hall) and Keith Charles (Mathew St Patrick) in *Six Feet Under*, where we have followed David's struggle to reconcile his homosexuality with his faith (Singleton 2005: 161–73) and the couple's adoption of two brothers, to the sexual escapades of the five guys from Pittsburgh in *Queer As Folk*, male homosexuality is enjoying a visibility as never before (as long as there is not too much canoodling to offend the straight male viewer). Political visibility afforded to gay men in the wake of the HIV epidemic and AIDS crisis has given them a platform in which to forge representation. But this is no easy matter. Referring to HBO's award-winning adaptation of Tony Kushner's *Angels in America*, Stacey D'Erasmo speaks about the urgency for representation, but also – and more importantly – for finding appropriate representation for groups previously underrepresented:

> At such a moment there isn't time to wait for general audiences to understand the importance of two gay men in a room, talking. You have to deploy images that can't be ignored: towering angels, galaxy-changing orgasms, history split in half roaming loose around the world. It's like that. It's that big. Visibility is a tricky thing: is someone visible when you can point her out in a crowd, or when you understand what her life feels like to her? (2004: 26).

Is this, then, a golden age for gay-TV? Many TV execs would say yes (Andrews 2003: 30). And certainly there is visibility as never before, and 'something [has] taken root across the spectrum of TV' (D'Erasmo, quoted in McCroy 2004: 26). But the question of appropriate representation still looms large – especially for lesbians.

And this leads nicely to The L Word...

This collection opens with the question of lesbian visibility and the 'consequence of living in a representational desert' (D'Erasmo 2004: 26). Ilene Chaiken, executive producer and writer for The L Word, was inspired to create the show to challenge stereotypes and to fill a representational void: 'I was seized with the urge to tell my stories' (McCroy 2004: 20). Yet critics have been divided over its portrayal of lesbians. While our glamorous LA babes may work to dismiss the stereotypical image of lesbians 'as not cute, not funny, asexual, unfashionable, way too pious, totally uncool' (Andrews 2003: 34), 'they are all so exquisite ... that [they play] into another stereotype – and male fantasy – of the lipstick lesbian' (Stanley 2004: E30). One does not have to look too far to uncover the reason for this paradox. On the one hand the show is original for being the 'first full-on post-*Ellen* lesbian-focused dramatic TV series ever' (Polly 2004: 20), but on the other, it must have crossover appeal, drawing straight viewers, to ensure economic survival for the cable network (Lowry 2004: 52). Competing agendas go to the heart of Eve Kosofsky Sedgwick's assessment of *The L Word*'s uneasy representational politics, reprinted (2004: B10-B11) in full as the Foreword. Her conclusions communicate a central concern that runs through this collection, setting an agenda that each author wrestles with – namely: visibility is one thing. But at what price does that visibility come? And what form should it take?

Sarah Warn takes up this very point in the Introduction. Shaped as a personal journey, she speaks of her initial excitement at the prospect of a show dealing with lesbian experience. Articulating her hunger to see representations of women like her on television she shares D'Erasmo's 'ferocious desire not only to be seen in some literal sense ... but to be seen with all the blood and angst and magic that we possess' (2004: 26). But Warn understands only too well the pleasures and perils involved in what it means to the lesbian community starved of representation on TV. And despite her reservations, she fervently believes that *The L Word* initiates a long overdue conversation. Viewing figures may now be declining but, as she contends, this does not adequately reflect the community created by the series. In this way, and like *Sex and the City* before it (Jermyn 2004: 201-218), *The L Word* might have something important to tell us about contemporary television viewership in terms of interactive engagement and communities created by and in the viewing experience.

Grounded in these questions of visibility and representational form, Part 1 focuses on contexts that give meaning and structure to *The L Word* in different and diverse ways. Diane Anderson-Minshall, the Executive Editor of *Curve*, delighted about the revolutionary possibilities of having a show about lesbians on primetime TV, is nonetheless wary. It is not enough simply to represent lesbians; instead 'there has to be something of substance behind the presentation to turn television into a revolutionary act.' Following on is Paula Graham with her observations on the lukewarm reception to *The L Word* in the UK. Given the politics of pay-TV and the strong tradition of public service broadcasting, *The L Word* has found it difficult to find a British audience. Not only this, she argues, but the show seems out of step with the current ideological and political climate in Western Europe. The following chapters shift the agenda to focus more on production and cinematic antecedents. Guinevere Turner, interviewed by Sarah Warn, talks about writing for *The L Word*. Turner made her name with *Go Fish*, along with L Word director Rose Troche, back in 1994. The film proved a milestone for New Queer Cinema, and this valuable link between NQC and *The L Word* is explored by Michele Aaron. Here Aaron looks at the legacy of NQC for a show like *The L Word* as she wrestles with the radical versus popular potential of lesbian TV.

Developing further the issue of visibility, and the tension created in the very marketing of *The L Word* as 'a manifesto of lesbian liberation and visual candy for men' (Stanley 2004: E1), we come onto another 'L' word – Looking. Part 2 interrogates the politics of looking. Laura Mulvey long set the agenda for understanding how women are subject to a patriarchal gaze within mainstream media, to reveal how visual pleasure is set up to objectify the woman and foreground her 'to-be-looked-at-ness' (1985: 305–15). Steamy scenes of women having sex, lithe female bodies entwined, girls in daring lingerie caught making out – such sights of sexy Sapphic acts have led critics to accuse *The L Word* of playing into straight male fantasies, 'a form of heterosexual foreplay' (Stanley 2004: E1). Authors here set out to problematise this whole notion of looking – what it means to look, to be looked at, and the possibility of looking differently. Susan Wolfe and Lee Ann Roripaugh rehearse anxieties over subjecting the lesbian body to a voyeuristic (and decidedly hetero-orientated) gaze. But identifying a self-reflective meta-narrative allows them to posit an alternative viewing position foreclosing easy definitions of the gaze. Dana Heller offers another perspective on the lesbian look and looking. Based on Stendhal's Syndrome, these 'transformative moments of sublime looking and ecstatic contemplation ... produce shock and disorientation' when the woman looks. Concluding this section is Mark W. Bundy's lyrical observations on how the lesbian body is seen as monstrous within our culture. He makes this revelation shocking as he turns the queer eye back on the patriarchal gazing of the lesbian body.

Authors in Part 3 pick up the gauntlet laid down in Part 2, as they focus on the question of making visible new and genuinely empowering representations from *within* a representational system ingrained in heteronormative thinking. Grounded in Judith Butler's recent thinking on the politics of norms, Samuel A. Chambers interrogates the politics of norms in *The L Word* to polemically argue that, while important in changing the script, the series remains firmly rooted in heteronormativity. Offering an alternative position, Lorna Wheeler and Lara Raven Wheeler train attention on the politics of representing lesbian sex on *The L Word* entrenched in the lesbian sex wars of the 1980s and 1990s, as they chart a shift from a more conservative second-wave feminist approach to representing lesbian sexuality in the first season to a decidedly more queer approach in the second. Next is Kim Ficera's humorous take on Alice Pieszecki's Chart, where she expresses her personal unease at seeing how incestuous the lesbian sexual world really is. Merri Lisa Johnson's third-wave feminist approach to the question of monogamy identifies a dense juxtapositioning of heteronormative and queer sensibilities around erotic partnerships and a lesbian polyamory. This is followed by Kathy Belge's take on what makes *The L Word* so darn erotic. By using the personal voice, her piece defies patriarchal definitions of desire and lust. This section ends with our contribution on the heterosexual dilemma faced by Kit Porter when drag king Ivan Aycock comes-a wooing. We contend such a queering of the heterosexual romance (temporarily at least) poses questions for the sexual politics of television representation concerned with romantic (heterosexual) love and female (erotic) desire.

As the first lesbian drama series on American television, *The L Word* does bear an unusually heavy burden for representing the lesbian community. There is pressure to meet the expectations of an audience who feel, in the words of Stacey D'Erasmo, 'not only unrepresented but somehow unrepresentable in ordinary terms' (2004: 26). Fending off criticism that the show fails to deliver enough diversity, Chaiken has said, 'I'm not intending to represent everyone. The characters reflect a community of women I know well – it just happens to be a largely affluent, attractive and well-acquainted women' (McCroy 2004: 20). Building on this idea of making visible the lesbian on television the final part develops thinking on what kind of representations are on offer. Investigating the treatment of female masculinities in the guise of soft-butch/inbetweener, Shane McCutcheon and drag king Ivan, Candace Moore and Kristen Schilt argue that 'while these images of female masculinity seem poised to represent a hip, new form of post-identity ... are [ultimately] reframed as gender-rigid [and] rendered safe for lesbian and straight viewers.' Next is Sarah Warn's interview with Katherine Moennig, where she discusses her approach to portraying androgynous soft-butch Shane. Following this is Shauna Swartz's piece on the presentation of Carmen de la Pica Morales' Latina identity, which Swartz argues emerges as little more than a fashion statement. Jennifer Vanasco writes about lesbian chic on The L Word. Long has the stereotype of the unfashionable lesbian existed, but The L Word banishes such notions to give lesbians 'a powerful presence in fashion' (Trebay 2004: 1) despite its appeal to mainstream notions of beauty. Biracial visibility is the subject of the next chapter. Here, Warn considers what Jennifer Beals, herself half African-American, half Irish-American, being cast in the role of Bette Porter means. Beals repeatedly couches her involvement on the show in political terms (Andrews 2003: 34), and Warn attempts to grapple with what that means for racial and cultural visibilities in contemporary America. Zoë Gemelli's contribution focuses on how the music gives visibility to a vibrant lesbian culture. Like Vanasco, Gemelli suggests how old stereotypes are fading and how The L Word is contributing to making lesbian culture something decidedly cool and hip. Concluding the fourth part is an interview with Erin Daniels who discusses her role as a lesbian and the success of The L Word both now and in the future.

Same text. Different voices. Each contributor is struggling to make sense of what The L Word means to our present zeitgeist, and to contemporary television culture and sexual politics in particular. Ever since Ellen DeGeneres publicly leapt out of her TV closet in 1997, a sustained discussion about lesbians on television has seemed a long time coming. In our toil to find appropriate methodologies, pertinent writing styles and different ways of talking about this dense media text, this collection alerts readers to the pleasures and perils of what lies beneath The L Word's glossy surfaces and the exertions involved in finding more hybrid, ambivalent and riveting representation beyond prescribed cultural scripts. Trying to dissect this pioneering show in all its complicated hues has authors rapt and confused in equal measures. Here we are reminded of what Stacey D'Erasmo says: 'The L Word suggests that L is also for limerence, that rapturous state of early love when the entire world is glowing and delectable' (2004: 26). And it is with this flush of possibility that we start the discussion.

Introduction

Sarah Warn

I was a high school junior when the first lesbian kiss on L.A. *Law* aired in 1991 to national debate; in college when a same-sex kiss between experimenting teenagers on *Picket Fences* in 1993 and on the popular sitcom *Roseanne* in 1994 caused such controversy that the network demanded creatively shot versions of both (the former in a dark room, the other showing only the back of Mariel Hemingway's head); and in graduate school when lesbians around the country gathered in bars and living rooms in the spring of 1997 to watch and celebrate Ellen DeGeneres's big coming-out on *Ellen*. In each instance, I remember exactly where I was when it aired, and how exhilarating it felt to see even a glimpse of someone like me on TV. Later, I was equally captivated by the low-key coming-out of *Buffy the Vampire Slayer*'s Willow Rosenberg (Alyson Hannigan) in 2002, and Jessie Sammler (Evan Rachel Wood) and Katie's (played by Mischa Barton) touching, tentative romance on *Once and Again* in 2002.

To those who are straight or white (or both), and used to seeing reflections of themselves every time they turn around – on the covers of magazines in line at the grocery store or at the doctor's office, on the big screen at the neighbourhood movie theatre, or the smaller screen at home on TV – it's difficult to adequately describe what it feels like to not see reflections of yourself anywhere. It's even more difficult to convey what it feels like when you do – the rush and jumble of emotion that is often all out of proportion to the actual event itself.

That's how I felt the first time I learned about The L Word, which was then titled Earthlings. It was September of 2002, and a paragraph announcing the series was buried in a larger press release from Showtime. I read it several times in disbelief. Someone was actually creating a show about lesbians? Fortunately, I had a creative outlet available: six months earlier, I had started an entertainment website for lesbians called AfterEllen.com as a weekend hobby (I had a full-time job in online marketing at the time), with a writer of one (me). So the next day, after I came home from work, I wrote a short article about the impending series, called 'Will Earthlings be the Lesbian Queer as Folk?' (September 2002), and posted it on the site.

The response was immediate, with other lesbians expressing a similar mix of excitement and scepticism upon learning about the series. Although my readership at the time was very small, women from all over the world found my article, read it, and forwarded the link to their friends, who forwarded it to their friends, and so on. I started to get more and more emails from women offering opinions, casting suggestions, and even complaints about the series – and it was still a year before the first episode debuted. I continued to write about the show as more information became available, and my traffic doubled, then tripled, and finally skyrocketed when The L Word finally aired in January 2004 (to this day, we see a traffic spike every time The L Word debuts in a new country).

Two and half years later, The L Word is about to air its third season, and my hobby has turned into a full-time business, with a dozen writers and over half a million monthly readers, many of whom initially came to read about The L Word, then stayed to read about everything else. It is a business that has literally been built on the lesbian community's interest in The L Word, even though the majority of topics we cover on the site aren't related to the series, and we offer criticism of The L Word as often as we praise it.

And there is plenty to criticise, as one would expect of any show that represents a previously underrepresented group. Although it hasn't had the same polarising effect on lesbians that Queer as Folk had on gay men when it debuted in 2000, or The Jeffersons had on African-Americans when it debuted in the late 1970s, The L Word has certainly had its share of controversial characters and storylines; I have a stack of emails, protesting Jenny's storyline and pleading to save Marina, to prove it. Besides these, the most common complaints made by lesbian viewers include the fact that the cast is mostly white and overtly feminine, and that the two bisexual characters are, well, not very bisexual.

But love it or hate it, this series represents the first – and so far, only – attempt to make lesbians, and to a lesser extent, bisexual women, the centre of attention. Instead of being forced to settle for one or two lesbian characters among a sea of heterosexuals, lesbians finally get to see their lives and relationships front-and-centre on The L Word, with the heterosexual characters and relationships on the periphery for a change. We finally have a group of people on television whose lives resemble ours – a more beautiful and successful version of most lesbians' lives, to be sure, but with conversations, interests, and friendships that resonate with many lesbian viewers in a way that the overwhelmingly heterosexual or blink-and-you'll-miss-it lesbian storylines on TV cannot.

This alternative perspective on life and relationships is also what attracts many straight women, and gay and straight men, to The L Word. Whether it's the conflicting demands of your personal and professional life, the fear and confusion of discovering your attraction to women, the desire to maintain your own identity in a long-term relationship, or the thrill of falling in love, The L Word succeeds because it portrays experiences that are specific to lesbians, and universal to all women (and men) at the same time.

This is not accidental. From the beginning, Showtime has emphasised the similarity of the gay women on The L Word to their heterosexual counterparts, as illustrated by The L Word's initial marketing slogan 'Same Sex. Different City', which sought to draw comparisons to the mostly heterosexual hit show Sex and the City. Promos for The L Word featured a montage of sensual scenes set to sexy music featuring conventionally attractive women interacting with one another in various sexual and non-sexual ways designed to attract both gay and straight viewers. It worked on the mainstream media, too, who eagerly ran cover stories featuring the women of The L Word.

If ever there was a series that had to be packaged just right in order
to succeed, it was The L Word: a show that featured characters to whom
few Americans could easily relate, engaging in sexual activity that had
never been shown on television before, and matter-of-factly discussing
topics that are considered controversial at best, offensive and profane at
worst. This might not have mattered if The L Word only needed to appeal
to lesbians, but it needed to draw a broader audience outside the gay
community in order to succeed. If the series had been packaged to more
accurately represent the lesbian community in all its glorious gender-
bending variety, we would have enjoyed it for a few weeks – only to see
it yanked from the schedule or limited to a one-season run because it
didn't draw a big enough audience (even with a cast of mostly lipstick
lesbians, The L Word still only achieved moderately successful ratings
when it debuted). The fact that the series was renewed for a second
season only days after its first episode premiered in January 2004 is
partly attributable to the fact that it did not show the full diversity of the
gay community.

But given all the unique obstacles The L Word had to overcome as
a pioneer – not only as a show about lesbians, but as a drama about
all women – on top of the obstacles that every new show faces, is it
any wonder that the characters on the series were generally written to
conform to traditional norms of femininity? In the pilot, when Tina
and her partner, Bette, are discussing whether to use a black donor in
their quest to get pregnant, Tina expresses concern that two lesbians
choosing to have a biracial baby is 'a lot of otherness to put on one
child'. While the veracity of Tina's statement in regards to having a
biracial child is debatable, the analogy is applicable here: to ask The L
Word to reflect the full diversity of the lesbian community when it already
has so many hurdles to clear just to survive is too much otherness to put
on one show – at least, initially. Other viewers would seem to agree: in a
May 2005 poll on AfterEllen.com only twelve per cent of the poll's 2,800
respondents answered 'Yes, I wish it was more realistic' to the question
'Does The L Word misrepresent lesbians?' Forty-six per cent answered
'no', and a full thirty-six per cent answered 'Yes, but who cares?' (Eight
per cent were 'not sure'.) This isn't a scientific study; it's just an online

poll. But it would seem to support the argument that while we might criticise (often justifiably) certain aspects of the series, for the most part, that doesn't prevent us from enjoying it.

The L Word is more diverse going into its third season, however, than it was when it premiered. In addition to the trans-character, Ivan Aycock (Kelly Lynch), who was in several episodes of the first and second season, Latina lesbian, Carmen de la Pica Morales, was added to the cast in the second season, with a bigger storyline involving her family in the third, and butch lesbian-turned-trans-character, Moira (Daniela Sea), appears in most of the episodes of the third season. No, it's still not as diverse as it could be, but it's far more diverse than anything else on television.

Equally as important as the diversity of characters is the diversity of storylines the series offers. Most lesbians on TV have been confined to coming-out narratives, and de-sexualised storylines revolving around parenting. From L.A. Law to Popular to ER, from the lesbian mothers on Friends to the bisexual teenager on One Tree Hill, mainstream television shows focus their lesbian or bisexual storylines almost exclusively on the coming-out process, and drop or diminish their storylines significantly afterwards, or saddle them with storylines revolving around taking care of children. Many series that have attempted to introduce a post-coming-out narrative, like Once and Again, Dark Angel, Relativity, K Street and Ellen DeGeneres' two sitcoms, were cancelled; those that were not, like Queer as Folk, The Wire and All My Children, quickly resorted to the ever-predictable (and boring) pregnancy storyline for their lesbian characters, as if there's nothing else for lesbians to do post-coming-out but settle down and have children.

This strategy 'visually asserts the absolute ordinariness of the family life as a precursor to the introduction of the gay theme' which functions to 'invite the "sympathy" of the viewer' before introducing their sexuality (Walters 2003: 221). In other words, the strategy is to make the lesbian characters so 'normal' and de-sexualised, viewers will almost forget that they're gay.

But The L Word, from its very first episode, has drawn us into the world of lesbian and bisexual life beyond coming out and giving birth, as it explores the ups and downs of the personal and professional lives of several women who are already comfortable with their sexuality. It gives us storylines like Bette's power struggle at the museum, her tenuous relationship with her older sister, and racial identity issues, as well as problems in her relationship with Tina; Dana's humorous attempts to determine her love interest's sexuality, and not-so-humorous attempts to balance her career with her personal needs; Alice's struggle to let go of a bitchy ex-girlfriend; Tina's determination to survive on her own; Shane's heartbreak over falling for a married woman, and her struggle to let herself care for someone again; Jenny's depression at dealing with repressed childhood memories, and her anger at being betrayed by her roommate, Mark.

The danger in focusing on life beyond the coming-out process, of course, is that you can make being gay look unrealistically easy to heterosexual viewers. Fortunately, The L Word makes such a conclusion impossible by including, but not overly focusing on, two coming-out storylines in the first season: Jenny's struggle to accept and understand her bisexuality, and Dana's struggle to come out to her family and her tennis sponsor. Next season that perspective will be provided by Carmen's storyline, as she takes Shane home to meet her family who don't know that she's gay. The series also includes representations of gay mothers through Bette and Tina's attempts to get pregnant, but doesn't make their roles as mothers their sole defining characteristic.

The L Word's most radical contribution to lesbian visibility on TV, however, is its least offensive on the surface: the sense of community it creates. Television has painted a lonely existence for lesbians – the handful of lesbian characters you do see only interact with straight characters, never with other lesbian and bisexual women (unless they're dating them). Even on Buffy the Vampire Slayer and Queer as Folk, two of the only series to successfully and integrally include long-term post-coming-out lesbian storylines, neither Willow and Tara Maclay (Amber Benson), nor Melanie Marcus (Michelle Clunie) and Lindsay Peterson (Thea Gill), appear to even know any other lesbians, let alone hang out with any. Simply by introducing the concept of a group of lesbians, The L Word more realistically portrays lesbian life than any other series to date, and offers an alternative view of lesbian life that doesn't cast us forever in the role of the outsider. The idea that lesbians could be the norm, that the world could revolve around us for a change, and that there could be a lot of us, that is what makes the show truly revolutionary, despite its flaws. Many of the best scenes on The L Word occur when the characters are simply hanging out together: bantering, arguing, advising, and teasing one another, while providing an undercurrent of support. Because despite all the high-profile romances on the series, it is friendship and a sense of community that forms the bedrock of the show.

Whether they would articulate it this way or not, many lesbians have been drawn to the series largely because of this sense of community – both on-screen, and off. For many, consuming The L Word is as much about discussing, analysing and re-enacting the series with friends and other viewers as it is actually watching the episodes. This has always been true of pop culture in America, of course – hit television shows have long been the subject of 'water-cooler' discussions at the office – but the unique combination of the isolation most lesbians feel (to some degree or another) living as an invisible minority, and the widespread adoption of the Internet in the last few years, has taken this interactivity to new heights, and the response has been overwhelming. From visiting popular L Word fan sites and sharing opinions on message boards and polls, to chatting with cast members on the official website after an episode, to writing and reading episode recaps and fan fiction involving the characters, and making and sharing music videos out of clips from the episodes, lesbians are getting together in droves online and offline to read and talk about The L Word, making it the first truly interactive television show for lesbians.[1] The show's ratings don't really reflect the very community it has created – the large numbers of women who gather each week during the season at one another's houses, or the local lesbian bar, to watch the episodes together.

While lesbian viewers are talking about the specific storylines and characters of the show itself when interacting with other viewers, they are more often responding to the issues it raises. While the series offers an often-entertaining, sometimes-frustrating fifty minutes of television each week, The L Word is perhaps more valuable as fertile ground for a long-overdue conversation about issues important to lesbian and bisexual women, from relationship problems to coming out at work to our place and visibility in American society.

This collection is designed to help further that discussion. In the chapters that follow, you'll find debate and discussion by academics and journalists on a range of topics related to the series – cultural reception, the lesbian look, questions of sex and sexuality, the lesbian body, monogamy, female masculinities, heteronormativity, queering desire, music, biracial visibility, gendered representation – as well as interviews and episode summaries. You may not agree with many of the authors' conclusions, but I hope they will at least help you to think about the series in a different way, as we prepare to watch, analyse, and argue over a new season of *The L Word*.

In accepting an award for her role on *The L Word* in late 2004, Jennifer Beals said, 'To know that you exist, and then to know that you exist in a larger, beautiful context, and then finally to know that we all exist as one larger, extended group is very fulfilling. To elucidate those connections ... is one of the things *The L Word* strives to accomplish' (Beals 2004). Years from now, we may look back and conclude that this ability to elucidate connections, to ignite and create a sense of community among lesbians around the world, is *The L Word*'s true legacy.

Reading The L Word is our contribution to that effort.

Note

1. *Buffy* fans were among the first to exploit the Internet's potential for this kind of interactivity in the late 1990s/early 2000s, as the number of Willow/Tara fan sites and message boards will attest, but the fact that the lesbian characters were secondary (and the series was sci-fi in nature) prevented it from developing the same following among lesbians *The L Word* has.

Part 1 Lesbians on tv

L*1*   Sex and the clittie

Diane Anderson-Minshall

I admit it, I was a child celebrity hound. A failed child actor, I knew then what I know now: celebrities are our American royalty. When I wasn't trying to get on TV, I was spending my waking hours watching television and developing intense relationships with the characters on my favourite shows. I realise now that I developed these intense relationships with fictional heroes of the small screen because television as a medium interjects itself into our lives with such a sense of immediate intimacy that children (heck, even some adults) aren't often able to distinguish where the box stops and real life begins. It sounds absurd, but it's still true that for many adults, the lives, the people, the stories we witness on TV become the foundation of our shared collective experience. We know that Ross and Rachel are not our friends but simply *Friends*, but that doesn't mean we don't feel every tingle when they touch, every ache when they part and every stomach-curdling moment when they argue.

Psychologists too have released a grouping of recent studies proving that people develop such intense relationships with people on TV that those characters act as our de facto friends, providing ancillary relationships that are so deeply ingrained in our psyches that when those people go away we actually grieve and when they reappear we feel intense joy. Don't believe it? Tell me you didn't feel something when Michael J. Fox turned up on *Scrubs*? Or when Laurel Holloman, the cute little, butchy lesbian from *Incredibly True Adventures of Two Girls in Love*, showed up on a little-known cable show called *The L Word*?

Of course it wasn't just Laurel Holloman that made dykes like me tune into *The L Word* last year. Like most of lesbian America I was jubilant about the pioneering nature of a television show that was made by, for and about queer women – a show that could imbue our lives with the same glitz and glamour (and all its inherent artificiality) that straight characters on other TV programmes experience. Timed just as *Sex and the City* was going off air, *The L Word* promised to be a provocative and sexual 'Same Sex. Different City' soap opera-type drama that was written and produced by a bona fide lesbian (Ilene Chaiken) and directed by another (Rose Troche). We thought it would be Sex and the Clittie. In the decade and a half since I came out, I've watched almost every single television programme that made mention of, portrayed or even offered a sub-textual hint at lesbianism (this includes a whopping number of TV in-jokes about men's fantasies and how two women together fulfil them). Most of my friends are the same way. But, *Buffy the Vampire Slayer* aside, we've never had a show to call our own. Until now. So it was with much anticipation, and a small dose of trepidation, that I tuned into *The L Word* to witness formerly straight Jenny boo-hooing about sultry heartbreaker Marina, to see blasé married couple Tina and Bette traverse the perils of conception, to revel in chirpy bisexual writer Alice as she charts the six degrees of separation surrounding the lesbian world.

Because I'm the editor of the country's largest lesbian magazine, I had the good fortune of watching all of the L episodes in advance and getting a weekly dose of inside information that the general public isn't privy to. My relationship to *The L Word*, because of that, is more complex than that of the average viewer, even though I engage with and relate to the show as intimately as other women do. In addition, as a professional lesbian, I'm supposed to be one of those editors who help generate the media buzz and Emmy attention that will eventually boost *The L Word*'s ratings and translate to new subscribers for Showtime. And indeed, that's what I did, what we did, and it worked.

Showtime's President of Programming, Bob Greenblatt, reported in *Television Week* (25 October 2004) that, though he wouldn't disclose actual viewer numbers (just how many Americans are tuning in to follow the lives and loves of nine LA lesbians) he would admit that The L Word audience is about three times higher in prime time than those of other Showtime original series. What Greenblatt said it came down to, though, the main goal behind the show, is 'making some noise'. Showtime, it seems, wants The L Word because of its very controversial nature. And it wants lesbians and straights alike to watch the show, to engage in these women's operatic lives and to debate the politics of lesbian portrayal ad nauseam when we're done.

What's perplexing though, is that while this groundbreaking drama is courting the lesbian market and the queer media buzz surrounding it, many of its female stars have become increasingly defensive about their own public personae. Though Rose Troche told TheLWordOnline.com that the writers of the show put together a 'top-secret real-life chart of which lesbians working on the show had slept with whom' and actress Erin Daniels (who plays closeted tennis player, Dana) hinted at lesbian trysts among the cast ('I'm sure there was all over the place. There always is!'), Showtime's PR machine has held a firm stance on the sexuality of their cast mates, telling reporters that only actress Leisha Hailey (who plays Alice) is openly gay.

When one of the heterosexual guest-starring actresses told me earlier this year that many of the regular cast members are lesbian or bisexual, she did so almost casually, as though so many of the women are so out in their daily lives that this straight actress had no idea they could be anything but in their public lives.

When asked to confirm this, the network was livid. Though several of the series' lead actresses may be queer in real life, as this guest star assumed, in public interviews, the actresses have been evasive or downright incensed over questions about their own sexuality. Their anger is ironic, though, given the show's outspoken lesbian content and its desire to market the acceptance of lesbian sexuality to mainstream media consumers.

Months later, Internet fan message boards were abuzz because straight but not narrow cast-mate Laurel Holloman seemed accidentally to have outed two of her L Word co-stars in an interview with PBS's In the Life. Fallout was scant; neither actress made any public admissions and the PR machine remained intact. What, then, is left to protect?

The question at the heart of the matter remains this: what does it mean to have a pioneering television series that seeks to empower lesbians peopled by actresses who are themselves gay but not willing to publicly come out (or be out)?

Though coming out is a personal choice that every queer individual must face on their own terms, when actresses who populate a TV series that markets directly to the lesbian community are evasive or hostile about their sexual orientation, it seems to be not merely an issue of privacy but one of exploitation. You're good enough to economically and politically support our TV programme, their actions seem to tell 'real' lesbians, but you're not good enough for us to join you in the larger struggle for lesbian and gay rights.

The denials of these actresses who want to have their cake and eat it too – they want us to long for them, lust after them, identify with them without ever publicly admitting their sexuality – seem to invalidate their very public presentation, offending us with their defensiveness and somehow diluting the show's relevance to lesbian and bi-women.

The psychological ramifications, I fear, are even worse. In an age where we intimately engage with our television shows and its stars, and we become friends with these people whom we invite into our homes week after week, one has to wonder what happens when those 'friends' of ours seem to live double lives: the free and openly queer women we see on TV and the closeted and defensive women we experience off-screen. Do we perceive their actions as internalised homophobia? Does their homophobia make us feel bad, threatened or wrong? Do we buy into their 'not that there's anything wrong with it' denials?

In the end, the controversy that producers of The L Word seek may be that which focuses around the boldness of having a show about lesbians on prime-time TV. That's a lofty and revolutionary goal already, to create a show all about us, but there has to be something of substance behind the presentation to turn television into a revolutionary act. The creators, producers and yes, the cast, of The L Word have a great opportunity to distinguish themselves, and to set a revolutionary standard (à la Archie Bunker from All In The Family or M*A*S*H) that will change television, and lesbian lives, forever. Let's see what they do with it.

L2 the L word
under-whelms the UK?

Paula Graham

In the USA, *The L Word* has been hailed as a landmark 'first ever' out lesbian TV show (depending on who you talk to, of course, and apologies to all you *Ellen* fans out there). The show seems to have caused considerable furore over the Atlantic but to have been received with little more than a cocked eyebrow among the British chattering classes, gay or straight – and it would appear to be the less-than-reconstructed straight men who have most taken the show to their hearts here. The UK tabloid press gleefully publishes tit and bum shots from the series (with 'click to enlarge' links in online editions) in a joyous fiesta of smutty drooling. I've lost count of the number of tabloid TV reviews which describe *The L Word* girls as the perfect male fantasy of lesbianism. Even the starchy and sarcastic *Radio Times* reviewer couldn't quite keep from dribbling.

This indifference on the part of *The L Word*'s target audience is rather unexpected given how well-received other witty, high-gloss US soapily satirical dramas and sitcoms such as *Sex and the City*, *Six Feet Under*, *Will & Grace* and *The Sopranos* have been over here, especially with women and gays. Indeed, Living TV expected it to appeal precisely to these groups. *Sex and the City*, in particular, inspired the same kinds of devoted activity in young, straight women and lesbians of all ages that cult shows such as *Buffy the Vampire Slayer* and *Xena: Warrior Princess* had produced in the same groups, including activities such as throwing dressing-up parties to watch the show together, complete with drinking games, fanfic, forums, chitchat – the whole nine yards. Flagship shows of Showtime's closest competitor, HBO, are frequently mentioned by critics in tandem with The L Word but, in terms of British reception, the similarities seem to end there. The L Word has demonstrated very little of the same sort of cult appeal among lesbians, straight women or gays and, indeed, has almost no profile on cult Internet portals.

On the face of it, this makes little sense. Why should British viewers, including many gays and lesbians, take the HBO stable to their hearts and yet accord the very first glossy lesbian show such a lukewarm reception? There may be many factors at play, including UK attitudes towards subscription TV, as well as the lack of novelty where overt representations of gay and lesbian life and love are becoming commonplace. But it seems to me that the answer may be rather more political – though not quite in the sense that one might expect. Before dealing with The L Word's 'other' political content, I'll overview some of the more usual ideological suspects and some extraneous factors which might affect the show's reception.

The politics of pay-tv

There's no getting around it, pay-TV is a bit of an issue for The L Word's target demographic in the UK. TV in the UK (particularly news and drama) has traditionally been seen as an important, educative part of the democratic process in promoting responsible awareness of social and political issues. The trivialisation of television content – particularly in news and drama – as a result of increasing commercial competition has long been a bone of bitter contention. Still worse, the near-monopolisation (some might say colonisation) of British pay-TV by the right-wing, pro-free-market, Murdoch empire is a thorn in the flesh of many chattering classes denizens who refuse to subscribe more or less on principle (not to mention having already paid for the BBC through the television licence fee).

This brooding resentment of Murdoch and all his works may be a factor in the lackadaisical reception of the show in the UK. The L Word made its UK debut on the subscription-only Living TV channel. Its more successful HBO competitors were all broadcast on terrestrial Channel 4, or on E4, which is available to UK digital users. Cult shows such as *Buffy* and *Xena* started (UK) life on terrestrial BBC Two and Five respectively. For terrestrial viewers, these high-quality and socially aware dramas are often the high spots of the week's available drama viewing (our home-grown TV being, on the whole, informative but hideously dull). Fewer than half of the homes in the UK have access to pay-TV (Ofcom Stats: http://tinyurl.com/at68v). What's more, subscription TV has most penetration in economically disadvantaged social sectors and is most frequently eschewed in precisely those socio-economic sectors targeted by The L Word.

This lesbian saw the first series on a DVD import played on my multi-region player last year (multi-region players being another luxury whose distribution has been somewhat restricted in the UK). The second series was broadcast on the UK pay channel Living TV during the summer of 2005, as part of a multi-million pound investment in rebranding the channel for a more sophisticated audience. The first series was also released in Zone 2 PAL (that's us Europeans) DVD on 20 June 2005 and reached the top ten in the DVD bestseller lists. It's quite possible that these impressive sales represent more straight male interest than lesbian, or even gay male, interest – there are probably not enough lesbians and gays to exert this kind of purchasing power. Salacious tabloid articles addressing heterosexual men also noticeably outnumber pro-feminist critical articles in the press. In fact, the show appears to appeal more to the typical consumer of pay-TV (blokes who like sport and pinups) than to the typical lesbian.

Lesbians greet the **L** word

Despite a gushing plug in 2004 from Rainbow Network (the UK's best-known gay portal) and the best efforts of *Diva* (the UK's premier – well only – lesbian glossy) with an L *Word* fanfare as centrepiece of a lezzies-on-TV Special Edition (2005), Brit lesbians don't seem to be demonstrating the kind of rapt attention one might expect. Googling-UK for L *Word* fansites and forums leads to rather a lot of dead links and/or sites actually based in America. This exchange from an online forum in Sheffield, a provincial Midlands city with a high lesbian quotient, seems a representative summation of lesbian apathy in relation to the show:

Nick2	*Do lesbians actually watch The L Word?* It looks to me like it's actually made for straight men to watch, a bit of a naughty treat late at night?
Carmine	Does anyone?
Tulip	I've never heard of this show. Is it English or American? If it's a US product I don't think they show it over here!
BoroughGal	It is American Tulip, and they did show it over there, on a channel called HSBO [sic] or something like that?
Spinny	It showing on liveing [sic] tv at the moment on a Wednesday at 10pm. I find it a good drama indeed.

(http://www.sheffieldforum.co.uk/showthread/t-44880.html)

So much for the stalwart efforts of *Diva* and Rainbow Network to spin up a bit of lesbian enthusiasm! It's possible that a lesbian or female response might become more discernible now that the DVD is available in the UK. The DVD has been out here for a few months now, however, and the show doesn't seem to have gathered a whole lot of momentum as a result.

Still, this editorial comment (published some time after the initial wave of editorial enthusiasm) from *Diva*, seems uncharacteristically pithy:

It's unlikely *Diva* will be revisiting *The L Word* or its stars in the near future. For one thing, lots of women (myself included) don't get cable and haven't seen it.

(*DivaDirect*, 'Letters to Editor:' http://tinyurl.com/ddkgm)

Lack of access, in itself, might be enough to prevent a show from becoming iconic more generally, but cult viewers will often positively enjoy digging stuff out of obscurity as part of the thrill of non-conformity. And, anyway, lesbians will notoriously watch pretty much anything with girls-who-love-girls in it. *Xena* and *Buffy* 'went cult' in spite of the former being run at some God-forsaken hour of Saturday morning on Five (access to which is impossible in some regions and erratic in others) and the latter being primly cut by Auntie Beeb (otherwise known as the BBC) and then shunted round the schedules in a customarily infuriating way by it's minority BBC Two hosts.

More mainstream means less lesbian-appeal?

In previous decades, *any* lesbian representation could be relied on to provoke passionate confrontation over its 'realism' or lack of it – and particularly as to whether it over- or under-sexualised lesbianism. Is a lack of British lesbian enthusiasm related, perhaps, to the show's mainstream Hollywood 'candy coat'? Probably not – there's no reason to suppose that UK lesbians are any more likely to care about this than their US sisters – as long as everyone has a good time.

Whilst *The L Word* is overt about its lesbian content and clearly foregrounds specifically lesbian issues as well as more general feminist ones, the drama revolves primarily around emotional dilemmas which most 'pomo' folk of any orientation can easily identify with. Straight women can also participate in lesbian dilemmas more immediately through identification with straight character Kit Porter's perspective.

The show is clearly constructed to allow pomo audiences who are neither lesbian nor gay to participate in the show's emotional dilemmas through a sort of modified 'window' effect. Window advertising is a postmodern technique developed to allow advertisers to reach gay and lesbian markets without alienating heterosexuals:

> [Gays] and lesbians can read into an ad certain subtextual
> elements that correspond to experiences with or
> representations of gay/lesbian subculture. If heterosexual
> consumers do not notice these subtexts or subcultural modes,
> then advertisers are able to reach the homosexual market
> along with the heterosexual market without ever revealing
> their aim.
>
> (Clark 1991: 188)

Nevertheless, straight women appear to prefer *Sex and the City* reruns. Gay men in the USA seem to have taken well to *The L Word*'s inclusion of relatively non-stereotypical gay male characters but Brit gay men appear, on the whole, to share their lesbian counterparts' lack of interest in *The L Word* along with their straight sisters' preference for *Sex and the City* or *Six Feet Under*. The flagship shows of Showtime's closest competitor, HBO, are frequently mentioned by critics in tandem with *The L Word* but in terms of British reception, the similarities seem to end there.

Under the circumstances, it seems unlikely that the show's California gloss or restricted access for UK audiences could account for its relative lack of success. Maybe we're just jaded from overexposure?

'Queer fatigue' – we've passed this way before...

Lesbians and gays on TV might be expected to provoke controversy in the straight press merely by virtue of showing lesbian or gay life and love at all. In the UK, this is no longer much of an issue, however. The nation is fairly well pickled in pomo and, these days, only 'outraged of Middle England' gives a rat's nether parts who sleeps with whom wearing what or how. Indeed, Brits easily take to their hearts the self-reflexive camp or cleverly understated HBO satires (so close to the celebrated 'British sense of humour'), but the more ponderous and literal style of *The L Word* tends to estrange the British love of sharp-edged (some might say cruel) ironic undercutting.

Tim Teeman and Stephanie Theobald's critical reviews sum up the perceived one-dimensional treatment of representational issues succinctly. Teeman's review for *The Times* is actually entitled 'The L Word needs to be more soap than sermon':

> *The L Word* is aimed more at straight women (for the clothes and bonding) and straight men (for the sex), rather than at lesbians. The message? You think that all lesbians are butch and badly dressed? Not these days, and certainly not in LA.
>
> (Teeman 2005)

I don't think *The L Word*'s candy coat matters too much.
Pushing lesbianism to the mainstream is all about Trojan
horses, i.e. strategy. Dress up lesbianism in Victorian boots
and corsets (see *Tipping The Velvet*) and you get primetime
space on the BBC. Make the chicks in *The L Word* shave their
legs and have some sensitive men hanging around and you
can get yourself a second series. Once your horse has slipped
through the paddock doors of 'the men upstairs', i.e. the TV
bods who decide what constitutes contemporary culture, then
you can ask why non-airbrushed chicks are unacceptable
– and, naturally, that's not only a lesbian issue.

(Theobald 2004)

There really doesn't seem a great deal to add to that – which might help
explain the lack of feminist debate and preponderance of overheated
drooling in *Sun*-reading het males. What's to debate? Lick that candy
coat!

There is also a distinct lack of novelty by now about queers getting
explicit on TV. We've had comic skits on the radio, such as 'Julian
and Sandy' in *Round the Horne* (BBC, 1965–1969), and posh queens in
period dramas such as *Brideshead Revisited* from time immemorial. By
the 1980s, we'd got much nearer the knuckle with stuff like a film
adaptation of Joe Orton's *Prick Up Your Ears* (1987), which included overt
scenes of sex in public toilets and with Moroccan teen trade. *Oranges
Are Not The Only Fruit*, broadcast in 1989, featured full-on sex between
teenaged girls. What's more, it represented Evangelical Christians as
a bunch of fanatical head-cases (an opinion shared by much of the UK
population). That caused a bit of a stir in the tabloids but it quickly blew
over because, on the whole, the Brits aren't really much flustered by
queers cavorting on telly – especially lesbians, who can always be relied
upon to appeal to straight men.

Then, in the mid 1990s, there were Warren and Ferdy in *This Life*,
the latter's encounter with a kilted plumber being notable at the
time. And, by 1999, we had pretty explicit under-age gay sex featuring
'rimming' – which came as a floridly interesting water-cooler moment
to British heterosexuals – in *Queer as Folk*. Again, it caused a bit of a

storm in a teacup which rapidly blew over but did wonders for the show's ratings and rapid rise to cult status. *Tipping The Velvet*, broadcast in 2002 by the relatively cosy BBC, featured, besides some routine naked lesbian romping and a lot of décolleté corsetry, butch-femme sex with a leather dildo and FTM cross-dressing, along with a thoroughly explicit smorgasbord of nineteenth-century sexual decadence – and was received pretty much in the spirit of bedroom farce by the queer-acclimatised denizens of 'Middle England'.

Whilst the Christian right in the USA has frequently been successful in campaigns to suppress sexually explicit – and particularly *homosexually* explicit – material, the UK public at large tends to regard the Christian right as a 'loony fringe.' Britain, as a nation, has long since accepted sexual scandal as a harmless form of public entertainment. In fact, the nation finds it howlingly amusing when, for example, a politician is caught in the act of auto-asphyxiating in a pink tutu and suspenders with an orange embedded where it shouldn't be *et cetera. The Guardian's* tongue-in-cheek summing-up of a mud-slinging match between the *Daily Mail* (the always-indignant mouthpiece of 'Middle England') and the stalwartly liberal BBC (this time on a royal scandal) hits the nail neatly on the head:

> The *Mail* versus the BBC is a masterly piece of news
> management – and it is less about genuine moral indignation
> than it is about newspaper sales.
>
> (Bell 2002)

Homosexuality on TV is now more likely to be deployed in a calculated bid to build ratings than to push the boundaries of gay representation. This has been precisely the strategy of Living TV in its efforts to attract more sophisticated female audiences recently. Terrestrial Channel 4 built its cutting-edge reputation through the 1980s and 1990s with a rampage of highly explicit and exotic queer documentaries and films and an almost obsessional coverage of transsexuality. On the strength of *Queer as Folk*, Russell T Davies has become a national treasure almost on a par with Sir Gandalf (Ian McKellan) himself. Davies, head writer and executive producer, wrote eight out of the thirteen scripts for the first series of the recent revival of the British sci-fi institution, *Doctor Who*. One of *Queer as Folk*'s central characters was an ardent fan of *Doctor Who* and this ironic (extra-textual) connection to one of our 'stately homos' is arguably part of the appeal of the new *Doctor Who* for British fans – gay or straight.

There is, of course, still bags of homophobia and discrimination in real life here – especially for lesbians – but on TV, homosexuality – especially lesbianism – is a sure-fire pull for sophisticated audiences. *The L Word* doesn't, therefore, attract a great deal of notoriety just by virtue of presenting lesbianism as a positive choice or by being sexually explicit. Brits, on the whole, really aren't all that bothered...

Beyond textual-sexual politics?

Differences in political climate and cultural attitudes in relation to sexuality and scandal may not be the only political differences between the UK and US which have a bearing on the reception of *The L Word*, however. British lack of enthusiasm may have a profoundly political element with its roots in an entirely different set of political agendas.

Lesbianism in Britain has characteristically been strongly associated with anti-capitalist movements in the UK right up until the end of the 1980s. Many European lesbians are still active in left-wing social movements. *The L Word* is clearly aimed at the cosmopolitan 'chattering classes' in the UK – Living TV's target demographic as well as that of Showtime/MGM. In contemporary Western Europe the chattering classes (gay or straight) are at best ambivalent and often fairly strongly opposed to a corporate-led globalisation of free-market ideology (known to economists as 'The Washington Model'). Closer to home, they feel a great deal of discontent about the marketisation of the British economy and work practices. Indeed, educated Brits are decanting alarmingly to France and Spain (which still have a social-democratic take on life). Those who remain are likely to feel very uncomfortable about their own complicity with hyper-capitalist cultural practices, and are either sceptical or outright dismissive of a perceived vapid obsession with celebrity, money and glamour in American culture.

Hollywood is notoriously liberal – but it is a liberalism steeped not only in implicit masculinism but also in economic free-market ideology which is not shared by all Americans and certainly not by the majority of contemporary Western Europeans. And I've yet to meet anyone who identifies herself as lesbian who isn't bitterly opposed to Britain's implication in the illegal occupation of Iraq. The strong influence of right-wing evangelism in the Bush regime is a factor, rather than a defining characteristic, of resentment in Europe towards America's current regime, even for queers. We're really a great deal more bothered about retaining our threatened public services and US foreign policy than about the USA's internal politics.

This American attitude towards the EU (and the Rest of the World) was rather inescapably brought to my attention when I tried to load the official Showtime site during the course of researching this article. I found the way barred. The official site (http://www.sho.com/site/lword/home.do) can only be accessed from a North American IP. According to the small print (after I accessed the site through a US proxy – well, DUH!!!) there seems to be some anxiety not only that us foreigners might be bootleggers unrestrained by our louche governments but that we might also be a bunch of wild-eyed terrorists on the US export-ban list too. HBO and NBC apparently have no such reservations about allowing European rabble to access home pages for *Six Feet Under* or *Will & Grace*. Is Showtime trying to get rid of European audiences?

The representational regime of *The L Word* is also rather off-putting to British audiences. To maximise its appeal, the show adroitly sidesteps conflicts over sexuality and representation by studiously trying to be all things to all (reasonably hip) people. The majority of its US and UK lesbian fans are clearly prepared to take a postmodern view of the anorexic and waxed feminisation of its heroines, their highly privileged lifestyle and apparent oblivion to a wider world. Nevertheless, the show *does* have a rather earnest political agenda underneath its lip-gloss. Whilst clearly intended to be lightly humorous in tone, it shows little of the cleverly controlled play of satirical humour in tension with compassionate insights into human weakness offered by shows such as *The Sopranos*, *Desperate Housewives* and *Six Feet Under*, or the camp send-ups of self-absorbed rich kids' conspicuous consumption and allegiance to the cult of celebrity in *Will & Grace* or *Sex and the City*, which ironically acknowledge their own complicity with these agendas. *The L Word* has the surface appearance of self-reflexivity but it demonstrates little real distance from its subjects. Issues are dealt with on a shopping list and the drama is too often palpably little more than a vehicle for these issues. I keep expecting Bette Porter, in particular, to break diegesis and frame post-feminist observations to camera, *Alfie*-style, followed by a 'press the red button now' poll.

The rueful critical distance of such shows as *Will & Grace* or *Six Feet Under* is reasonably in tune with the ambivalence many Brits feel about their love of glossy Hollywood shows and their discomfort with the inroads of the free-market ideology to European socio-economic regimes and socialist cultures which these shows effectively represent. The more intimate, lesbianised, representational order of *The L Word* offers little distance to its lesbian viewers. Its protagonists *are* feminised, lip-glossed, air-brushed, stick-insects – but as Theobald (2004) points out, these are not issues specific to lesbianism in particular but are general to the representation of women. The same criticism could be levelled at *any* of the glossy American shows which have become popular here, with the possible exception of *Xena*.

The more disturbing element of *The L Word*'s political quietism for British audiences may be unrelated to gender or sexual morality, and more to do with the show's location within the wider politics of Bush's America. There are few episodes I recall in which an overtly political statement stands out as dominating an entire episode – and which actually picks a side – except one in the first season in which the girls are arrested for confronting a far-right picket of an art show featuring sexually explicit material ('Locked Up', 1:12). And the last episode of the second season, when Gloria Steinem takes to the stage at the Ms Foundation benefit ('Lacuna', 2:13). The position of the narrative and meta-narrative is, for once, absolutely clear. The 'moral' right is repressive, violently aggressive and fundamentally dishonest. The only question on which the narrative offers ambivalence is as to whether the lesbians should counter a right-wing smear with counter-smears. It would seem that the fundamental political point of *The L Word* is that it exists in Bush's America at all. This is an issue of limited interest to most European lesbians, of course.

The show's largely unquestioned allegiance to hyper-capitalist 'lifestyle' identity is, I think, still more problematic to European audiences. Halfway through the second season, Alice Pieszecki remarks to her lover in passing that, just *possibly*, it's wrong to invade Iraq to secure their consumerist lifestyles. However, both characters are clearly infinitely more interested in the question of whether dildos are appropriate in lesbian sexuality than whether consumerism should define lesbian identity ('Late, Later, Latent', 2:9). The ethics of killing hundreds of thousands of innocent civilians in the process of securing a lifestyle identity based on a wardrobe full of uncomfortable shoes is framed more as a five-second meditative exercise than an actual question. There's certainly no commitment here. To the British, a large proportion of whom object more or less strenuously to the Iraq war and half a million of whom hit the streets to protest against it in the largest demonstration Britain has seen for a couple of centuries, this appears lame, insular and self-obsessed.

The second season has clearly made more of an effort to widen its critical frame and Bette also expresses some mild resentment to the punishing exercise regime required to maintain an entirely unrealistic body shape for her age, height – or any other physical parameter you'd care to name. Again, this goes nowhere, however. After throwing a teensy paddy, Bette obediently does her butt-crunches. Well, dear God, the alternative (a substantial female body confidently occupying space on its own terms) is apparently inconceivable. Perish the thought that we would become (gasp) *unfashionable!*

The glossier end of UK LGBT (well-heeled and largely male) Millivres culture remains entranced by US gay political culture – but they're not much interested in lesbians anyway. *Diva*, Millivres' 'sister' publication for lesbians (*spookily*) shares this Amerophiliac obsession with candy g-strings, celebrity dykes and a firm avoidance of 'feel-bad' controversy – but even here, reception of *The L Word* has been muted. For the wider community of queers, lesbians, gays and straights of the no-logo-inclined chattering classes of Europe, an invitation to align oneself with a queer politics in which identity *is* little more than a lifestyle choice clothed in edible knickers might be expected to fall on relatively stony ground.

L 3 Interview with Guinevere Turner[1]

Sarah Warn

In the 1990s, openly gay writer/actor/director Guinevere Turner's starring role in the 1994 hit film, *Go Fish*, which she co-wrote and produced with director Rose Troche, made her into one of the lesbian community's poster girls, so it seems natural that she would be involved with Ilene Chaiken's groundbreaking lesbian series *The L Word*, where she has served as one of the show's writers and an occasional guest star (as Alice's bitchy ex-girlfriend, Gabby). On the day of the release of the first season of *The L Word* on DVD, Turner talked to me about the show's writing process, her inspiration for some of its first-season plotlines, and how scenes sometimes change from page to screen.

AfterEllen.com: What's the writing process like on The L Word?
Guinevere Turner: We start off by all getting together and just talking for hours, and from that we develop six or seven episodes, which we then go off and write. Then we get together to brainstorm the next six or seven episodes, everyone goes away to write again, and then we rewrite, etc. Usually you end up learning so much about the people in the room because you're sharing such personal stories. We start out with eight or nine writers each season, and then the core melts down to me, Ilene and Rose for the rewrites.

Where are you at with season two?
Ilene is directing the season finale this week. We finished the official writing in June, but the nature of TV is that there is a lot of changing. My job is done unless I'm up there acting, but Ilene called me in late summer and said, 'Please come up and brainstorm with me, because we have to make these radical changes to the end of the season.' So then it was a whirlwind of ten days of writing, writing, writing, and then I'm done again. The process has become easier this season, because we already know the characters and the actors, and what they can do.

Ilene mentions in her pilot commentary on the DVD that several of Bette and Tina's insemination-related scenes are loosely based on her own experiences. Are there any stories in the first season that are based on your life?
Lisa [Devon Gummersall], the lesbian-identified man, is based on a story I heard about a guy who was so lesbian-identified that he was mad he wasn't allowed into the Michigan Womyn's Music Festival. That whole character came about because I was trying to explain to some of the staff what the Festival was, and in the process I mentioned this guy Lisa. And the executive producer was like, 'A dude named Lisa? I love it! Let's make him a character.' That's sort of the way characters evolve.

That's what fun about my job – just talking to lesbians gives me ideas. Although people do say to me, 'If I see that on The L Word, I'm going to kick your ass!'

What was your inspiration for the Dinah Shore episode in season two?
The whole idea for the Dinah Shore episode came about because I had been there for the first time the year before, and I thought, 'This scene is so intense and so lesbo, it would be great to do an episode about it.' I always had this idea about Dinah Shore that it was this older lesbian, golf getaway for couples, but when I was there, I was like, 'This is Spring Break!' There were women racing through the halls with beer at 4 a.m., and I thought, 'That's fun! That would make great TV!'

What was your favourite scene in the first season?
The scene where Kelly Lynch sings the Leonard Cohen song to Kit. I just loved how Kelly inhabited that character, and how Pam as a straight

woman tried to keep the boundaries, but there was this sweet romance between them... And Kelly's just hot in her boy drag. We all just loved Kelly, and Ivan, and we immediately wanted to know how many scenes Kelly could do.

One of my other favourite scenes is Alice's flashback in the Dinah Shore episode, about how she first fell in love with a girl. I can completely attribute that to Leisha Hailey's genius; I think it's so funny. I'll confess that that wasn't what I originally had as a flashback for Alice – it was originally her and a girl at a football game, under the bleachers. The joke of that scene was that they're really drunk and they make out, and then the girl pukes on her.

Alice's mom mentioned that story in the car...
Yeah, that was the vestige of what was written. But Leisha really wanted to do a musical thing so we just rewrote it for her, and it worked so beautifully.

All of the coming-out flashbacks were really good...
They were really fun to write. We were worried initially that you wouldn't know the characters well enough yet to really care about their coming-out stories, but I think it turned out well.

Are there any scenes you'd do differently if you could go back and rewrite them?
I always wanted the Lisa character to be more Goth, anarchy, punk-like, and less like the soft, crunchy type Lisa sort of bled into, like the male nanny that Freddie Prinze Jr. played on *Friends*. Because I think Lisa ended up seeming more like a scammer, rather than someone who was coming from a genuine place. So I would have rewritten that.

And in the episode where Jenny goes on a road-trip and does mushrooms, there was something about the kid she was with – in my head, he was younger and more vulnerable, but the actor played him so huge that it came off goofy, when it was supposed to come off more sweet. But that's what I've learned in writing for TV: there's so much that goes into it long after the writer has done her job, you just have to let go of it and let things develop the way they develop. It's a good lesson.

There was a subplot in 'Losing It' (1:6) involving the Asian girlfriend (played by Taayla Markell) of Bette and Tina's sperm donor, Marcus Allenwood (Mark Gibson), who came across as an inexplicably crazy stereotype of an Asian woman. A lot of viewers were offended by that, especially since, so far, she is the only Asian woman on the series. What was up with that?

That wasn't really how I wrote the character, but that's the funny thing about TV... what the actress and the director brought to it turned it into this way overblown hysterical character that it wasn't meant to be. That whole thing is a little painful for me that it turned into a hysterical woman of colour. I came across a blog on the Internet where the woman was ranting about what a racist I am, because of that character, and it was painful to read.

Who is the most difficult character to write for?

In season one, Tina was the most difficult, because her character lives so much in relation to Bette. We were always looking for ways for her to have her own identity, but we never seemed to quite get there, story-wise. I just worried that we were making her character boring, and she deserved a lot more than that – and she gets a lot more than that in season two.

Who is your favourite character?

Alice is the easiest and most fun to write for, because she's funny, and I know Leisha will bring humour to anything I write. But also because she's an easy character, lower on drama and higher on quips. She gets to be the voice of the single woman about town, and it's fun.

What kind of reaction have you gotten to Alice being bisexual, since some lesbians have issues with bisexuality?

I think people forget she's bisexual. Our joke about her character is that she always says she's bisexual, but she really isn't, she just wants to be like, 'I'm open to anything,' because she's that kind of person. Except for Alice's stint with Lisa, which goes so wrong, she doesn't ever really act on her bisexuality. And Jenny's bisexuality so overshadows hers that any anti-bisexuality sentiment goes towards Jenny.

Does Jenny get less annoying in the second season?
Suffice it to say that the staff of The L Word is well aware of how annoyed the community was by Jenny's indecisiveness in the first season, how watching her you're just like, 'What do you want already?' So we tried to take her in another direction in season two.

I did really like the final scene with her, Anne Ramsay [who plays Robin] and Gene [Feinberg (Tygh Runyan)] all playing Scrabble together. I just think it's really sweet. Probably there was a fear there that there was going to be a three-way there, but I just like how that turned out. Anne Ramsay did a great job with her character.

Are you surprised at how popular The L Word has become?
I'm thrilled. The Internet creates a whole new level of fans, it's great. I wish people wouldn't post spoilers, but just the fact that people are already thinking about season two is exciting.

Besides the lesbians, the group that really seems to love the show are straight women. Straight women and my dad. He just really likes the show. He's always emailing me to ask what's going to happen in season two, with questions like, 'Is Jenny ever going to decide she's gay? Why did Bette cheat on Tina?!' It's really funny.

Note
1.   Originally published on AfterEllen.com, November 2004.

New queer cable?

the L word, the small screen and the bigger picture

Michele Aaron

Is *The L Word* the latest ripple emanating from the wave of 'new queer' films that excited lesbian and gay audiences, and some of their best friends, in the early 1990s? Does it represent a high point in the mainstream's toleration-cum-group hug of gay lives, or a familiar exploitation of girl-on-girl action for the no-less titillated straights? Has it exposed the limits of cinema as radical but popular entertainment form or tapped the latent queer potential of flexi-format television? Is there more to cunning Showtime's stunning Linguists than first meets the... er... eye?

When proudly quirky and queer-themed fare, like *Paris Is Burning* (1990), *Poison* (1991), and *Swoon* (1992), reaped awards on the film festival circuit, B. Ruby Rich (1992: 32) heralded the emergence of a New Queer Cinema (NQC). Joined by such films as *Tongues Untied* (1990), *Young Soul Rebels* (1991), *R.S.V.P.* (1991), *The Hours and Times* (1991), and *Khush* (1991), and work by, among others, Derek Jarman, Gus Van Sant, Gregg Araki, Sadie Benning, Su Friedrich, John Greyson and Monica Treut, lesbian and gay film-makers and their audiences were finally being recognised and responded to. The films themselves were most similar, it seemed, in their commitment to being different. In their range of subjects, styles and social investment, thick with self-consciousness even at their shallowest moments, they vied with political correctness, with

gay history, with homogeneity. What they shared, then, as both Rich
and J. Hoberman (1992: 31) implied, was a kind of insouciance. This
insouciance represented, for me, an air of defiance binding the films
together in a socio-critical oppositionality that was distinctly queer
(Aaron 2004). In exposing the various levels (aesthetic, narratival,
contextual) upon which this defiance was enacted, the characteristics
of this new queer vision could be distinguished. These characteristics
distilled the films' radical aspirations even as they afforded their more
popular pleasures. And it is this play-off between the radical and the
popular that haunted the evolution of NQC and the queer narratives,
like The L Word, that have come in its wake.

What I want to do is to apply some of these characteristics of NQC
to The L Word as a way into understanding the series in terms of the
recent 'queering' of western culture. In using The L Word to evaluate
the legacy not of New Queer Cinema per se but of the lesbian and gay
community's recent, supposed, gains, that NQC made manifest, we
can better judge The L Word's critical, rather than just clitoral, value,
offsetting its success against both its radical antecedents and its more
popular, its 'queerlite', appeal.

Firstly, then, the NQC films, in giving voice not simply to lesbians
and gays but to the more marginalised subgroups within the lesbian
and gay community, defied the conventions of popular or acceptable
subjects. From the poverty of the Hispanic and African-American gay
youth in Paris Is Burning, to the interracial romance in Young Soul Rebels,
to the HIV+ heroes of Araki's The Living End (1992), to be queer was
always more than a question of sexual preference. NQC embraced
the complexity of the community, it sought out the alienated, the
discordant. Now, if The L Word does nothing else, it at least represents
the previously non- or mis-represented lesbian community. Indeed,
it doesn't just give lesbians a voice; it gives them a Planet. And the
Planet is populated by a wide array of women: there are students and
sportswomen, hairdressers, lawyers and writers. So how come they are
all so damn similar? Though there are many voices in The L Word, they
are hell-bent on harmony. (How fitting, then, that the band 'Betty', with
their a cappella n' rock, should accompany season two.) The differences
and dissonance within the community have been remixed into the

now compulsory metrosexuality of the universal narrative. In making the lesbian protagonists privileged white folk (or near-white folk) in their beauty, booty, and access to the best of friends, sex and gourmet coffee, the women are neither representative nor realistic – this is a TV show, after all – but they still manage to be compelling. With the programme's high production values, its skilled writing and direction, the characters invite identification and empathy as well as voyeurism. They are over-glamorous, under-stressed, and enjoying a seemingly endless work-break, but they still manage to credibly convey some of the angst of twenty- and thirty-something urban professionals. *The L Word* also injects a measure of sophistication into such mainstream fare by confronting some of the thorny issues of our times: promiscuity and monogamy; coming out as a rite of passage versus the commercial lure of the closet; interracial relationships and identity; gay marriage and gay parenting. This is certainly not the way that we live – East London, say, seems a long, long way from Lala land – but it does approximate the way that we love: sometimes messily and sometimes mindfully and often less well-managed than our wardrobes.

The NQC films frequently defied positive imagery. They were unapologetic about their characters' faults or even crimes. They beautified their villains more than they vilified their acts. *Swoon*'s child murderers, for instance, were softly spoken, well-groomed romantics, naturally inclined to the black and white indulgences of Kalin's art film rather than the sullied connotations of its courtroom recreations. Sin certainly remains sexy in *The L Word* – the steamiest storylines followed the adulterous misdeeds of Bette Porter and of Jenny Schecter – but the universal narrative is also the moralistic one. Both Bette and Jenny suffer for their weaknesses. For Jenny, her affair leads to trauma if not personal breakdown as she tries and fails to choose between her impossibly sweet boyfriend, Tim Haspel, and the irresistible gatekeeper to the Planet, Marina Ferrer. For Bette, repentance will saturate her characterisation for almost the entire second season: the pained strained face of temptation in season one turning into the near hysteria of her purgatory in season two. Television's serial dramas need their rogues and heroes but with *The L Word*'s soapy allusions, it is also, inevitably, self-cleansing. Season two will end with Bette and Tina

Kennard firmly reunited as a couple and committed for the long term, as parents. Helena Peabody, the (familiarly evil British) interloper, is clearly categorised as the baddie: by Bette, by Tina and by her own mother (tongue). Cheating on the one you love, The L Word tells us, is wrong. Sleeping around is fine as long as it is temporary or, as Peggy (Ma) Peabody (Holland Taylor) so perfectly puts is, it produces great art. The show moralises while it jokes with popular morality or, and we are back to the cunning of the series' creators, it moralises in order that it can get away with intervening into popular notions of morality.

Unlike New Queer Cinema, then, The L Word admires, indeed exploits, positive imagery. Television programmes, and serialised programmes especially, do more than seek the audience's approval, they require it for their own existence. The oft-cited 'glance' at TV as opposed to the 'gaze' at cinema, encapsulates not only their respective spectators' difference in intensity but also in commitment. TV audiences must be rendered more than merely entertained, they must be made addicts: they must keep tuning in, in large numbers, for a series to endure into another season, that is, for the network and advertisers to allow this to happen. And it is in the second season, I would suggest, that The L Word reaps the benefits of its earlier conformity, its (lip-to-)lip service to the stock stuff of soap-cum-soft-core serial-drama. The L Word's genre-hybridisation is far from standard fare, but its novelty points more to necessity than to the rampant innovation of its creators, despite what their NQC credentials – the film-makers often broke with formal and narrative conventions – might imply. The notion of queer television has, for some, proved oxymoronic. This is not only because TV inhabits the everyday through embracing its common denominators – precisely the terrain against which queer agitates – but because its serialised narratives, its dramas, comedies and soap, have depended on 'normative developmental narratives of sexuality' (McCarthy 2001: 599) and as such militate against queerness.

The L Word, at least, tries to balance its normative romance trajectories of the Bette-Tina and Dana-Tonya/Dana-Alice relationships with the more random or individualistic investments of Shane, Kit or Jenny. But it is in its expansion of understandings of desire and memory, of the referential and the reverential, and, especially, of family that it makes its queerest connections. While Jenny's flashbacks more than grate upon an otherwise grateful spectator, they sit within the series' fascination with the past that connects Alice's chart to Kit's former glory to Shane's mystery. The show's extolling of art and its investment in community and community action (through Tina's work in season two, and the direct action protest at Bette's gallery in season one) clearly locate The L Word as an AIDS-era cultural product. In this way the series again connects with its new queer heritage, for NQC has been seen as triggered by the queer culture of AIDS activism (Arroyo 1993: 70–96; Pearl 2004: 23–35).[1] 'The queer present,' according to Rich, 'negotiates with the queer past, knowing full well that the future is at stake' (1992: 32). When season two ends with the group of friends gathered around to welcome the new, and crucially non-biological, mother Bette and her and Tina's mixed race newborn, The L Word queers the family, the final frontier of normativity, in a gesture that is more than oppositional, it's downright revolutionary.

The New Queer pedigree of The L Word comes from its association with some of the film movement's talent and success. Rose Troche and Guinevere Turner, who co-created the milestone 'NQ' Lesbian feature, Go Fish (1994), are both involved with the writing of the Showtime series and Troche is one of The L Word's main directors. In addition, the episodes 'Lynch Pin' (2:4) and 'Liberally' (1:10) were also directed by NQC directors (Lisa Cholodenko and Mary Harron respectively) and some of NQC's actresses appear in the series (Guinevere Turner in a minor role, and Tina is played by Laurel Holloman, who starred in Maria Maggenti's 1994 film The Incredibly True Adventures of Two Girls in Love). The L Word also references its queer film heritage. The prison seduction in season one was an homage to Jean Genet, and in particular to his 1950 film Un Chant d'amour (although, according to Jennifer Beals, bless, it was the jail scene in Fassbinder's Querelle [1982] that she was recreating [see, Stewart]). This classic of queer cinema focused on one inmate's sexual obsession with another in the dark vaults of a men's prison, and provided the inspiration, too, for the portion of Hayne's Poison (1991) that he set in the same location.

In engaging with and reworking this cinematic past, The L Word fulfils another characteristic of NQC. On the one hand, then, it would seem to share its queer sensibility, on the other, it is doing something quite different. Rather than queering the straight past – as Jarman's *Edward II* (1991), Kalin's *Swoon* and Münch's *The Hours and Times* do in (re)instating the homosexuality of some of their historical characters – *The L Word* inserts lesbianism into the queer past. In other words, it is not just homophobia that it is reckoning with but the masculinist discourse of queer itself. Indeed, homophobia is far less a source of fear or force of oppression in the series than is sexism. Dana might worry about the reprisals of coming out of the closet, from her family, from her fans, but ever more apparent in the series as it progresses are the problems that confront women historically, globally and in the everyday.

In the second season the show gets to be more profound and, not a coincidence, more political and, for this spectator at least, the wait – which was hardly all that painful – pays off. The women move beyond the one-dimensionality of, say, Shane who can't but fuck, and Kit, who can't but fuck up. And Jenny even becomes marginally less irritating. But, surprisingly, it is not the show's queer credentials that afford this politicisation. In fact, do the L *Word* women even mention the Q word? This doesn't depoliticise the show, it just locates it on a different plane of politicisation: feminism. The firmly feminist politics of the show gain momentum throughout the second season, aided by resident straight boy, Mark Wayland. His character and learning curve shift the issue of the ethics of male voyeurism away from the reception to the content of the show, and reprioritise its function within a literal undressing of masculinist assumptions. Subtlety aside, the last stages of the season see the creators getting to realise some of their feminist fantasies, and score a few strikes against George W. Bush at the same time. The Planet, hosting the memorial service for Bette and Kit's father, now has its favourite clients sitting around chatting with Gloria Steinem, an old friend of his. The group may chat about sexual preferences, but when they all toast 'choice', there is no doubt about the show's political affinities (Steinem has been an outspoken supporter of abortion and opponent therefore to Bush) or how they are creeping in within the lesbian project.

One of several problems noted of NQC was the absence of women from the roll call of acclaimed directors, and of lesbian experience from its many varied narratives. As Amy Taubin would note in the early 1990s alongside Rich, queer in the new queer films 'is figured in terms of sexual desire and the desire it constructs is exclusively male' (1992: 33). In the realm of television, there was little difference. As Cheryl Gudz (2003: 11) rightly noted 'queer tv' means gay white male TV, as Queer Eye for the Straight Guy and Queer as Folk make only too obvious. Its generic, narrative and stylistic flexibility associates The L Word more compellingly with other queer-influenced 'quality' or cinematic TV dramas, like Six Feet Under, rather than with the 'queer TV' phenomenon that framed its production and reception. The L Word's steering clear of queer, then, at least on the face of it, is far from coincidental, and the unspeakable represented by that 'L' in the show's title alludes not simply to the absence of lesbians within straight culture but within the 'new' queer culture too.

Notes

1. Several filmmakers like Kalin, Greyson and Haynes, were explicit about this association with AIDS activism.
2. Both Ellen and Will & Grace gestured towards the potential of the queer family but neither realised it. See, Castiglia and Reed 2003: 158–88; McCarthy 2001: 604.

Part 2 Looking

L 5   The (in)visible lesbian

Anxieties of representation in the L word

Susan J. Wolfe and Lee Ann Roripaugh

As Eve Sedgwick observes in 'The L Word: Novelty in Normalcy', Showtime's series creates a lesbian ecology – '[a] visible world in which lesbians exist, go on existing, exist in forms beyond the solitary and the couple, sustain and develop relations among themselves of difference and commonality' (2004: B10). However, Sedgwick also points out that to meet this 'obvious and modest representational need' the show must also enact a Faustian bargain because television is a genre which ultimately caters to the desires and expectations of mainstream audiences. As noted in The Advocate by Showtime President Bob Greenblatt, 'The L Word has not only proven itself to be a signature show for Showtime but also one that has captured the imagination of a large mainstream audience with its bold, sexy storylines and talented cast' (Anon 2005).

Not surprisingly, The L Word has elicited highly ambivalent and hotly debated responses among its lesbian viewers, revealing intense anxieties regarding lesbian identity and representation, as evidenced by the wildly disparate reviews published after the show's debut in early 2004. The show's detractors, for example, criticised the show as shamelessly pandering to the male, heterosexual gaze. Winnie McCroy, in her review of The L Word in New York Blade, 'L is for Invisible', stated:

If lesbians have to choose between remaining invisible to the mainstream, or being represented by Showtime's clipped and plucked lesbians, I choose invisibility. After all, real lesbians will still remain invisible, at least until our lives become more than a marketing tool or cottage industry or pud fodder for Joe Sixpack.

(2004)

Similarly, Malinda Lo, in 'It's All About the Hair: Butch Identity and Drag on *The L Word*', laments the lack of 'hair diversity' on the show:

[If] we are committed to fighting discrimination and stereotypes about women in general – not only lesbians – it is not enough to have a show full of slender, beautiful, femmy women who just happen to be lesbians. We really need to have a few butch haircuts too.

(April 2004)

Conversely, proponents of the show praised it as 'ghetto-busting' and focused on its deconstruction of 'negative' lesbian stereotypes. Stacey D'Erasmo, in her review from the *New York Times*, 'Lesbians on Television: It's Not Easy Being Seen', hailed the show as:

a breakthrough in the annals of television's fantasy life. Being an L myself, a member of a group that has had a spotty presence on the small screen, I can testify with authority to the despair of bouncing along a life of risk, mystery and heartbreak only to turn on the TV and see two women in bad pantsuits gingerly touching one another on the forearm. *The L Word* tosses those pantsuits to the wind, and good riddance to them. A mini-series of one's own is progress, undeniably.

(2004)

Along similar lines, Jacqueline Cutler noted in '*The L Word* Breaks Lesbian Ground' that, 'Indeed, clichés are avoided. There are no plaid flannel shirts or fat, hairy women in sight' (2004). And in a *LesbiaNation* article

appearing on the verge of the second season première, 'The L Word: Paragon Paradox', Shona Black, fending off criticism of the show, exhaust-
edly queried, 'Have we not reached a point where we can admit and celebrate the fact that women can be just as shallow as men, that lesbians
appreciate some eye-candy just as much as the next guy?' (2005).

While these reviews demonstrate conflicting responses to the
show, they also reveal a consistent sense of anxiety about lesbian
representation: assimilationist visibility vs. marginalised invisibility,
identitarian 'authenticity' vs. Revlon revolution 'passing', second-
wave vs. third-wave feminism, lesbianism vs. post-lesbianism, and
policing of commodified mainstream image making vs. the policing of
negative stereotypes. Interestingly, these anxieties have also surfaced
repeatedly in the past decade's scholarly discourse on lesbian identity
and representation. In her book The Lesbian Menace, for example, Sherrie
Inness (1997) critiques the phenomenon of the 'frilly lesbian' in popular
women's magazines – a representation which she argues is calculated
to reassure a heterosexual viewing audience that lesbians are, indeed,
just like them. Inness writes:

> Viewers are given a fantasy image of lesbians, which is as
> unrealistic as the image that all lesbians are ugly. Also, using
> models who look stereotypically heterosexual pretending to
> be lesbians provides titillation without threat as there is an
> implicit understanding that these are not 'real' lesbians.
>
> (65–6)

Along similar lines, in an analysis of cinematic conventions governing
lesbian representation in eighties cinema, Judith Halberstam complains
that, 'the butch character is played as a shadow of her former self'
(1998: 217), going on to state that:

> The shades of butch are still readable (Patrice Donnelly as a
> jock, Mary Stuart Masterson as a rough-and-tumble southern
> dyke), but their embodiments are definitely feminized.
> Wherever a novel has been turned into a film (Fried Green
> Tomatoes, Desert Hearts), the characters in the novels who were

coded as butch have been noticeably softened into femmey butches or soft butches.

Halberstam goes on to assert that 'the butch is a *type* of lesbian as well as a lesbian stereotype.' This erasure of the butch from 1980s lesbian cinema, Halberstam argues, seriously undermines lesbian visibility within these films – rendering lesbian erotic relationships as ambiguously submerged, or virtually indistinguishable from platonic friendship and thus invisible, as in the case of *Fried Green Tomatoes* (220–1).

Conversely, post-lesbian scholarly perspectives reveal anxieties about identity and representation that centre primarily around a perceived need to uncouple lesbian and feminist identities, as well as a desire to dismantle, usurp, and transgress against prior generations' identitarian formations of lesbian identity. (And perhaps tellingly, it is these former incarnations of lesbian-feminist identities which have been frequently caricatured and perpetuated as 'negative' stereotypes by mainstream media.) In *Not My Mother's Sister: Generational Conflict and Third-Wave Feminism*, Astrid Henry writes:

> as in straight third-wave writing, young dykes tend to portray
> the previous generation of feminists as frumpy and unsexy.
> The word 'frumpy', like 'dowdy', suggests a look that is not
> only unsexy but out of fashion. Fashion plays a central role
> in staging this generational divide, both in terms of literal
> fashion – that is, style of dress – and in terms of the desire to
> be 'in fashion' in a larger sense.
>
> (2004: 124)

Charlotte Ashton notes the same trends in 'Getting Hold of the Phallus: "Post-Lesbian" Power Negotiations', stating that, 'With big hair, short skirts, lipstick and lycra, post-lesbians are holding up a mirror to the mainstream and reclaiming the components of "passing" as totems of transgression. Or, put another way, as overheard at a chic London dyke club: "This is the Revlon revolution, Sister!"' (1996: 163). Going on to argue that the Revlon revolution comes at a cost, however, Ashton claims that:

> The reason for post-lesbianism's current popularity with the
> mainstream media lies in the fact that it doesn't *look* or *act*
> any differently from other forms of accepted femininity. For
> as long as men can look at post-lesbians and see sexy women
> they want to fuck, and who indeed might even fuck them
> back, they will not consider that they have been forced to
> concede any ground.
>
> (172)

Rather than resisting commodification as a form of exploitation and
invisibility, though, post-lesbianism embraces its subversive potential.
In 'Lesbian Bodies in the Age of (Post)mechanical Reproduction', Cathy
Griggers writes that we are:

> bearing witness to the military becoming lesbian, the mother
> becoming lesbian, straight women becoming lesbian, fashion
> and Hollywood and the sex industry becoming lesbian,
> middle-class women, corporate America, and technoculture
> becoming lesbian, and so on. That is, the lesbian body of
> signs, like all minority bodies, is always becoming majority,
> in a multiplicity of ways. But at the same time, in a multitude
> of domains across the general cultural field, majority bodies
> are busy *becoming lesbian*.
>
> (1993: 184)

Clearly, *The L Word* emerges as a site of contestation for precisely
these types of anxieties regarding lesbian identity and representation.
Perhaps more interestingly, however, it could be argued that the
show itself *enacts and critiques* these anxieties of representation during
moments when the show turns the lens in on itself through the use of
meta-narrative, or the insertion of what Candace Moore (2005) refers
to in an *AfterEllen.com* piece as a *meta-eye*. These moments of meta-
narrative serve to complicate and implicate acts of representation,
acts of performance, and acts of consuming/viewing, thereby creating
a self-reflexive commentary on the anxieties of lesbian identity and
representation that is, ultimately, quite nuanced and rich.

From the outset, viewing and voyeurism play a significant role throughout the first two seasons of The L Word and, indeed, the show seemingly attempts to distinguish between negative vs. positive modes of representation and viewing through periodically framing the episodes with opening credit vignettes with distant narrative connections to the episodes themselves. These opening credit vignettes often depict abject circumstances, such as the exploitation of young women via lesbian pornography, lesbian self-denial and self-hatred, and homophobic discrimination or violence, among others. On occasion, the vignettes also seem to function as overtly constructed and explicitly fictionalised representations of lesbian identity, including scenes from movies, dreams/fantasies or fiction.

The enclosure of the episodes within these framing vignettes does several interesting things: on the one hand, the framing vignettes create the illusion of a lesbian third space. Within the protective folds of these framing vignettes, the episodes themselves – particularly in juxtaposition to the overt (and frequently negative) constructedness of the vignettes – are privileged as positive and 'authentic' lesbian representations. Furthermore, the vignettes immediately place the audience member in a voyeuristic relationship to the episodes via the implication that they are being allowed a titillating glimpse into a fictional 'inner sanctum,' so to speak.

By the same token, the very constructedness of the opening vignettes cannot help but signal the presence of meta-narrative devices within the show – serving as a constant reminder that what the viewer sees might *seem* like the 'real deal' but is, in fact, a deliberately constructed fiction as well. This perspective prevents the potentially salacious voyeur from becoming too comfortable about peering into this fictional 'inner sanctum'. Viewers who hope to lapse into a complacent and pleasurable voyeurism will instead find themselves repeatedly bumping up against the boundary of the television screen and reminded that what they are viewing is a representation which serves as a sort of screen or shield to the real. In this sense, the screen almost serves as a symbolic fencing device, separating viewers from characters in much the same way that voyeurs are separated from the fictional lesbians they attempt to spy upon, forced to view them through windows and lenses. The use of the opening vignettes, like the examination of the role of the voyeurs in the episodes, establishes from the outset that the act of viewing is a complex activity that is never innocent, passive, or neutral.

Meta-narrative, or the introduction of the *meta-eye*, is even more explicitly introduced in the pilot episode of *The L Word*, when the character of Jenny Schecter – at this stage a heterosexual, engaged woman – glimpses two women having sex in her next-door neighbour's pool. Fascinated, Jenny crouches down in order to remain unobserved herself, and then spies on the women through the slats of her fence. The audience is thus immediately implicated in a voyeuristic observation of lesbian sex, rendering the act of viewing as both titillating and inappropriately transgressive. Furthermore, the camera not only cinematographically forces the viewer to spy on the lovers through Jenny's point of view, but to also spy on Jenny spying on the lesbian lovers. What is particularly fascinating about this scene is that the fence through which Jenny spies does, in fact, form a visual fencing device, and what she, as an outsider, sees through the slats of the fence (along with the viewer, through Jenny's point of view) is only a partial, obscured, and incomplete image.

Similarly, the scene eventually evolves into one of *mistaken identity* when Jenny later describes the women in the pool to her fiancé, Tim Haspel, and asks if his next-door neighbours are gay. Assuming that Jenny is referring to long-term partners Bette Porter and Tina Kennard, Tim, at first incredulous, is then turned on by the idea, and encourages Jenny to continue her narration. He seems particularly aroused by Jenny's interest in what she describes as the blonde woman's 'really beautiful breasts'. The women in the pool that Jenny describes, however, are not Bette and Tina (as Jenny and Tim imagine), but rather Bette and Tina's friend, Shane McCutcheon, enjoying an afternoon fling in Bette and Tina's pool with an anonymous woman. In this sense, lesbian identity is foregrounded as slippery and difficult to pin down or essentialise, and what the viewers think they have seen may not in fact be what they've actually seen.

Furthermore, this act of viewing has profoundly disturbing and unexpected effects on both Jenny and Tim. For Jenny, what she has witnessed functions as a lesbian primal scene of sorts – opening the door to latent desires which first initiate a full-blown homosexual panic but later culminate in her affair with Marina Ferrer. Tim, on the other hand, learns that he gravely mistakes his own (imagined) sexual desires when he casually appropriates Jenny's interest in the lesbians to fuel his own fantasy fodder. Later in the season, when Tim accidentally walks in on Jenny having sex with Marina ('Lies, Lies, Lies', 1:4), he (predictably) doesn't find the scene remotely sexy, but rather feels upset, betrayed, excluded and emasculated. Thus, as viewers, we witness fantasy and reality colliding in ways that do not necessarily mesh with one another, while simultaneously being reminded that what we are witnessing on the small screen is also a representation, or form of fantasy.

Another rich instance of meta-narrative which similarly questions lesbian identity and representation occurs during a strip club outing when the friends arrange to take the pregnant and grieving Tina out for a lap dance in order to distract her from her painful break-up with Bette ('Lap Dance', 2:3). Upon their arrival at the strip club Tina, who is dubious about the evening's agenda, says that she thinks it's hideous, but Alice Pieszecki gives her a little pep talk. 'Well, they're all different, you know,' Alice says. 'Some have real boobies. You just keep looking. You'll find something you like.' Her comment seems to adumbrate two key strands of representation which are explored in this particular meta-narrative. On the one hand, the visual juxtaposition of the strippers on stage with the cast members is immediately striking. Once again, the artificial constructedness of the dancers – their bodies, costumes and rhetorical gestures of seduction – is acutely highlighted in contrast to the bodies, costumes and casual posturing of the show's cast members in such a way as to privilege the show's characters as 'natural', positive and authentic representations of lesbian identity. Furthermore, the entry of the characters into the male-dominated space of the strip club – with all of the concomitant rights and entitlements symbolically contained therein (i.e. symbolic power of the gaze, symbolic power of choice and symbolic control of capital) – seems to playfully enact a post-lesbian appropriation of the phallus. Playfulness is key here, as if there's no need to take the phallus too seriously, and while the characters enjoy the show and distribute tips to the dancers, they nonetheless continue to talk and carry on among themselves. In other words, their narratives are foregrounded and continue to unfold against the backdrop of the dancers. This is in stark contrast to the male clientele of the club, who all appear to be grimly riveted to their seats and tractor-beamed onto the stage – held in thrall to the dancers and rendered semi-paralytic by their own gazing. The presence of these submissively cow-like male viewers at the strip club once again seems to unflatteringly implicate an 'outsider' or purely voyeuristic gaze – brushing it off as both laughably reductive and impotent.

At the same time, anxieties of lesbian representation do not go uninterrogated here. Before they go out to the strip club, for example, the women have dinner at a Chinese restaurant, where Tina foregrounds salient issues about representation, lesbian visual pleasure, political correctness, and power when she states, 'I don't think women, especially lesbians, should exploit other women.' Shane likewise interrogates assumptions regarding agency and sexual abjection when she counters, 'Well, the strippers I know do it because they love it.' Also as before, the highly constructed performances of the fictional dancers on stage inevitably serve as a reminder that the characters we are viewing on the screen are likewise actresses who are similarly performing roles for an audience. In another interesting layer of meta-narrative, when Tina is finally cajoled into accepting a lap dance, her friends immediately observe that the woman she has chosen resembles Bette. Tina's wistful expression during the seductive lap dance seems to suggest she is pretending or imagining that the dancer is, in fact, Bette. Later on at home, Tina attempts to masturbate, but the imaginary representation fails her and she ends up weeping instead. Like Tina, we learn that the dancer is an inadequate substitute for Bette, who is more than just her body. Viewing has stimulated a desire which cannot be satisfied by a visual fantasy, and once again, the failure of a representation to stand in for the real is thematically underscored.

Perhaps the most overt instance of meta-narrative, however, occurs in the second-season storyline involving the character of Mark Wayland – a would-be amateur film-maker who, after becoming Shane and Jenny's roommate, embarks upon a film project titled *A Compendium of Lesbianism*. This project involves videotaped interviews with Jenny, Shane, and their friends, as well as tape taken from 'strategically and respectfully placed' hidden cameras planted throughout the house without their knowledge. On the one hand, Mark's intrusive presence in the house as a narrative embodiment of the male gaze can be read, in part, as a response to first-season criticism that the show pandered too much to the imagined needs of this gaze. The hidden cameras seem to serve as a reminder that perhaps the viewer and not the 'panderer' bear responsibility for the acts of gazing. Interestingly, though, while the non-consensual nature of Mark's film is characterised as violating, his obsessive viewing and interaction with the women nonetheless has a transformative effect, in that his film starts to become less prurient and more 'anthropological'. Early in the storyline ('Lynch Pin', 2:4), Mark explains his desire to pin down lesbian authenticity in his documentary – a discussion that perhaps explores criticisms of inauthenticity raised by viewers during the first season of The L Word. He says he can't quite figure out the 'lesbian thing' but, with access to 'real' lesbians, he's determined to 'put his finger on it anyway'. Here, Mark's ludicrous assertion seems to foreground the impossibility of representing a non-existent, essentialised lesbian identity. When he questions Jenny's long hair and remarks that she doesn't exude that 'thing', Jenny – in a gesture that also seems to be a calculated response to first-season critics – gets a short haircut.

In episode nine ('Late, Later, Latent'), Mark emerges as misguidedly earnest when he pitches his film to his repulsive sidekick Gomey (Sam Easton) and their sleazy financial backer. A Compendium of Lesbianism, Mark enthusiastically gushes, is replete with insights into lesbian life: 'The women talk all the time, it's not all just about sex it's about a way of life, they have a culture of their own, it's revelatory, it's anthropological.' In response to Mark's description of his film's aims (aims which would seem to echo the representational aims of The L Word itself), the financial backer becomes incensed, screaming, 'Red-blooded men don't give a fuck about this anthropological bullshit.' Rather, 'They want hot lesbian sex and they want it now.' Gomey suggests that Mark is turning into a homosexual and indeed, by this point, Mark has a decidedly queer crush on Shane – a crush that reverses the stereotypical fetishising of hyper-feminine lesbians in favour of a model that seems to have overtones of male homoerotic desire and therefore speaks to the potential of trans-semiotic queering.

While Mark emerges as a not entirely unsympathetic character, his intrusive and non-consensual viewing has serious consequences for which he is ultimately held accountable. Given that network executives insisted on writing in a straight male character for straight male audience members to relate to, it is probably no coincidence that the scripts render this character, a creative intrusion, as a vehicle by which to examine and critique the theme of male intrusion. In particular, in 'Land Ahoy' (2:10), when Jenny discovers that Mark has been taping the house without permission, she confiscates his video camera and lures Mark to her room. Having scrawled 'Is This What U Want' in black magic marker on her naked body in a disturbing sexual parody, Jenny then turns the tables on Mark and issues one of the show's strongest feminist speeches. Training his video camera on him, she demands that he ask his younger sisters about the very first time they were intruded on by a man or a boy. Asked by Mark why she assumes his sisters have been intruded upon, Jenny replies, 'Because there isn't a single girl or woman in this world that hasn't been intruded upon, and sometimes it's relatively benign, and sometimes it's so fucking painful. But you have no idea what this feels like.' Later on, when Mark tries to make amends to Jenny, insisting that she and Shane have made him a better man, Jenny takes a radical feminist view, arguing that women, and by extension the show itself, are not responsible for educating men: 'It's not a fucking woman's job to be consumed and invaded and spat out so that some fucking man can evolve' ('Loud and Proud', 2:11). Furthermore, Mark then dramatically removes his clothes to demonstrate his vulnerability, asking Jenny if that's what *she* wants. Jenny's explanation points out that making any female body available to the male gaze poses a danger which he, as a man, has never experienced. At the same time, on the level of meta-narrative, the statement also reflects the inherent difficulty of representing lesbians (or any women) on the screen because female characters are always open to exploitative readings:

> What I want is for you to write 'Fuck Me' on your chest. Write
> it. Do it. And then I want you to walk out that door and I want
> you to walk down the street. And anybody that wants to fuck

you, say, 'Sure, sure, no problem.' And when they do, you
have to say, 'Thank you very, very much.' And make sure that
you have a smile on your face. And then, you stupid fucking
coward, you're gonna know what it feels like to be a woman.

Given the relative lack of viable lesbian protagonists in mainstream
media, *The L Word* has good reason to be anxious over its portrayal
of lesbians; as the first show of its kind, the show bears inordinate
responsibilities and impossible representational burdens, particularly
when it must perform competitively to ensure its continued existence.
As Stacey D'Erasmo ruefully confesses in 'Lesbians on Television: It's
Not Easy Being Seen':

> A peculiar consequence of so rarely seeing your kind on
> television, in movies, in plays, what have you, is that you
> can become, almost unwittingly, attached to a certain kind
> of wildness: the wildness of feeling not only unrepresented
> but somehow unrepresentable in ordinary terms. You get so
> good at ranging around unseen (and finding less obvious
> characters to identify with, from Tony Soprano to Seven of
> Nine) that it can feel a little limiting to be decanted into a
> group of perfectly nice women leading pleasant, more or less
> realistic lives. You can think, ungratefully: Is that all there is?
>
> (2004)

Perhaps inasmuch as certain burdens of representation are impossible
to meet within the scope of a single television show, arguments about
whether or not *The L Word* attains any sort of representative 'normalcy'
with regard to lesbian identity are moot. However, through the moments
of self-reflexive meta-narrative under discussion here and present in
numerous other examples, *The L Word* ultimately makes a sophisticated
attempt to acknowledge, speak to, and address these anxieties of
representation in ways that are ultimately both savvy and subversive.

L 6   How does a lesbian look?

Stendhal's syndrome and the L word

Dana Heller

Since its US première on 18 January 2004, The L Word has mindfully explored the complexities of lesbian visibility and vision, the risks and pleasures of seeing lesbians in the world and of seeing the world as lesbians see it. The latter perspective, I would argue, is the Showtime series' unique contribution to television history although, at this early stage in the show's evolution (the second season having concluded in the USA at the time of writing), such an accolade may be somewhat overhasty. However, it is certainly not premature to say that the creators, writers, and cast of the series understand the high-stakes game of representation and visualisation that this lesbian-themed drama invites cable subscribers to play. In an interview on the radio talk show, Fresh Air (2004), Jennifer Beals points out that the show's function is 'to represent people who don't often see themselves represented, and certainly not represented in a multiplicity'. Writing in the New York Times, Stacey D'Erasmo, a self-acknowledged 'L', describes the consequences of being one of the people to whom Beals refers, someone who lives in 'a representational desert'. In D'Erasmo's words, 'a tremendous urgency develops, a ferocious desire not only to be seen in some literal sense… but to be seen with all the blood and angst and magic you possess' (2004).

Indeed, reviewers and critics have paid considerable attention to the question of how effectively the series responds to the 'ferocious' representational desires of lesbians and non-lesbians alike. While many have praised *The L Word*'s long-overdue representation of a community of mostly gay women that is racially mixed, ethnically diverse, sexually switch-hitting, and ambiguously gendered (as in the case of the characters Lisa [Devon Gummersall], a self-avowed male lesbian and Ivan [Kelly Lynch], a drag king), others have criticised the series for pandering to the soft-porn voyeuristic fantasies of straight men (McCroy 2003; Sedgwick 2004: B10–B11). And more than a few have remarked on the characters' unrealistic glamour, their excessively luxurious lifestyles, and their impossibly svelte figures, prompting comparisons to another all-female fantasy television ensemble, the heterosexual women of *Sex and the City*. In short, consensus seems to have taken shape that while *The L Word* has much to offer audiences in terms of narrative pleasure and responsible cultural diversity, the series is otherwise entirely consistent with the television industry's emphasis on conventional femininity and its portrayal of women as non-threatening (read non-butch) objects to be visually enjoyed by some imagined mainstream (read non-queer) cable audience.

The problem with this line of criticism is that it tells us more about television critics' enduring suspicion of mass culture's oppressive objectification of women and dishonouring of genuinely lesbian desires than it does about the far more subtle and intriguing developments of character and plot that fashion *The L Word*'s *musée imaginaire* of stylish West Hollywood dykes. Undeniably, most episodes provide plenty of eye-candy, or ample opportunity for the contemplation of lesbian bodies as works of art. But even sweeter, one might say, are the transformative moments of sublime looking and ecstatic contemplation that produce shock and disorientation, a temporary state of madness comparable to the condition known as Stendhal's Syndrome.

But how does this comparison make sense within the mise en scène of *The L Word*? A direct answer to this question is issued early in the first season when Bette Porter, a central character of the series, unexpectedly finds herself face to face with a photographic work of art, behind which stands an infamous history of relentless, worshipful seeing and re-

seeing ('Longing,' 1:3). The photograph, by Carla Marie Freed, depicts
a nude woman – the artist's lover and perennial subject of twelve years
– positioned at centre, her body commanding the length and breadth
of the photographic frame, her eyes fixed forward. Off to the side
a ghostly silhouette of the artist is barely visible, frozen in the act of
looking at her subject. The ambitious director of a small California
art museum, Bette is a level-headed administrator of the arts, and yet
this near life-sized photograph – its direct, visceral intensity – catches
her off guard. Bette is emotionally unravelled before the image. Struck
speechless, her eyes welling with tears, she dissolves into a rapture of
intimate recognition and sorrow. And in this moment, as television
viewers observe Bette observing the image of a woman observed by an
artist who frames herself within the passion of a lesbian subject-object
predicament, they may feel that they have jumped through the looking
glass, Alice-like, into a wondrous space where distinctions between
observer and observed tend to collapse in the process of truthfully
training one's eyes.

But the story does not end here. Later in the episode the narrative
cuts back to Bette as she regains her composure after beholding the
photograph. The scene unfolds in the hotel suite of Mrs Peggy Peabody
(Holland Taylor), the wealthy and eccentric art connoisseur who just
purchased the Freed photograph for her private collection and unveils
it to Bette after learning that she, too, is an admirer of the artist.
Earlier, Bette had proven her spunk to Peabody by presenting herself,
unannounced, at the art patron's hotel suite with hopes of procuring
a major exhibition of her collection for the California Arts Center. The
two women engage in animated conversation, during which Peggy
unhesitatingly admits that she was a lesbian once, in 1974, a fact that
Bette admits would qualify her as a 'hasbian'. Peggy finds this hilarious,
and after Bette's emotional meltdown over the Freed photo she seems
sincerely moved. 'You can't imagine how jealous I am of you right now,'
she confides in Bette. 'You – you know Stendhal?' 'The French art critic,'
Bette readily acknowledges. 'He went to Florence,' Peggy continues.
'He saw the Caravaggio.' Bette, recognising the story, chimes in and
completes it. 'And then he burst into tears, and then he fainted. The
work of art was so beautiful and moving, he couldn't withstand the

impact. The Stendhal Syndrome.' Here, Peggy begins reciting from
Stendhal's diary – from memory, I might add:

> My head thrown back, I let my gaze dwell on the ceiling.
> I underwent the profoundest experience of ecstasy I had
> ever encountered. I had obtained that supreme degree of
> sensibility where the divine intimations of art merge with the
> impassioned sensuality of emotion.
>
> ('Longing', 1:3)

Not bad for a hasbian. But in any case, this scene has haunted my
viewing of the series. I was reminded of it time and again throughout
the first and second seasons as the meaning of Stendhal's Syndrome
continued to reverberate, a resonant metaphor for one of The L Word's
central motifs: the emotional, physical, and spiritual state of panic and
delirium that results from honestly opening ourselves – and our eyes
– to the richness of human sexuality in general, and to the humanity of
lesbians in particular.

Such shocking and deliriously Stendhalian moments define the
peculiar 'L' world conjured by The L Word. Or so it would seem, judging
from the recurrence of provocative point-of-view shots and voyeuristic
subplots, all typically signalling revelation and transformation, which
mark the series. For example, take the pilot episode, in which viewers
are introduced to Jenny Schecter. Jenny, an aspiring fiction writer from
the Midwest, is relocating to Los Angeles to join her boyfriend, Tim
Haspel. After meeting her at the airport and delivering her to their West
Hollywood bungalow ('It's very traditional,' Jenny naively remarks), Tim
returns to work as coach of a university women's swimming team while
Jenny begins setting up her writing studio in the newly renovated garage.
She hears some commotion outside and steps into the backyard. From
behind the slats of a fence – a white picket fence, no less – she sees the
notorious heartthrob Shane McCutcheon and her companion strip off
their clothes and dive into a neighbour's swimming pool. The women
begin to engage in sexual play as Jenny, instantly mesmerised by the
scene, hunkers down to conceal herself from view. When Tim arrives
home, Jenny's detailed account of the girl-on-girl action she witnessed

becomes grist for their sex. However, the more twisted significance of
Jenny's field observations (and the irony of her description of the home
she and Tim share as 'traditional') begins to unfold precisely from
this point, as Jenny finds herself irresistibly drawn to the enigmatic,
statuesque Marina Ferrer and an unwitting player in a Sapphic drama
that she had initially eyeballed from a 'safe' distance.

But this is not to say that *The L Word* stoops to cheap voyeurism.
To understand why this is not the case, consider more closely Bette
Porter. One of the first season's dominant subplots focuses on Bette's
professional struggles as an openly gay museum director who seeks
to challenge the way that her board of directors and patrons perceive
the representation of human form. After her meeting with Peggy
Peabody, Bette manages to expropriate the show, *Provocations*, from a
larger museum and convince the CAC's sceptical board of directors
that it will put their museum on the map. However, true to its name,
Provocations contains works of a graphic sexual and sadomasochistic
nature. The exhibition sparks protest from the religious right and
social conservatives who deride the 'art' as filth and accuse Bette of
peddling pornography. At work and at home, where Bette's partner of
seven years, Tina Kennard, suffers through a failed pregnancy, Bette
becomes the target of hate and harassment. Yet through it all she
tirelessly defends the First Amendment and champions the function
of art in a free society to make available diverse, albeit sometimes
disturbing, imagery. Bette's efforts climax during a televised debate
on the commentary program *Insight*, in which she takes on the right-
wing pundit, Fae Buckley (who, in a salutary nod to lesbian film history,
is played by Helen Shaver, the star of the 1985 film *Desert Hearts*). As
Buckley rails against the exhibition's blasphemous content, Bette
counters. 'It's relevant because we have to have other perspectives. Not
everyone is of the Christian faith; not everyone believes in Heaven or
Hell. Art reflects that. It's a ... mirror of the world we live in' ('Liberally',
1:10). Here, Bette's promotion of art as a 'mirror' of a diverse world,
inclusive of multiple viewpoints, speaks to the principle aim of the
series: to provoke larger points of view, or more nuanced, focused ways
of seeing lesbians.

On the opposite side of the issue, Fae Buckley unabashedly associates the pornographic nature of *Provocations* with Bette's lesbianism. In this way, the debate scene indirectly references the battles waged in the early 1990s by the National Endowment for the Arts against the Helms Commission's charge that it had financed obscenity by funding artists such as Robert Mapplethorpe, Holly Hughes and Karen Finley. However, in the series' trenchant twist on the culture wars, Bette learns of the nasty skeleton that Fae Buckley's political zealotry closets. With the help of local activists, Tina unearths an obscure child-porn video, 'Here Cums the Principal'. The video stars Buckley's runaway teenage daughter, China (Michaela Mann), whose police records reveal that she had been sexually abused by her father in a recurrent pattern that Fae Buckley apparently could not or would not stop. This windfall discovery places the opening sequence of the episode in context: a porn shoot in a San Fernando Valley high school bathroom that, according to the screen caption, took place one year earlier ('Liberally'). Two teenage girls in school uniforms put on make-up before a mirror. The camera pulls back to reveal a film crew and equipment. The director calls for 'the pussy light' and then commands the girls to begin making out in a scene that involves the sudden intrusion of the principal, a blowjob, and a 'facial' cum shot to which China is told to respond with the words, 'That was great.' The cold, mechanised behaviours of the cast and crew and the use of industry jargon suggest that the opening sequence is presented as a disturbingly realistic portrait of sexual exploitation and dehumanisation, one made even more jarring because of viewers' inability to place it in a narrative context until the revelation of the video.

Moreover, the discovery of the porn video introduces an ethical dilemma into the plot, one that speaks to Bette's character as well as to the series' fraught relation to the cultural politics of visibility. Although the board of the CAC grants her permission to use the video against Buckley, Bette's ethical instinct is to avoid the exploitation of personal misfortune for political gain. Oscar (Zak Santiago), a Latino social activist, urges her to reconsider: '[Our] people don't know how to play this game ... We take the high road, we wind up in the ditch ... We have to get into their closets. We cannot afford to keep on being so high-minded. Because we're getting killed.' Thus persuaded, Bette brings the video to the debate but refrains from using it until she sees that Fae Buckley is intent on destroying her before the public. 'I understand why Miss Buckley is so sickened by the porn industry ... I mean, it's brutal, especially for the poor children ... There is a world of difference between complex, provocative art and the tragedy of the porn industry.' But before she can introduce the damning piece of evidence, Buckley spots the video and automatically apprehends Bette's tactical manoeuvre. Over a series of jump cuts that alternate between the televised debate and China, whom we see again in her porn role and prostituting herself on the streets of LA, Fae Buckley launches into a vicious religious counter assault, one that ends with her proclamation that Tina's miscarried pregnancy was God's revenge for their sinful, homosexual lifestyle. Bette, shocked and visibly defeated, dissolves into tears.

An interesting device of this episode is its representation of screens within screens, or its juxtaposition of media texts (the pornographic film and the television debate on the limits of pornography and art) within the main screen of *The L Word*. Again, 'Stendhal's Syndrome' aptly describes the state of disorientation that these competing spectacles induce, as their correspondence troubles the conventional boundaries of private and public, personal and political, pornography and religion, and exploiter and victim. In this way, China's manufactured lesbian performance before the film camera parallels her mother's manufactured missionary performance before the television cameras, the implied question being which one is more obscene. Bette's one-word response to Fae Buckley answers this question. 'Monster,' she cries when Fae, realising that she went too far, tries to put her arms around Bette in an almost maternal gesture of consolation. Bette's physical repulsion renders that gesture perverse; her denunciation accords Fae a place beyond the limits of respectable representation.

In this way, the *Insight* debate is staged as a commentary on the ubiquitous glut and blurt of screens that arrest our attentions and determine what may or may not fall within our sights. Such visual engagements frame social identities and fix concepts of 'normal' sexuality, morality and aesthetics within ideological narratives that grant little space for the imaginative revision of the world. Bette's effort to compel alternative ways of viewing *Provocations* is foiled by Fae's pre-emptive labelling of her as an unsightly object – a damned pornographer. Oscar's cynicism appears justified, as Bette's hesitancy in exposing Fae's hypocrisy results in her own erasure. Bette's faith in the visionary dimensions of visualisation – what Ludwig Wittgenstein called 'seeing by seeing' (1967: 77) – turns out to be no match for Fae's faith-based politics of personal annihilation.

Race also plays a part in Bette's broad vision of the world and informs her attempts to instil it in others. She is racially mixed, half African-American and half white. During the first season, Bette's character develops in ways markedly relevant to the shaping of racial identities in the USA, not simply in terms of how racial categories are assigned, but in terms of how race contributes to the myriad ways that lesbians see themselves in relation to the communities with which they identify. These identifications may be multiple, organised around context-specific bonds that privilege one vector of social identity – be it race, sexuality, gender, or class – over another. Bette sees herself as someone capable of living comfortably with these contradictions, yet in several episodes her confident self-image is unmoored. Fae Buckley achieves this in the television studio, moments before the debate, when she obliquely remarks on Bette's 'in-between' skin tone and how hard it will be for the make-up people to 'find' her colour. In the pilot episode, Tina is miffed when Bette engages an African-American sperm donor without first consulting her, a response that Bette interprets as a rejection of her racial identity. And in a later first-season episode, Yolanda (Kim Hawthorne), an African-American woman in Bette and Tina's group therapy, accuses Bette of suppressing her race and posing as white to the group. Bette is vindicated when she learns that Yolanda has been suppressing her sexuality and posing as heterosexual to the group ('Listen Up', 1:8). In these instances, Bette struggles against interpretations of her identity imposed from the outside and insists on being understood, in her own terms, with all her 'blood and angst and magic'.

Bette's professional battle in many ways mirrors the personal battle waged by Jenny, who gradually comes to share *The L Word*'s moral centre as she discovers and struggles with her sexual attraction to women. As figures initially positioned at opposite ends of the lesbian visibility spectrum, Bette and Jenny's development invites comparison within the series. The correspondence is further encouraged as Jenny's encounter with Stendhal's Syndrome is narrated alongside Bette's. Both characters become subject to overwhelming passions unleashed by an overdose of seeing. For Jenny, this begins with a phone message from Tim – now her fiancé. He invites her to join him for a beer at the local café, the Planet, which is managed by Marina, Jenny's secret lover. Their affair has already been discerned by several of the Planet's regular patrons, and Jenny, fearing that the gossip will overtake Tim, makes a beeline for the Planet. Arriving, she enters upon a scene that arrests her in her tracks: Tim and Marina are at the pool table, laughing, their arms draped platonically around one another. The sight of them together sends Jenny into a confused delirium. Her vision begins to blur as her eyes move from Tim to Marina's face. We see them across the room from Jenny's point of view, calling out her name with puzzled expressions. Overwhelmed, Jenny collapses into a dead faint on the floor.

At home later that night, Jenny claims that she is suffering from low blood sugar and angrily derides Tim for flirting with Marina. Viewers, however, are privy to the fact that Jenny's swoon is the fundamental physiological response to the stress produced by the blurring of sexual identity categories, the crack in her illusions of clarity, the collision of contradictory visual-emotional sensations, the shock of seeing by seeing. In the episode's closing moments, as Bette and Peggy (back at the hotel suite) recall Stendhal's experiences in Italy, Peggy's recitation from his diaries provides a voiceover to cut scenes of Jenny leaving her house and determinedly walking toward the Planet. The café is closed and dark, it is late. Jenny enters and finds Marina sitting alone in her office. After pleading with her to keep their intimacy disguised from Tim she admits, in a disconsolate whisper, 'Every time I look at you, I feel so completely dismantled' ('Longing', 1:3).

Dismantle: 'to take to pieces; also: to strip of dress or covering' (Merriam-Webster). This, I would argue, is a word well chosen, one intended to remind us not only of passion's power to unglue us but its power to reveal us to ourselves, to show us what we look like from the inside. Indeed, *The L Word* persistently dismantles the conventional social dynamics of looking in ways that challenge typical assumptions about pleasure, politics, and power. For example, toward the conclusion of the first season we see Tim dismantled when he returns home unexpectedly to retrieve his stopwatch, only to catch Jenny and Marina in the act of oral sex ('Lawfully,' 1:5). As Tim approaches Jenny's studio, he sees them framed through a glass window and stands paralysed before the scene, his expression changing from one of puzzlement to shock to outrage. From Tim's point of view, we see the two women clad in flimsy black lingerie. Marina is going down on Jenny whose legs are splayed, her head thrown back in an expression of ecstasy as she cries, 'Oh, fuck... oh... oh yeah... wait, right there...' Tim is unable to wrest his eyes from the women. Looking up, Jenny sees him and quickly covers herself as Marina hurriedly collects her clothes. Tim picks up the manuscript that Jenny and Marina had been discussing, a short story written by Jenny and entitled, 'The Demons that Haunt Me'. He throws it at her and leaves.

Interestingly, although this critical moment of voyeuristic invasion mimes the conventions of industrial pornography (anticipating the video production scene in the 'Liberally' episode, and looking forward to the second season's major subplot involving hidden video cameras in Shane and Jenny's apartment), the narrative turns the presumed dynamic of male pornographic spectatorship on its head. Rather then directing the full force of his anger and humiliation on Jenny, Tim accepts her apology and agrees to marry her post haste. Rather than becoming aroused by the girl-on-girl primal scene that he has witnessed, Tim fails to get an erection and cannot make love to Jenny on their honeymoon night. He abandons her in the hotel before she wakes, realising that he can no longer be with her. Speeding off in his car he is pulled over by a police officer (Phil Hayes) whom we recall from the episode's opening sequence, a scene set in a West Hollywood diner in 1976. Here, the same officer, Sammy, hungrily solicits a blowjob in the diner's bathroom and then arrests the 'fucking faggot' who unwittingly performs the act. Twenty-eight years later, after listening to Tim's account of Jenny's infidelity, Sammy offers Tim some sage avuncular wisdom:

You know, we spend our whole lives watchin' porn. We never
see the warning. There it is. You know that scene, where, uh,
two women are getting it on? Guy comes in, he's all hard,
y'know, he's gonna give it to 'em, he's gonna *fuck* 'em good.
We think that's what those chicks want ... That's not what
they want ... That's why this country's homosexuals are so
dangerous.

('Lawfully')

Emboldened, Tim confronts Marina in the following episode ('Losing
It', 1:6). 'What is it you do? You girls?' he asks. 'Should I even care? Does
it even count?' Marina responds dispassionately: 'Well, you were there.
You saw how much it counts.' Here then is the point: seeing Jenny's
pleasure compels Tim to consider not what his eyes caught, but the
knowledge that has unexpectedly caught and changed him. In the end,
both Sammy and Marina direct Tim's attention to the critical difference
between watching and *seeing*.

The question of how lesbian bodies count, and for whom they
count, is extended and painstakingly explored in the second season's
narrative that introduces Mark Wayland, a straight male and aspiring
documentary film-maker. He moves in with Jenny and Shane, who
have become housemates after Jenny's break-up with Tim. When the
women come up short on rent, they place an ad for a third housemate
and begin screening candidates. In the course of interviewing, Mark
arrives at the door with a video camera perched on his shoulder
('Lynchpin', 2:4). Handsome and glib, he proceeds to film the
interview, explaining apologetically that he's 'chronicling'. Jenny and
Shane are mildly irritated, as shown in video format through Mark's
viewfinder. They pointedly ask him what sort of living arrangement
he's looking for. Here, Mark hands the camera to Shane and asks her
to film his response. Reluctant at first, Shane gradually obliges as
Mark admits that his ambitions to make a truly moving documentary
have taken a back seat to his current occupation, producing direct-to-
video films with titles such as, 'Wild-Ass Catholic School Girls'. Jenny
and Shane are incredulous, but despite his intrusive entrance and
dubious employment, Mark manages to win the women over with his

earnestness and his ability to produce enough cash to cover six months rent up front.

What Shane and Jenny do not know is that Mark sees them less as fellow artists than as objects of erotic and aesthetic fascination. When a group of friends assemble next door to skinny dip in Bette and Tina's pool, Mark calls Jenny aside and asks if she, too, is gay. He puzzles over what it is that makes lesbians recognisable – visible – as lesbians, what unique quality they exude. 'I don't know,' he muses. 'I'd say it has something to do with their attitude. It's not that they're masculine, or anything, 'cause actually some of them are pretty feminine. You know? It's … they have these … haircuts.' Jenny grows discernibly impatient with him, as Mark adds, 'I'm gonna try and put my finger on it.'

'Good. Tell me when you do, Mark,' Jenny says, as sounds of raucous laughter and splashing water issue from next door. When Mark glances over toward the pool, Jenny hits him in the arm and scolds him, 'Don't look … that's naughty.' As she walks away, Mark appears visibly conflicted between his desire to look and his recognition that his gaze is somehow unwelcome and invasive. However, upon considering that his new housing situation promises a wealth of educational information about the unseen lives of lesbians, and after failing to solicit their full cooperation in a video project documenting their adventures as housemates, Mark installs hidden cameras throughout the house – including the bedrooms – and determines to make a *cinéma-vérité* documentary that will make lesbians wholly visible and reveal the truth about what makes them lesbian.

Throughout the second season of *The L Word*, Mark secretly films and studies the daily comings and goings of the mostly lesbian household in an intense effort to unlock their mysteries and get inside their sexuality, which he initially assumes is the essence of their being. But late one night in his studio, as he sits before his monitor watching Shane engaged in detached, emotionless sex with a woman she barely knows, Mark is visibly moved by the pathos and complexity of Shane's character ('Labyrinth', 2:5). His violation continues and is ultimately revealed near the season's conclusion, when Jenny inadvertently happens upon Mark's video equipment and tapes of Shane confessing her love to Carmen de la Pica Morales, the woman Jenny has been dating ('Late, Later, Latest', 2:9). However, regular viewers know that Mark's project was in jeopardy long before this revelation, a result of his increasingly conflicted and compassionate attachment to his subjects, in addition to his weakening ability to rationalise for 'art's sake' the daily exploitation of Shane's all too human longings, intimacies and foibles. Showtime's official website for The L Word neatly summarises the trajectory of Mark's development in terms that suggest the visionary aims of the series, signalling that his character is changed when he 'starts to see the world through lesbian eyes'. The script affirms this in a scene where Mark apologises to Jenny and tries to assure her of the change in his perception of lesbians, and the corresponding transformation that has taken place in him ('Loud and Proud', 2:11). 'When I moved in here, I was the type of guy who was capable of doing shit like this,' he claims. 'But I am not that guy anymore. I know that I've said it before, but you and Shane have made me a better man.' Jenny angrily counters that it is not her job to make him a better man, nor is it the responsibility of women to be invaded and consumed by men so that they can 'evolve'. She leaves the room and Mark follows her, pleading with her to stop as he hurriedly undresses. Standing naked and exposed before her, he asks, 'Is this what you want?' In this way, once again, The L Word turns the tables on conventionally gendered and sexualised structures of power and spectatorship, as Mark's reckless eagerness to make a 'moving' documentary results in his own moral and ethical dismantling, compelling him to look into himself.

For The L Word, which arises in response to the television industry's long-standing effacement of lesbians from the popular scene of representation, the dismantling of visual relations really does count. It has to, especially when we consider that television has so far presented lesbians mainly to be watched, but not seen. 'Visibility is a tricky thing,' D'Erasmo ruminates. 'Is someone visible when you can point her out in a crowd, or when you understand what her life feels like?' (2004) Bette's dismantling before the photograph of love's eternal eye, like Jenny's dismantling before the protean nature of desire, and like Mark's dismantling before the image of what one life feels like, accords value to Stendhal's Syndrome as a figuration of the revolutionary powers of seeing – and understanding – in ways that connect us to one another reflectively. And my guess is that if *The L Word* has a lasting contribution to make to queer cultural history, it will be to advance our awareness of one of the most pleasurable and dangerous L words of them all – just look.

L7 Lipstick leviathans

Demonologies of the lesbian body in the L word

Mark W. Bundy

Only the devil can eat the devil out.

Sylvia Plath, 'Poem for a Birthday' (1981: 135)

... our blood flowed fast now, darkening, already inventing a new language for desire.

Rikki Ducornet, 'Voyage to Ultima Azul, Chapter 79' (1994: 162)

The secret is out. West Hollywood is heaving with vampires: lithe, voluptuous, lethally beautiful creatures who prowl the glittering filth of empty boulevards and who penetrate club after club, savouring the slow burn of a sharp, insatiable hunger. These are abiding, careful monsters – a velvet hybrid of sophistication and audacity, longing and apathy, seduction and dismissal. They are the newest generation of Los Angeles lesbians, and they are not your mother's queers. A few 'L' words come to mind that quickly conjure up some ambassadorial names for these sexy outlaws with ties to blackest supernature: Lilith. Lamia. Lorelei.

Legion.

And it isn't just bloodsuckers hitting all the girlbars in the city: we're overrun with succubae, harpies, psychic vampires, sirens, banshees, viragoes, werewolves, djinn, medusas, voodooiennes, and, outnumbering all the others by far – demons.

1. Gustav Doré, *Furies*.

All because of a cable television show about women having sex with women

Season one of Showtime's The L Word invokes seven devilishly lesbian and/or bisexual hipsters: Bette Porter, Tina Kennard, Alice Pieszecki, Dana Fairbanks, Shane McCutcheon, Marina Ferrer, and Jenny Schecter – a powerhouse coven of beauty, fashion savvy, professionalism/ rewarding careers, artistic and cultural sensibility, money, rising fame, and blistering hot sex; these ladies smoulder and glide, suede like, through a fantastic 'lesbohemia' of their own design. However...

Méfiez-vouz des appearances

Never trust appearances – especially not what you see on television, and definitely not how you see television depicting the City of Angels (where I happen to live, and where real angels indeed fear to tread... the freeways, mainly). As I became more and more obsessed with viewing (and re-viewing) season one of The L Word, I was haunted by certain key indelible impressions about elements, characters, moods, and motifs of the show that both fascinated and frustrated me – not unlike tasting the chronic ghost of a beloved's incomparably hot *and* tragic 'farewell' kiss that can spontaneously disrupt one's level of control of the mouth/ body, emotions/memories, and power/control. First, let me say that the arc of episodes 1–13 possesses and is possessed by a series of visual and narrative delights that are equally sinister and ebullient, extraordinary and mundane, iridescent and monochromatic – with many episodes often revealing, as poet César Vallejo might describe it, 'the horrible, the sumptuous, the slowest,/the august, the fruitless, the ominous, the convulsing, the wet, the fatal,/the whole, the purest, the lugubrious,/ the bitter, the satanic, the tactile, [and] the profound' (Ducornet 1999: 107). What follows in the rest of this chapter is a hellish perspective of season one of The L Word as a metaphorical/symbolic reading of the seven main characters as 'monstrous women' and an attempt to venerate some of the series' breakthrough achievements throughout season one: to seize intensely erotic moments and saturate them in rapture, to extract a fusion of disparate emotions, and to articulate fresh imagery in each episode validating the commitment of cast and crew to the success of the show; for Executive Producer Ilene Chaiken and for writers such as Rose Troche:

> to create a fictional world with rigor and passion, to imagine
> a character of any sex, place, time, or color and make it
> palpitate and quiver, to catapult it into the deepest forests of
> our most luminous reveries, is to commit an act of empathy.
>
> (Ducornet 1999: 115)

> It's unbelievable what the female body goes through.
>
> (Bette Porter, in 'Listen Up', 1:8)

'Ovoid, lunate, opalescent life – fuck./You miss your mouth almost entirely now./Over forty varieties of lipstick...' (Maso 1996: 182). The title of this article, 'Lipstick Leviathans', came together for several reasons: first, I'd known my topic and I wanted to deliberately juxtapose something overtly 'sweet' or traditionally 'feminine' with the concepts of the demonic, the wicked, and the possessed; secondly, I realised that the phrase 'Lipstick Leviathans' provided a pretty striking echo to the tag a lot of us queers love to hate – 'Lipstick Lesbians'– and, finally, I

2. (above left) Gustav Doré, *Arachne.*
3. (above right) Gustav Doré, *Destruction of Leviathan.*

knew that there were factions of viewers of the show that argued fiercely for one particular side of an ongoing argument or the other: some say that 'the girls' of *The L Word* are all much too 'femme', too beautiful, too thin, etc., while others say that the show is in fact still representing a group of 'real' lesbians who just happen to look, dress, talk, and behave in a more roundabout 'feminine' fashion – this debate will continue inexorably, but the idea that the mere mention of the word 'lipstick' in the middle of a dialogue about lesbians can cause an eyebrow to arch and twitch is more than enough for me to sprout a sly grin and a pair of horns. Now, then...

Leviathan: (Hebrew, 'that which gathers itself together in folds')... hmmm – a shy or tidy vagina? Oh, wait, there's more... in the Enoch parables, Leviathan is the primitive Female sea-dragon and monster of evil; in Rabbinic writings, she is identified with Rahab, angel of the primordial deep, and associated with Behemoth... cf. Isaiah 27:1 where Leviathan is called 'that crooked serpent', an epithet which recalls Revelation 12:9, where Satan is dubbed 'that old serpent' (Davidson 1967: 173).

The concept of linking lesbianism (or any modes of queerness, for that matter) with demons and/or monsters is just... 'wrong' – especially to demonise our seven remarkably lovely, charismatic, effervescent lesbohemians, right? NO. There are (at least) three good reasons to approach the topic of Demonic Dykes on *The L Word*.

1) To create a newer, bolder counter-narrative that flows against the endless stream of violence, hatred, and ignorance that has been directed toward the queer community by any self-righteous bigots who have demonised us, made us into monsters, condemned us to their version of hell, and forced us into actually hellish ghettos.

> Just consider what it would be like – to simply embrace your 'demonhood'.

Remember when 'Queer' was a word that, when hurled across the street at you, stung hot and pulsing like venom for hours? We took back that word, fairly recently. *We own it.*

That sting is, generally speaking, gone. What else could we change, here and now?

> I dare you

2) The line between sexuality/desire/longing and behaviour/acting out/ transgression is so damn fine on this show, you'd need to either be an angel or a corpse not to have performed some of the 'monstrosities' that engender themselves quite frequently throughout season one.

3) Ultimately, regardless of the passion, friendship, love, and trust that the seven women enact, some of them very clearly represent, at least symbolically, major figures of mythological, religious, and socio-cultural female monsters and demons; further, 'Lies, Lies, Lies' (1:4) explicitly manipulates overtly demonic imagery, the invocation/ repetition of specific demon names ('Abraxas'), and the theme/ suggestion that Jenny's 'phase' of bisexuality (*marcher à voile et à vapeur*, French slang; (lit) 'to work by sail and steam') and her acute infatuation with Marina – a sirenic/vampiric lesbian, *qui est de la maison tire-bouchon* (more French slang, meaning 'who is of the lesbian world' – (lit) 'who is of the corkscrew house') might be caused by 'demonic possession' (Maso 1996: 22, 24).

I. Vox Erotica

Before considering the 'demonic' or darker aspects of some of The L Word's characters' behavioural patterns and monstrous dynamics, this section will attempt to briefly mirror just an essence of some of the deeper emotional and sensual pleasures that the show offers viewers, leading up to a discussion of when the show turns from an often witty, urban, lesbian nod to the hetero-vitality of Sex and the City to just plain 'Your Ex in My Kitty'.

> And looking up I see through veils and veils of mad desire:
> the hanging gardens
> a grove of mangoes
> blooming breasts and thighs
> a pomegranate. Like Magic.
>
> Carole Maso, Aureole (1996: 92)

'Mapping' the demonic/possessed lesbian body is no ordinary cartographer's task; demons nest within various spaces of the body, and 'the cities of the interior are vast and do not lie on any map' (Winterson 1987: 152). Thus there is no occult atlas from which to extrapolate specific zones of possession, which forces us to return to the employment of rudimentary research materials: anatomy, psychology, behaviour, and tracing the alphabet along the contours of each part of the possessed body. Often, more than any other force, language coveys the power of desire, renews the spirit, but denudes the heart and betrays the body.

> *Verweile doch, du bist so schön.*
> Stay with me, you are so beautiful.

> All beauty, promise, shining – she looks out as the woman –
> delirious – *you are beautiful*, she whispers, manages to stutter.
>
> (Maso 1996: 7)

> Beautiful my desire, and the place of my desire.
>
> (Roethke 1975: 198)

Guide me. Make me dazzle. Grinding glowing bones to stars
and salt and sea, guide me. Show me.

(Maso 1996: 54)

Language is a skin: I rub my language against the other. It is
as if I had words instead of fingers, or fingers at the tips of my
words. My language trembles with desire.

(Barthes 1978: 73)

Somewhere between the swamp and the mountains.
Somewhere between fear and sex. Somewhere between God
and the Devil passion is and the way there is sudden and the
way back is worse.

(Winterson 1987: 68)

II. Vox Mystica (Demons and Other Monsters)

How to repulse a demon (an old problem)? The demons,
especially if they are demons of language (and what else could
they be?) are fought by language.

(Barthes 1978: 81)

The central image of the demonised lesbian/bisexual appears in 'Lies,
Lies, Lies' (1:4) with the opening vignette showing a woman holding an
ancient Ecuadorian idol of a minor demon (possibly a representation of
Fourcas or Abraxas). Later in the episode, Jenny reveals her secret affair
with Marina to Nick (Julian Sands), her former professor:

Jenny: I don't know if it's love. It might be sort of like this,
         you know, fantastic, sort of like, demon possession
         sort of thing.

Nick: It's exotic. Demon possession. That's it – that's what
         you have to take and run with ... when you write about
         Marina, you must dig, you must delve, you must open
         up and eviscerate everything.

Near the end of the episode, Jenny has a dialogue with herself/her demon, and a graphic overlay of writing across the screen starts up, in sync with her words:

> I'm sitting in this chair writhing in agony a demon a minor demon is pinning me there fucking with my head. 'Abraxas,' he says. 'I'm Abraxas, the demon of lies and deceit. What do you want to know about lies, my dear?' I'm not a liar. I try again to get up this time I'm flayed splayed I feel myself screaming. 'I'll tell you about lies. There are white lies and black lies... and many shades of grey lies. But some lies are justified: lies told out of kindness, lies that preserve dignity, lies that spare pain. Everybody's a liar...'

In 'Lawfully' (1:5) Tim finally catches Jenny and Marina having sex. He also discovers Jenny's manuscript, which is entitled 'The Demons That Tempt Me'. They, of course, have their huge meltdown scene, which is both tragic and pathetic at once. Interestingly, the episode does not leave off with talk of demons or monsters at that climactic moment. In a bar scene, while Shane is playing pool with Clive (her ex-street-hustling partner and friend played by Matthew Currie Holmes), he lets her know that he has found a place to stay – with a clique of very wealthy Hollywood gay men that she does not approve of – she gives him a lecture that flips the gender of the queered monster on its head: 'You are going to be the latest boy-toy to a bunch of Hollywood fags who are gonna pass you around and suck you dry. They're vampires, man, and you should know that.'

Shane, the *louve*. The She-wolf. A 'loner' of sorts, but *never* lonely.

'She belongs to whoever wants her' (Maso 1996: 91). Shane, though, seems to be the 'free spirit' of the group for most of the first season and does have her demons from the past: her history of soliciting on Santa Monica Boulevard suggests that her oldest demon is 'Naamah' – in the cabala, Naamah was one of four 'angels' (recall that all demons are fallen angels) of prostitution; one Rabbi called her the mother of demons, and another Rabbi believed she was 'the great seducer not only of men but of spirits and demons [and, women, perhaps?]' (Davidson

1967: 203). Shane's more pressing concern is her relationship with Cherie Jaffe (Roseanna Arquette), which has turned suddenly and unexpectedly into love: something Shane has never had to deal with so intensely (if at all) before, and something that both terrifies and thrills her – exactly the kind of work performed by the demon/angel of Fascination, 'Tablibik.'

While these two particular 'Demon/Angels' may not sound familiar, most of the remainder of demons/creatures to be mentioned should be fairly recognisable.

The succubus is a female monster that usually takes her victims while they are asleep, though she may attack at any time, according to legend. Succubi seduce their prey before draining them of their life, or, if they are a vampiric succubus ('Bruxas'), of their blood. In 'The Pilot', Bette and Tina take on the roles of vampires and/or succubi – only they are performing a seduction/operation on a man for a different agenda. Tina wants to get pregnant... other options look grim; and then Bette and Tina hit it off with a guy. Things get rolling, and when he pulls out a condom, they both insist (smiling nervously at him) that it isn't necessary. A few seconds later, and his clothes are back on – insulted, frustrated, and 'violated' (clearly this has happened to him before), he's ready to give his speech and storm out:

> Man, that's great. Why is it whenever dykes wanna have sex
> with a guy, it's only 'cuz they're trying to steal his sperm?

Other forms of evil female figures include sirens (water creatures who lure men to death by drowning because of their beauty and/or the beauty of their singing), lamias (succubi-vampires who take the form of a beautiful woman but are serpents within; lamias are reported to be bisexual, having intercourse and making victims of both men and women) – you could say that Marina is a siren and a vampire; Bette and Tina are succubi, Jenny is a special breed of succubus, called a neuralger (they visit people's sleep to inflict headaches). *Lord knows she visits me.* Alice, in my opinion, is not truly 'demonic' – mildly vampiric/sadistic, perhaps, for ripping out Lisa's (her lesbian-identified-boyfriend) heart; Dana is a Lamia for what she did to Lara. And Shane is a little bit of a vampire, a little bit of a succubus – but mostly werewolf. Altogether, though, the bonds of passion, long-time friends, and fabulous sex under the glittering Los Angeles horizon – they just might be enough to beat away any demons that happen to hound all of our heels.

> Love, they say, enslaves and passion is a demon and many
> have been lost for love ... we fear it. We fear passion and laugh
> at too much love and those who love too much. And still we
> long to feel.
>
> (Winterson 1987: 155)

So, are lesbians really 'demons' in disguise? Of course not. At least I don't think so. But who am I to say?

I'm only sure of one thing – I'll see y'all in Hell, and soon.

(You know – that new club in Hollywood. It's pretty hot.)

Note

This article is dedicated to my amazing sister, Sherry Sokol – neither lesbian nor demon – who personifies so many 'L Words': *Loyalty. Laughter. Life-giving. Loved and Loving. Luminous. Lively. Lucent. Listener. Lovely. Liberated. Lasting.*

And, for the many years of your endless support and encouragement – I love you, Sher.

> For Your Beauteous
> Language is a rose, a woman, constantly in the process of
> opening
> thank you
>
> (Maso 2000: 75)

Part 3 Loving

L8 Heteronormativity and the L word

From a politics of representation to a politics of norms

Samuel A. Chambers

Television should be watched – and written about – as television.

Lawson 2005: xxi

Theory can only be judged by what it enables, by what it opens up and closes off.

Grossberg 1992: 13

The L Word's significance lies in its very existence. On one level, this claim proves irrefutable: who could deny the political and cultural impact of airing a show centred on the lives of lesbians, and portraying the main characters (their relationships, their experiences, their struggles) in a positive, healthy light? Even a cursory glance at the recent political history of gay and lesbian television, and the portrayal of queer issues on television – from the cancellation of thirtysomething, to the protests that stopped a gay kiss on Melrose Place, to the firestorm over Ellen DeGeneres' (and Ellen's) coming out – demonstrates the political import of The L Word, a commercially successful show soon to enter its third full season, all with relatively little backlash or scandal.

If one takes for granted the show's weight in portraying the lives of lesbians, then the political question quickly and easily shifts to an analysis of that portrayal, i.e. how *well* does the show *represent* the lives of lesbian women. Unsurprisingly then, a rich debate has already arisen to address the question of representation on the show, one that I feel certain will continue (productively) into the future. Despite my belief in the validity of this question, in this chapter I will not merely eschew the debate over representation but will directly reject it. And despite my belief in the importance of The L Word for even being aired, I will offer a polemical critique of the show.

First, I contend that the identity politics that centres the debate over representation tends to constrain the political possibilities both for the show and for writing about it. I therefore urge a shift away from the question of representation and toward a queer politics that considers the problem of norms. This shift facilitates my critique (a sympathetically motivated critique, but a critique nonetheless) of the show. Focusing on the first full season, I argue that the narrative structure of The L Word – despite (and perhaps because of) its central cast of characters – often serves to perpetuate, preserve and sustain the normativity of heterosexuality. In short, one might best describe the show aporetically: The L Word is a heteronormative show about homosexuals.

Beyond representation; Or, everyone in LA is beautiful

Much has been written, posted, probably even texted about the question of representation on The L Word. In this chapter, however, I wish to take a detour around the politics of identity and the question of representation. For the purposes of my argument, the problem with representation is (at least) twofold. First, the representation game, as we see in discussions of The L Word, can never be brought to a close. The game usually runs as follows. In the first round, The L Word wins an enormous number of points by having so many lesbian characters. In the middle rounds that follow, points are consistently lost for the show, since that group of lesbians is overwhelmingly white and overwhelmingly feminine in appearance, dress and behaviour. Late rounds may include more losses (for subtle critiques, e.g. over class) or

•

small gains based on tertiary characters. And sometimes moves will be made to stop the game after round one, by claiming that the gains here are so important that nothing else matters (Warn 2004a).

In the end, we emerge with no clear winners or losers in the representation game – both sides admit that in the case of *The L Word*, we have a cast of 'Beautiful People' (Warn 2004a; Lo 2004b) – since we never find a perfect solution to the puzzle. The predicament can be articulated as follows. If *The L Word* cast of lesbian and bisexual women had included a balanced (proportionate to some statistical average) number of butch and femme characters, and then gone on to pick a handful of racial minorities – perhaps one African-American, one Latina, and one Asian-American – to round out its representation of lesbians, then it would have run headlong into another waiting 'representation' critique. To put it simply, a multicultural pastiche would prove utterly unrealistic, both for the setting (West Hollywood) and for the group of friends. How many of us are a part of, or know a group of friends that are as close as Dana, Alice, Tina, Bette and Shane, in which the group is evenly populated across lines of sexuality, gender-identification and performance, race and class? We know the world does not work that way. Thus, *The L Word* will be (rightly) criticised for being too white and too femme, but if it had not been, it would be (rightly) challenged for its departure from any semblance of reality.

Second, and more significantly, the question of representation only gets at one small dimension of the politics of gender and sexuality. Representation can have an important political impact – here we might think of the common thought-experiments concerning how the world would be different if, for example, women comprised fifty per cent of a given country's legislative body – but it has no necessarily determinant effect on the *norms* that both structure the political world and saturate society. 'Representation' in the sense I have been discussing it here (i.e. not political representation in an electoral democracy, but in terms of TV characters representing reality) can provide absolutely no political guarantees. Norms of gender and sexuality may be changed by a show about lesbians, or they may not. To get at this political level of the show, requires both a different approach to it (no longer fixated on representation) and a clearer conception of norms.

To elucidate the nature, power and importance of norms, I follow Judith Butler's recent work in *Undoing Gender*. She writes:

> A norm is not the same as a rule, and it is not the same as a law. A norm operates within social practices as the implicit standard of *normalization*. Although a norm may be analytically separable from the practices in which it is embedded, it may also prove to be recalcitrant to any effort to decontextualize its operation. Norms may or may not be explicit, and when they operate as the normalizing principle in social practice, they usually remain implicit, difficult to read, discernible most clearly and dramatically in the effects that they produce.
>
> (2004: 41)

Norms must not be conflated either with any sort of specific, politically enforced edict (a rule or a law) or with a statistical average; they are related to, but always distinct from both of these. A norm is not a piece of legislation (though it may be sustained by legislation), and it is not merely 'what people do' (though it is usually, also, 'what people do'). A norm implicitly, and sometimes explicitly, demands, presumes, expects and calls for the *normal* (see Warner 1999). This means that norms construct and continually reinforce (even if only in the background) our idea of 'the normal' – a process or power often referred to as *normalisation*. This is the power that repeatedly judges and marks us in relation to an idea of normality. It evokes the statistical bell curve, with a median point at the top of the bell that contains 'normal' identity/behaviour, and with marginal tails that hold the abject, deviant cases. Normalisation affects those at the margins in often obvious ways, by marking their existence as other. But it also impacts those near the centre of the curve, since they must *remain* 'normal'. (If this point seems counterintuitive, just ask the 'cool kids' in school if they find it easy being the cool kids.)

As a constitutive element of culture, television participates in both the fashioning and refashioning of norms. To make this connection clear it must be stressed that a norm is not a structured, static position; rather, norms are always produced socially and they remain variable, *contingent.* Norms have no independent or transcendent standing: 'the norm only persists as a norm to the extent that it is acted out in social practice' (Butler 2004: 46, 48). Their status as norms depends upon their daily reproduction and implementation, even while they somehow always exceed those particular instantiations. One can clearly extend this logic to the politics of television, since one of the daily practices through which norms are continually reproduced, must also be discursive practices that include cultural objects – media and television. Television must be thought of not merely as a 'representation of reality' – a reality ostensibly 'out there' beyond the screen – but as a cultural practice that produces and reproduces the norms of gender and sexuality that *are* our lived reality (both political and social).

To reduce the politics of television to the politics of representation would be precisely to mistake TV for nothing more than a mimicry of a reality that supposedly exists in a separate realm. But television, like any other cultural artefact, participates in the constitution of our reality (Hall 1980: 128–38; Lawson 2005: xvii–xxii; Lavery 2005: 19–33). We cannot therefore analyse television solely by checking its adequacy against an idealised standard that somehow stands apart from the show in question (since norms do not work that way). Thinking politics in these terms more clearly illuminates *the politics of television*. Television, to put it starkly, proves political because of the way it participates in the reproduction of norms (and therefore culture, and therefore reality). This explains why quite often important critical work on gender and sexuality gets done on shows that are not 'gay shows' at all: *Six Feet Under* exposes the workings of the closet, with only one central gay character (Chambers 2003: 24–41); *Star Trek* can be seen as exploring the taboo against same-sex desire through the metaphor of alien species (Capsuto 2000; Ferguson 2002: 181–95); *Desperate Housewives* subverts traditional gender roles while working from precisely within their terms (Chambers 2006). And the converse may be true as well: there is nothing inherently radical or subversive about a show that centres on gay characters.

In the case of *The L Word*, we find narrative structures that actually mimic and help to reify the structures of heteronormativity. If we insist on moving away from a politics of representation and toward a politics of norms, then it becomes clear that one cannot make political judgements about a television show based solely on its 'identity-ingredients' (e.g. how many straights, how many gays, how many blacks, how many whites?). Only when trapped within the narrow frame of identity politics would we wind up with the crude reduction – lesbians are good, straight guys are bad – that marks the 'final rounds' of the representation game.

A queer politics of norms proves much 'wider' because it can assess a show on different terrain. Thus, exploring lesbian relationships (from friendship to sex to business to politics), challenging societal presumptions about gender and sexuality through the portrayal of lesbian characters and their interactions both with one another and with society as a whole, and articulating a normative vision of gender and sexuality that surpasses heteronormativity can all be described as 'good things' (socially progressive, politically democratic) to the extent that they do the important and productive work of cultural politics. On the other hand, practices that reify the structures of heteronormativity – by either mimicking the heterosexual norm or upholding patriarchal visions/assumptions – these practices may, and should, be criticised for their conservative and freedom-limiting effects. The key for my analysis is this: one can, and indeed one must, analyse The L Word in terms of this politics of norms, regardless of how we assess it with respect to the politics of representation. This demonstrates precisely why shows that are not at all 'gay shows' can often prove quite successful in subverting the heterosexual norm, while, at times, so-called 'gay shows' will wind up (perhaps unwittingly) maintaining heteronormativity, e.g. Will & Grace (Lawson 2005: xx; Havrilesky 2004).

Both criticisms and praise for The L Word miss their mark to the extent that they remain trapped within a politics of representation and fail to take into consideration the question of heteronormativity. The profound importance of Sarah Warn's work on The L Word cannot be denied; it provides the starting point for any serious consideration of the show (Warn 2002, 2003, 2004a, 2004b, 2005). And this is not to mention Warn's broader work on gay and lesbian entertainment. I focus on Warn's arguments precisely because of their prominence and significance. And, on my reading, Warn's approach to the show proves problematically narrow, not because she fails to see the weaknesses in the show – Warn does a wonderful job of remaining balanced in her treatment of *The L Word*, despite the obvious fact that she is a fan – but because she fails to assess the show in terms of norms. In the debate she stages with Malinda Lo over 'butch representation', Warn's opening tactic is to take the position of moderation: 'to ask *The L Word* to reflect the full diversity of the lesbian community when it already has so many hurdles to jump just to survive is too much otherness to put on one show' (Warn 2004a). One could certainly debate this point – Lo does – either on its own merits, or in terms of the extent to which it mimics conservative political responses to gains in civil rights for lesbians and gays; 'don't go too far, too fast' has been a constant conservative refrain in the face of civil rights advances, whether it be challenges to segregation in the US South or claims for gay marriage in recent years.

The political pitfalls of taking the representation tack emerge clearly if we follow its logic to the concluding point: '*The L Word*'s biggest achievement is simply in improving the visibility of lesbian and bisexual women on television by leaps and bounds, which will make it that much easier to challenge traditional concepts of gender and appearance in the future' (Warn 2004a). But, put simply, this logic will not hold. It *might* be the case that having a show about lesbians will help to challenge gender norms, but it *might also* be the case that having a show about lesbians will make it *harder* to challenge gender norms in the future. There is no way we can tell what happens to norms of gender, or to norms of sexuality, simply by checking the sexual orientation of the main characters. If a show about lesbians reinforces heteronormativity; if it preserves traditional conceptions of femininity; if it maintains binary gender; if it rejects queer sexuality, then it cannot be blithely assumed that it will prove progressive in terms of the politics of gender and sexuality. The argument that lesbian visibility is progressive by definition can be challenged if we shift (read: broaden) the frame of analysis to a politics of norms. This frame reveals that there is nothing automatically positive about having lesbian characters maintaining given norms of gender, not to mention potentially mimicking heteronormative structures. The claims for lesbian visibility do little, if anything, to assess whether the show challenges heteronormativity or upholds its structures.

For her part, while often debating with Warn within the terms of the politics of representation – by calling attention to what is missing in the representational spectrum – Malinda Lo regularly gestures toward the politics of gender norms. She does so by emphasising that the debates over representation have a great deal to do with the show's refusal to question gender:

> What these discussions boil down to is not whether The L
> Word represents all lesbians – it simply cannot do that, being
> a thirteen-episode Showtime television drama – but whether
> The L Word is willing to engage with issues of gender. [As one
> of her friends put it:] 'They're willing to talk about sexual
> orientation but not about gender. They clearly did not want to
> blur any gender lines.'
>
> (Lo 2004a)

Making the crucial distinction between sexual orientation and gender could mark the first move toward interrogating the heteronormative nature of the show – exploring the norms of gender and sexuality as they are instantiated in particular episodes, finding out whether the show subverts heteronormativity by calling the so-called naturalism of heterosexuality into question, or reifies heteronormativity by imitating its terms (see Halberstam 1998). Yet Lo fails to carry out this analysis, and thus her critique falls short exactly because it stays within the terms of identity politics. She writes: 'Like many viewers who posted their thoughts online, my friends and I felt that the inclusion of men in numerous sex scenes ... pandered to a straight male audience and was outright offensive to lesbian viewers' (Lo 2004a). I am fully sympathetic to Lo and her friends' general reaction; I share it. But I do not think that Lo's heading title, 'Too Many Straight Men', quite captures what is sometimes so very wrong with the show (see also Lo 2004b). The problem that Lo puts her finger on cannot be boiled down to a problem created by the appearance of men. The presence of men no more sustains heteronormativity than the presence of lesbians undermines it. We must get to the question of norms, which far surpasses games of counting heads, to ask after much deeper questions concerning constructions of gender and sexuality. The weakness of the show does not arise from 'having men around', since, in the world, men (and even straight men) are 'around' quite a bit. Neither inclusion nor exclusion can decide matters here. (To put it crudely: have the guys around, just don't have the threesomes.)

Reifying heteronormativity; or, lesbians are hot

The structure, focus, dialogue and stories in the show, not the mere presence of men (or representation of lesbian identity), lead to heteronormativity. I will take as my frame the first full season of the show, focusing particularly on the opening episodes. In doing so, I seek to analyse the initial presentation of *The L Word* to its audience, in order to capture the impact of the show on norms of gender and sexuality. (Some would suggest that the show does not find its lesbian audience until the end of the first season, and that the second season proves much 'queerer' for this reason. But in the terms I am working with here, a show that speaks only to a gay audience loses much of its potential to challenge heteronormativity and therefore cannot be all that queer. Heteronormativity cannot be subverted merely by being evaded or ignored. The first season therefore remains crucial in the sense of how it *engages* with the dominant norms of sexuality and gender.) I will argue specifically for four distinct, but certainly intertwined, manifestations of heteronormativity: the bizarre fixation on straight sex, the (re)production of heterosexual desire, the presumption of a straight audience (in the form of a 'student'), and the consistent construction of narratives of straight romance. In all of these areas, *The L Word* produces the paradox I mentioned in my introduction: it takes a cast of mostly lesbian characters yet still manages to mimic, support and even reify the norm of heterosexuality.

Straight sex

I am not the first to comment on the (straight) sex in *The L Word*, but it cannot be ignored and its importance should not be downplayed. Well before the pilot episode initially aired, when it still had the bizarre working title of *Earthlings*, the show drew constant comparisons to *Queer as Folk*. The latter show proved groundbreaking not only for centring on the lives of a cast of gay characters, but also for its direct, honest and some might say graphic portrayal of gay sex. For the first time on television, viewers had the chance to see not just gay characters, but male-male desire, eroticism and a rather broad spectrum of sex acts. And *Queer as Folk's* pilot episode was filled with lots of sex; sex that delighted most of its gay fans, surprised many of its gay and straight viewers, and shocked a portion of its straight audience. When *The L Word's* own pilot finally aired, many viewers keenly anticipated a chance to see, finally, lesbian sex.

Those viewers had to wait. The pilot has plenty of sex, just not very much between two women. The first sex occurs between the only straight characters on the show, Jenny Schecter and Tim Haspel, and while lesbians have a 'presence' it occurs only through Jenny's fantasy. In terms of supporting heteronormativity, this last fact proves much more significant than the fact of the straight sex itself, since lesbian sexuality has long *had a role* in the structure of heterosexual fantasy and the circuits of desire. So-called 'lesbians' have been an object of heterosexual desire in popular culture and pornography for quite some time. Two straight people having sex doesn't tell us much about heteronormativity, other than the fact that some people have opposite-sex desire. But by including lesbians in that circuit of desire as objects of fantasy to supplement straight desire, this first sex scene fully supports the heterosexual norm – not merely by ignoring lesbianism but by giving lesbians a specific, secondary place *within* the heterosexual norm (see Butler 2004).

Perhaps readers might see this as an 'over-reading' of a simple sex scene? To dispel this sense one only needs to continue watching the pilot. The second sex scene repeats the first in structure, only adding the variation of beginning with oral sex. Now the first sex in general, and the first oral sex in particular, belong to the straight couple. The point, it would seem, has been made. But just in case it has not, the pilot episode takes one more step into the fantasy life of the straight male. When viewers of *The L Word* finally get their first full sex scene with two women in it (the earlier make-out session in the pool served only as a turn-on for Jenny), they have to abide the inclusion of a man. Almost everything about this scene proves hard to believe: that the show would even include this ultimate straight male fantasy, that Tina Kennard and Bette Porter would choose this route to conceive their baby, that as intelligent citizens of LA, they would have unprotected sex with an utter stranger (that the guy really drives a motorcycle). The scene could serve at least two plausible purposes, both of which reify heteronormativity.

First, it sells the show to a straight male audience (see Lo 2004a), and this marks a crucial difference between The L Word and its constant companion in comparison, Queer as Folk. Queer as Folk's primary audience is gay men, with a secondary audience of straight women, and this latter group need not find the main characters attractive as objects of desire. The L Word's perceived secondary audience is straight men, a group that within the structures of heteronormativity has taken lesbians as objects of a certain kind of desire. To include scenes that make lesbians attractive to straight men cannot be explained away in marketing terms (even if that explanation proves valid), since this move undercuts significantly any plausible chance the show might have of challenging heteronormativity. The threesome scene proves this point, for another reason: it serves to mask the one example of lesbian sex in the pilot. By cutting from the sex scene between Marina Ferrer and Jenny, to the threesome with Bette and Tina, the pilot sneaks in lesbian sex, covering it up with the classic example of heteronormative fantasy.

Eventually, of course, The L Word offers numerous and repeated portrayals of lesbian sex, even lesbian sex that excludes both straight participants and straight voyeurs. Yet reminders of the implicit message that lesbians are sexy, attractive objects of desire, even for straight men, crop up repeatedly, whether in the form of the straight man observing lesbian sex ('Lawfully', 1:6) or in the representation of lesbians in/as the pornographic model, e.g. the 'lingerie sex' between Marina and Jenny that Tim walks in on ('Losing It', 1:7). These reminders reinforce the message of the pilot – that lesbians are attractive, desirable, feminine beauties (cf. 'Let's Do It', 1:3) – and they help to blunt any challenge that lesbian sex might pose to the preservation and exaltation of heteronormativity.

Straight desire

This message is subtly reinforced by the show's construction and production of desire. Desire proves essential to the politics of heterosexual norms, since heteronormativity operates by way of excluding the possibility of same-sex desire; it manifests itself in the world through the constant presumption of opposite-sex desire and heterosexual identity (Butler 1999). It follows, then, that shows centring on gay characters, much like the individual and social practice of 'coming out', hold the potential to undermine heteronormativity by questioning this assumption. Thus, 'gay TV' can undo the heteronormative supposition and belief that remains dominant in the world, much as it can be reversed within the context of a lesbian and gay community; within these situations the presumption might be that everyone is gay. In a sense this happens on *The L Word*: anyone who patronises the Planet (Marina's coffee shop) or attends a party hosted by Bette and Tina is more likely to be gay than straight, and this is the view taken up by most of the gay characters.

This makes it all the more surprising and disquieting that the show can so consistently both presume and produce straight desire. Viewers see this most clearly through the triangular relationship among Tim, Jenny and Marina. The appropriately titled episode, 'Longing' (1:4), foregrounds this issue nicely. As Jenny has begun her affair with Marina, we see Tim as utterly clueless about his own betrayal. Tim positively and repeatedly encourages Jenny to spend time with, to befriend the very person with whom she is cheating. It simply does not enter Tim's head that Jenny might betray him by sleeping with a woman. Even when Jenny changes her appearance rather drastically, dressing up to go out with Marina, Tim simply finds it attractive. Jenny makes herself up to be the object of a woman's desire, yet the effort only serves to reinforce straight male desire. Tim operates in the world of binary sexuality produced by heteronormativity, i.e. if Jenny has sex with him, she cannot be a lesbian, and thus she cannot desire Marina. The irony, of course, stems from the fact that Jenny's desire for Marina positively oozes from the screen, and Marina's passionate focus on Jenny proves obvious to anyone *not* utterly blinded by the heteronormative logic of exclusion – the logic that unilaterally and universally prevents straight women from having sex with other women. Tim's making Jenny into an object of straight male desire reinforces the message that lesbians do not, will not endanger the heteronormative order.

It would be possible, of course, through a more self-reflective portrayal, for the show to be making fun of Tim and thereby questioning his heteronormative assumptions. Unfortunately, *The L Word* rarely, if ever, achieves such self-reflection; it thereby misses the mark of critical parody and serves conservative ends. Thus, within the very same episode, we sink to deeper heteronormative depths (and, in inverted fashion, we reach greater heights of irony). While Tim harbours no jealousy toward Marina, Jenny *does*. Despite the fact that Jenny has no reason to think Marina is bisexual, she immediately grows jealous of Marina's interactions with Tim. The heteronormative presumption of straight desire proves so strong that even though Jenny herself is sleeping with Marina, even though she knows Marina is gay, she worries that Tim wants Marina as well. Heterosexual desire moves in a circle here, both presumed by the characters on the show and reinforced by their actions. This is the circle in which actions both follow the edicts of a norm *and* instantiate that norm.

One might try to explain away these examples as the product not of heteronormativity, but of a relationship in crisis (e.g. Jenny's jealousy masks her guilt, Tim's naïveté hides an underlying knowledge of Jenny's betrayal). Yet the show presumes straight desire in other ways and it continues to construct straight desire well after Jenny and Tim's break-up. Despite the fact that Jenny cheated on him with a woman, Tim finds a way to be comfortable with Jenny's living on the premises and bringing over dates. Somehow lesbian desire fails to appear as a threat to Tim, even though it clearly is one. Tim shows no jealousy toward the women Jenny brings home to have sex with, but he immediately reacts with anger and frustration when she merely *receives a phone call* from an old boyfriend ('Lies, Lies, Lies', 1:5); and he becomes temporarily insane when she brings home a guy ('Limb from Limb', 1:13). Thus, the narrative consistently communicates the notion that lesbians pose no threat to heterosexual male possessiveness. Therefore, Tim does not really 'lose' Jenny to Marina; he rejects her for her betrayal. And Tim's actions say that, if Jenny is a lesbian, it does not matter that he loses her anyway; he competes for her only with men.

Here, The L Word conveys a vision of the world much like the one in which we live; in it, only gay people ever consider the possibility that someone else might be gay. This structure preserves heteronormativity, since the world will continue in the foreseeable future to be populated by a large majority of straights, and smaller minorities of gays, lesbians, transgender people, and others who are queer with respect to the norm. By reproducing heterosexual sex and reifying heterosexual desire, The L Word obviously fails to challenge heteronormativity.

Narratives of straight romance

Worse, it fails in other, more subtle, perhaps more insidious ways. When the show is not explicitly working with a heteronormative frame of sex and desire – that is, even when it deals explicitly with sex and relationships between women – it often goes well out of its way to replicate a narrative structure of heterosexual romance. The first scene of the pilot offers just the most obvious example. The scene opens at the epicentre of domesticity, in the bathroom off the couple's master bedroom; there, Bette and Tina learn that Tina is ovulating. The scene perfectly imitates, in generic fashion, the hundreds of scenes from movies and television in which the wife happily discovers that she is pregnant, or the recently married couple heroically decide to do the most romantic thing of all, 'make a baby'. The opening scene only falls short of the straight romantic script when, rather than having sex (can't have that), Bette says instead, 'You get dressed; I'll drive you [to the clinic] on my way to work.'

Perhaps this interruption at the end could be read for its disruptive potential, making the scene a politically powerful parody of the straight script, rather than a mere repetition. 'Let's Do It' (1:2) rejects this reading outright, by *repeating* the same scene, only this time Bette and Tina *do* have sex at the end (as they have decided to do the insemination at home rather than at the clinic). Thus The L Word opens both of its first two episodes with a narrative so familiar to its viewers as to be beyond cliché; it tells those (straight) viewers that lesbians are just like 'us'. They desire nothing more highly than reproductive sex in the family bed.

Unlike *Queer as Folk*, which opened with daring portrayals of gay *desire* and eroticism, *The L Word* tames the lesbian sex, even before it portrays it. After all, Bette and Tina's attempt to make a baby at the beginning of 'Let's Do It' marks the first uninterrupted sex between two women on the show. Where the pilot and other episodes throughout the first season tell the straight male viewer 'lesbians are hot', this episode says, again to a straight audience, 'Worry not, there is nothing scary or even all that different about lesbian sex.'

To fortify this case, the first season consistently returns to clichéd heteronormative narratives that will strike the straight viewer as comforting and familiar (see Havrilesky 2004). Thus, we have some of the obvious cases: the ultrasound scene with Bette and Tina ('Lies, Lies, Lies', 1:4) and the marriage announcement from Dana and Tonya (Meredith McGeachie) ('Limb from Limb', 1:13). The former proves to be so tired as to be uninteresting, in any context. The latter not only mimics heterosexual marriage, but also runs the risk of trivialising gay marriage, since Dana announces her 'engagement' to a woman that she hardly knows and that both her friends and the viewers can hardly stand. (And here I simply put aside the huge debate over whether gay marriage in general can be thought to queer marriage, or ape heterosexual marriage. See Sullivan 1996; Warner 1999.)

None of this is to say that lesbian desire can be portrayed as a single, monolithic entity, nor is it to deny the possibility that same-sex desire may participate in power relations related to those of opposite-sex desire (see Bersani 1995). As has been shown, however, *The L Word* often mimics heterosexual symbolic structures on the *primary* level, thereby closing off any portrayal of same-sex desire or lesbian eroticism. This reflects the privileging of straight male desire, and the male gaze within the order of heteronormativity. The conveyance of (same-sex) female desire has the potential to disrupt this order; hence the disappointment that a show about lesbians so rarely depicts lesbian desire.

Teaching to straights

This failure can be directly and easily linked to missed opportunities in exploring lesbian sexuality. Dana's relationship with Lara Perkins

(Lauren Lee Smith) offers the most lucid example. Like Justin Taylor (Randy Harrison) on *Queer as Folk*, Dana is the sexually inexperienced character in the group, one through whom the audience could potentially explore lesbian sexuality. *Queer as Folk* used the relationship between Brian Kinney (played by Gale Harold, a much older, much more experienced gay man) and Justin (an inexperienced, but not necessarily innocent seventeen-year-old) to, for lack of a better word, 'teach' the audience about gay sex. Like Justin, Dana is learning about her own sexuality in the context of a same-sex relationship. But instead of exploring the sex between Dana and Lara – with all the nuances, complications, discoveries and embarrassments it might entail – The L Word chooses to provide yet another mimicry of straight narratives. The viewer does not witness the first sex between Dana and Lara; instead, the scene opens with the two of them in bed just afterward. There we witness the rehearsal of another worn-out dialogue, as Dana expresses her embarrassment and disbelief at something that has 'never happened to her before'. The references to straight male impotence scenes can be missed by absolutely no one, even though those references make no sense (how could Dana possibly be impotent?). We learn later, in the safe space of discussion in the coffee shop, that Dana had experienced female ejaculation, but the intimate sexual encounter has now been reduced to comedic relief and the moment to investigate both the logistics and the meaning of sex between women has been lost.

The L Word does offer its share of 'teaching' about lesbians; however, it confines that teaching to a narrow, often desexualised teaching to straights. Thus, in the pilot we have the scene in which Jenny meets Tina, and Tina explains that she has quit her job to stay at home to have a baby. Jenny reacts with awkward surprise, as if she cannot process how this could possibly be. Tina explains. That is, she points out to Jenny that women (even lesbian women) can, indeed, have babies (even without men). But this explanation proves necessary only if one makes the rather ignorant and certainly heteronormative (if not homophobic) assumption that a baby can *only* and ever be brought into the world by 'a man and a woman'. That is, this embarrassing and cumbersome 'explanation' that Tina offers to Jenny might be helpful to those state and federal legislators across the USA who are most convinced that 'families' cannot be constructed with gay members, but it seems hard to see why Jenny or the audience would require it. Perhaps this scene could have a more critical edge if it served to expose precisely the ridiculousness of the heteronormative idea that women cannot have babies (or that lesbians are not women). To achieve that effect, however, would require Jenny to look a bit stupid – rather than funny and cute.

Presuming an unreasonable level of ignorance (appropriate only to rather dense straights) appears elsewhere. Take the example of Dana showing up to a cocktail party with her doubles tennis partner, named Harrison (Landy Cannon) ('Pilot' 1:1). The viewer has almost no reason whatsoever to suspect that Harrison is straight. First, we know that Dana is gay, so if she attends a cocktail party with a man, there is a decent chance he is gay. Secondly, Harrison does not look much like a typical straight male: his outward appearance, dress, manner and behaviour all read as more likely gay than straight. But if that were not enough, Harrison *hits on* Tim. Tim may be clueless about it (see above), but it proves obvious to the viewer. Still, in the face of all this (just in case) Dana later makes certain to say explicitly that Harrison is gay.

The act confirms the heteronormative operational principal that one can only be gay through an unambiguous, affirmative declaration. This aspect of heteronormativity serves to closet, in many aspects of their lives, even those lesbians and gays who have no desire or intention to keep their sexuality a secret. It demands of gays what would never be expected of straights: to outwardly declare their sexuality, or be prepared to have everyone assume wrongly about it. And, of course, in the face of being forced by heteronormativity to announce their sexuality much more often than anyone would want to, lesbians and gays will then be accused of making too much of it, of 'shoving it in our faces'. If the world were not so thoroughly and consistently heteronormative, if it did not shove heterosexuality in *everyone's* face, *all the time*, then there would be no need for gay people to continually make it known that they are gay (Sedgwick 1990; Halperin 1995; Chambers 2003: 24–41). By refusing even the slightest degree of subtlety about sexual identity – and one should not forget that Dana finally comes out in a full-page magazine spread, the loudest declaration possible – the show reinforces heteronormativity in yet another way.

Television and the subversion of heteronormativity

In demonstrating the show's maintenance, preservation and furtherance of heterosexual norms, I have attempted to make my critique of *The L Word* as lucid, stark and forceful as possible. Nevertheless, this critique would prove misdirected if it implied, and misread if it were taken for, a dismissal of the show. Norms are not the sort of thing that one can avoid, transcend or otherwise get outside of. This crucial fact about norms has two entailments. First, the subversion of heteronormativity must come from within its terms. Second, to ignore heteronormativity entirely would be, in its own way, to sustain it by letting it go unchallenged – something that other 'gay shows' often do (Chambers 2003: 24–41). By refusing to construct a 'homosexual utopia', *The L Word* holds the potential to offer genuine challenges to heteronormativity, and occasionally does just this, especially around the character of Bette and her family and work conflicts.

The ongoing battle against heteronormativity – whether it comes in the form of legislative politics or the cultural politics of television – requires a two-pronged approach. Challenges to heteronormativity must be foregrounded and acclaimed (even if they appear where least expected) in order to increase their chance to become successful subversions, while failures to confront heteronormativity must be called out and questioned, discussed and debated (even if *they* occur where least hoped or planned for). My effort here clearly operates within the second prong of this battle: *The L Word*'s problematic reification of heteronormativity cannot persist un-interrogated. The show deserves criticism on this account, that is, within the politics of norms, even if it makes a contribution in the politics of representation. Yet it seems crucial to read this critique, and to read the show itself, as part of this larger struggle against the power of heteronormativity. And this leaves open the possibility that future, or even concurrent, readings of the show may highlight its confrontations with heteronormativity. In any case, neither strand of critical work can afford to be cut at this point, since the project of challenging heteronormativity cannot be abandoned.

L 9

Straight-up sex in the L word

Lorna Wheeler
and Lara Raven Wheeler

Bette is fucking Tina. Candace is fucking Bette. Helena is fucking Tina. Alice fucks both boys and girls. Shane is fucking everyone. Teeth on nipples. Lean bodies sliding in rhythm together. The sexy power of the pregnant woman. Golden showers, bondage, dildos. Body stacked on body. Will she? Won't she? Did she already? Pressing, forcing, selling, playing. She wants it. She doesn't.

Educating, disturbing, and arousing its viewers, *The L Word* plunges into lesbian sex with abandon in its first two seasons. Still, there is a chasm of difference between how sex is portrayed in the first season and in the second. In season one, the characters in this television drama demonstrate a remarkable lack of sexual restraint in their unabashed enjoyment of the body, yet are almost prudish about which sexual acts they will do and with whom. The second season, in marked contrast, shows very little sexual activity, yet it seems to embrace as many so-called radical practices as it can in the small amount of footage allotted to the subject. We argue that this shift marks a change from a relatively conservative, second-wave feminist identity politics to a more contemporary and lively queer approach. We will explore how the plot's unfolding performs different political positions in the history of queers as we illustrate the major sexual themes in this drama: danger, power and play.

Particularly in terms of sex, The L Word alternately normalises and differentiates the lesbian, shifting from a theoretical perspective steeped in 1980s identity politics to a more inclusive and current queer approach toward the end of the second season. When considering the gay, lesbian, bi and trans communities' cultural and political histories, theorist Annamarie Jagose describes the gay political movement of the 1980s as primarily assimilationist and committed to the idea of a cohesive gay identity: unique from but parallel to that of straights (1996: 30–43). During this time in the gay liberation movement, the differences between gays and lesbians in terms of race, class, nationality and gender were de-emphasised in order to present the image of an integrated and cohesive group. As shown by television programmes like Queer Eye for the Straight Guy and Will & Grace, where the constant theme is we're just like you, only a little more fashion conscious, Hollywood at least is still deeply committed to assimilation.

In the 1990s, a nascent queer theory became popular in academia, but this broad approach to sexuality was born on the street. Beginning with the AIDS epidemic, perhaps earlier, people started questioning the usefulness of identity categories. In attempting to locate high-risk populations and disseminate information regarding the disease, AIDS educators quickly learned that gay and lesbian are complicated terms entrenched in the oversimplified binaries gay/straight and male/female. Here identity politics fail, thus marking the need for extending the definitions of sexualities to be more inclusive. Enter queer (Jagose 1996: 19–21).

Queer is more than just an umbrella term for gay/lesbian/bi/trans. It recognises the dangers of exclusion and acknowledges the limitations of strict gender and sex oppositions. Most queer theorists have abandoned the explanation of homosexuality or lesbianism as a natural or inherent condition and are fully committed to the idea that sexuality, like gender, is socially constructed (Butler 1999: 18–21). Jagose describes queer as focusing 'on the mismatches between sex, gender and desire', (3) thus making room for those who have been relegated to the margins of gay and lesbian discourse. Since queer sets itself against the normative, whatever that may mean at any given time, the gender rebels, butch/ femmes, cross-dressers, transgendered, as well as some gays, lesbians, and heterosexuals may identify as 'queer'.

Ladies of the 1980s

In comparing the first season of The L Word to its gay male counter-part, Queer as Folk, the sex scenes are almost Victorian. Whereas Queer as Folk walks a line close to pornography, one cannot really see what is going on between the women in the first year of The L Word. There is a dearth of hands or mouths actually touching bodies, leaving the viewers to rely heavily on their imaginations. Additionally, in a surprising number of the encounters, the women are shown enjoying orgasms with a remarkable distance between their bodies and no indication of what is bringing them to ecstasy. It is our conjecture that this distance is part of the normalising element of The L Word. In this space between lovers' bodies, the lesbian sexual act is made obscure and thus reassuring. Thankfully, this assimilationist urge is mostly abandoned in the second season, where there are far fewer sex scenes but the sex that is shown is more visually descriptive and adventurous. Who is doing whom and more notably what is *not* being done reveals a tired identity politics in the first season. Truly radical sex is not shown – it would be both a threat to the assimilation goals of the identity-bound lesbian and a turn-off to the more conservative viewer. Even penetration is never portrayed or even implied by any lesbian sexual encounter on the programme. Sadomasochism, or SM, is common enough in the lesbian community. But there is not the faintest whisper of leather in this season outside of Shane's signature armcuff, which only appears to be decorative. Sex toys are notably absent except in one unusual scene (but more of that later).

Another nod to conventionality and sexual silence in the first season: unspoken but omnipresent is a dearth of sexual reciprocity and the portrayal of top/bottom positions as being cemented to one's identity. When every sexual couple shown has a permanent top and a permanent bottom, the characters are not only sutured to their genders and to their sexualities but even to their sexual roles. What might be 'top', that is more assertive sexually, is conflated with 'stone', a woman who is *never* a sexual recipient. This is reminiscent of the heterosexual myth about lesbian sex where the same woman must be 'the man' in every sexual encounter. Though Bette orgasms, she does so with no indication that she is being fucked – she appears to be stone until Candace Jewell enters the picture. Marina is never touched sexually and even appears to never orgasm: another stone. Yet this dynamic is never mentioned. Marina never asks Jenny to touch her, nor does Jenny wonder if perhaps she ought to reciprocate. Likewise, Shane is never shown receiving sexual attention. She, like Marina, Candace, and Bette (in her relationship with Tina), performs sex: meaning, she only gives pleasure. Fuzzy verbal acknowledgement of top and bottom positions finally comes in season two, with Dana claiming to be a top ('Loyal', 1:8) although she certainly was a bottom with Tonya. This inclusion suggests a queering of sexuality, both in Dana's role flexibility and in the acknowledgement of this aspect of lesbian sexual culture.

The differences between seasons one and two on *The L Word* are so strong as to make the seasons seem almost like separate shows. While sexual reciprocity within a coupling is still largely absent in the second season, the sex scenes are more explicit and more varied, and involve a panorama of sex toys and sexual practices. There is a daring in season two that is refreshing, as the writers move away from rigid sex stereotypes and toward a queer approach to filming sex. Playing into this transition from assimilationist to queer are three captivating scenes that embody the themes danger, power and play.

Dangerous liaisons

A close analysis of the portrayal of danger on *The L Word* would not be complete without an examination of one of the first season's hottest couplings, that of Jenny and Marina. A classic interlude is their *second* restroom encounter, this time at the Planet ('Lies, Lies, Lies', 1:4). Characteristic of other scenes with this pairing, the camera brings the viewer deep into Jenny and Marina's eyes. It enables the spectator to linger in the stolen humid moment and experience for themselves that thrill of electricity present in their illicit encounter. Jenny's eyes widen at the sight of her lover's beckoning, then narrow, and then shift to Tim as she feels the burden of her expected fidelity. A swallow. A shrug. Three seconds pass before Jenny saunters away in Marina's wake. When she enters the bathroom, we see her movement through the mirror, a tease that the viewer may not truly see this encounter. Anticipation is met however when we slide into Marina's stall with Jenny. A red brassiere, a leather skirt, unbroken silence – all the trappings of an almost anonymous fuck. This penetrating scene offers no penetration. After Jenny's one fumbling grope toward Marina's crotch, she succumbs to what appears to be her sexual role as a bottom. Marina pushes her skirt up and seems to be rubbing her clit. Cut.

This is dangerous sex. This is hot sex. But what really are they doing? The *sex* is not made obvious. At least in this first season, *The L Word* refuses to answer the question, *what do lesbians do in bed?* Perhaps its answer is to imply lesbians don't do it in bed. By and large, the dykes, the lesbian tourists, and even the bi-curious women are all doing it straight up. Although at first glance it may appear trifling, filming lesbian sex in the more active positions of sitting or standing indeed affects representation. We believe that portraying lesbians in less passive, conventional sexual positions both marks lesbian sexuality as something 'other' than heterosexuality; and also as an act so subversive that it has to be done fast, wherever and whenever possible. It is necessarily transitory, even for the long-term couple. This portrayal punctuates a belief that lesbian sex is hasty and subversive – and therefore hotter than heterosexual sex. The first lesbian sex we see in the pilot occurs in a swimming pool in an upright position. Even when Bette inseminates Tina, despite the practical aspects that recommend a horizontal position, they are indeed having sex upright – again ('Let's Do It', 1:2). Indeed, coupling unusual erotic spaces with active bodies lends a decisive air of exoticism and adventurousness. The sex scenes are fast and furious, and while part of the appeal must be in the adrenalin rush embedded in the stolen encounter, the subversion implied is undeniable – and is quite queer.

In addition to position, sexual location emphasises the danger of lesbian sex. Including the pre-show vignettes, one sees that lesbian sex occurs in bathroom stalls, in broom closets, in offices, at the tailor's, after-hours at fast-food jobs, at funeral services, under the table in restaurants, in swimming pools, in doctor's offices, in jail, and house hunting. The message is clear: if you see two women in reasonable proximity to each other, in any situation or location, *they might be fucking and you don't even know it.*

Additionally, the plot emphasises that sexual encounters between the female characters are dangerous to the social order, which serves both to affirm the straight viewer's idea of lesbians as dangerous (and therefore sexy), and to reinforce the lesbian viewer's self-image as extreme (and therefore sexy). Certainly Jenny and Marina are almost always standing up, in a hurry – and completely disregarding Jenny's engagement to Tim. Lesbians disrupt societal boundaries. They do not honour commitment. They have sex in public. They ignore polite behaviour. They do not really seem to care whether anyone notices, unless he is a husband or a desperate voyeur looking to get off on their encounter. Even more conservative Tina is not as offended as she ought to be at Helena's desire to make out in front of her children ('Luminous', 2:7). This element of dangerousness is the first thread we see of a queer approach to the series, and is woven through the first two seasons.

Power tools

Danger and power are certainly intertwined topics. But note that the danger we have explored so far has been predominantly societal menace – the perception that lesbians are threatening the social order. With *power*, we explore the way in which characters on The L Word form bonds of dependence and dominance. Exemplifying this dynamic is the relationship between Bette and Tina, culminating in what has come to be known as 'the rape scene' ('Limb from Limb', 1:13).

This scene is genuinely disturbing, a quality that actually brings it closer to a queer politic than any other scene in the first season. Here, we see The L Word definitively portraying sex, not as audience eye-candy but as critical to the plot, as a 'provocation' in itself. There is a power interchange inherent in sexual acts. What does it mean that the first season concludes with the escalation and distortion of this power dynamic into brutality? Its violence is undeniable yet mutual. Bette initiates sexual contact that is clearly unwanted when she rips Tina's dress, touches her breast, and attempts to fuck her. But then, when Tina flips on top of Bette and bites her, it is Tina who actually finalises the sexual encounter by thrusting Bette's hand to her crotch. This queers the pitch of the scene as it were, by muddying the definition of rape. Showing lesbian violence, particularly where both women might be seen as perpetrators and as victims, is a queer impulse both in its critique about the lesbian community and in its exploding stereotypes about sexual violence. There need not be a man present for violence to occur, and violence can sometimes be sexy. Whatever the viewer might think of the scene, it is undeniable that Tina flips from victim to eager participant. Is it rape at all when both at the end have ceased struggling against each other? We have come to the conclusion that, distressing and disturbing as this scene is, we would not call it rape. But neither is it a daring portrayal of sadomasochism, as Pat Califia clarifies:

> Sadomasochism is not a form of sexual assault. It is a consensual activity that involves polarized roles and intense sensations. An S/M scene is always preceded by a negotiation in which the top and bottom decide ... what activities are likely to occur... The key word to understanding S/M is *fantasy*.
>
> (2000: 167–8)

Certainly most SM encounters are more controlled, with safety rituals in place and a mutual understanding of the limits of the power play. However, the sheer sexiness of the power differential and of pain is acknowledged by the SM community while avoided by the early lesbian-feminists. In contrast to identity politics, and even Andrea Dworkin's anti-porn feminism (1987), a queer approach, such as the 'rape' scene takes, unflinchingly looks at the darker side of a community – ignoring desire for assimilation or acceptance to uncover and even embrace the grittiness of a range of sexual practices, not all of which we might find pretty. While it is not until the very end of the first season when The L Word makes its first attempt to represent the prickly subject of power and its 'outlaw' subculture, we appreciate the effort to extend and complicate lesbian sexual practices that do not tidily fit into vanilla categories.

Third-wave feminism, observes Astrid Henry (2004: 92–3), rebels against earlier feminisms in asserting theoretical difference – and sex has become the battleground. Interestingly, Bette's ensuing downfall mirrors the discrediting of second-wave feminism. Just as the intergenerational shift from lesbian to queer defines itself as a new embracing of sexuality, so Bette's transformation is also sexual with her developing affair with Candace. Bette can easily be seen as the 'old' lesbian, more mature than the others, if not notably older. Certainly, Beals' prior lesbian-iconic role from 1983 solidifies her identification with second-wave feminism. In fact, many 1980s lesbian feminists likely had their first screen crush on Beals playing the tough welder-by-day, undiscovered modern dancer-by-night, Alex Owens in *Flashdance*. Many a frontline lesbian second-waver swooned when Alex pulled off her welder's mask, revealing a mass of feminine curls. So Beals now plays Bette Porter, who, like a second-wave lesbian feminist from the 1980s, finds that succeeding in her career is paramount, and taking a highly public stand on her politics is a personal requirement. Her initial image is almost maternal – and very old school. It is almost as if *The L Word* writers, following on from a new generation of feminist writers, wanted to prove a sex-positive theory. When Bette succumbs first to an extra-marital affair, and then to a violent fuck with her wife, the viewer is ushered to the new millennium with the young queer lesbians: for all the political power of early feminism, sheer lust has the final word after all.

Bette is able to have the affair because she is in the dominant position in her relationship with Tina, financially and socially. Tina leaves Bette and enters a relationship with an even broader financial division, and even greater power differential. Helena uses her extreme wealth to buy herself the ability to perform sex in public without censure. She is an exhibitionist, but it is Tina's body she exhibits. Their relationship can also be read as embodying the complicated power dynamics that are just below the surface of each good fuck.

Come out to play

It is Dana and Alice who take sexuality to a hitherto unseen realm in the second season. Not only does the viewer witness refreshing play during and around sex – but the introduction of bondage and sex toys fills the significant first-season void. Alice and Dana's performance of their *Love Boat* fantasy during a cruise epitomises their relationship ('Land Ahoy', 2:10). It begins with both women clad in bikinis, with Dana striking a jaunty feminine pose. There is to be no doubt that the forthcoming transvestism is only role-playing. Once dressed as Captain Stubing, Dana uncomfortably grabs and pats the dildo that completes her uniform. Awkwardly standing to attention, she is clearly trying on an unfamiliar role. However, when Alice emerges as Julie the Cruise Director, the viewer can see the fantasy solidify for Dana. She moves from comic awkwardness to immersion in their creative scene upon sight of her lover – Julie now, no longer Alice. What crosses Dana's face is a combination of shock and arousal, and is very believable. Alice performing the straight girl is equally fascinating. She seems fully aware of the performance, thus resembling a drag queen more than the straight girl when she cries, 'O Captain, my Captain.' Both may be in drag but both rise to the challenge of their roles.

Rather than the danger that it was for Marina and Jenny, or the erotic aid for Helena, sexual interruption is comic relief for this pair. Their show hits the road when they are summoned to the real captain's table for dinner with no time to change. The sex play does not end when the couple exit their cabin; in fact, 'Julie' gives 'Captain Stubing' a hand job while dining. Returning to their cabin, we finally get a glimpse of the famed dildo in action – and it is not a tool for the light hearted. 'Realistic' (penis-looking) and generously portioned, the apparatus proves Alice is certainly a size queen.

While we are enthusiastic to see some fun, diversity and, dare we say it, penetration in these sex scenes, the dildo is by no means welcomed collectively in the lesbian circle, or even in *The L Word*. With the sole exception of the almost mockable scene between Alice and Lisa (Devon Gummersall), the lesbian-identified man ('L'Ennui', 1:7), the first season is notably bereft of sex toys. When they attempt to have sex on the yacht, Lisa stops Alice from putting her hand in his shorts, and produces instead a non-representational dildo. Alice replies: 'You've got to be kidding – you're a man. You've got the real thing.' Strangely, even though none of the lesbians on the show have yet used dildos, Lisa knows that it is a lesbian thing to do; and Alice so strongly identifies it with lesbian *lack* that she refuses to use it with Lisa.

With this scene, The L Word shunts public view of lesbian sexuality back to the early 1900s, when a lesbian's desire was defined around her lack of a penis, 'the real thing'. But one need not reach so far into history to find conflict between lesbians and penetration: as recently as the late 1980s, second-wave feminists were taking sides in a 'sex war' centred around penetration (Henry 2004: 131–5). Anti-pornography icon, Andrea Dworkin, explains why she believes *heterosexual* penetrative sex is to be avoided when she declares that '[the] normal fuck by the normal man is taken to be an act of invasion and ownership taken in a mode of predation: colonising, forceful (manly) or nearly violent' (1987: 63). However, this repugnance at the 'invasion' of penetration did not stop with acts performed by men. Esther Newton and Shirley Walton were not alone among lesbian theorists in their opinion that '[lesbians] should not engage in any form of "hetero" sex ... includ[ing] both penetrations, either by fingers or dildoes, and tribadism (rubbing the cunt against the partner's body) which can resemble the heterosexual missionary position' (1985: 250). The timidity about penetration displayed by The L Word recalls these proscriptive tenets. While the second season presents a peace offering to penetration by illustrating two women using a dildo, it is still a conservative statement that the *bisexual* requested and received it to the initial discomfiture of her lesbian partner. Even by the end of the second season, the dildo is still just a fake penis.

As if in a courageous attempt to deny this conservatism of the first season, season two starts out slowly and then soars into taboo sexualities with abandon. Dana and Alice's fantasy life is just the cream from the milk. Jenny and Carmen make an erotic moment out of peeing together ('Late, Later, Latent', 2:9). We see handcuffs and nipple clamps, even a fair (though limited) treatment of an SM dungeon where Jenny goes to revisit her childhood demons ('Loud and Proud', 2:11). The taboo of incest is crossed but not commented upon when

Shane brings twins back to the house to watch them fuck ('Luminous', 2:7). In addition to loosening the reins on conventionality, certainly the sincerity, or comfort levels of the actors has improved in the second season when they show more boldness and more heat. Where *The L Word* started out unconsciously portraying the same sex scene in episode after episode, by the second season it seems to glory in the lesbian's status as a sexual outlaw.

The L Word, as the first national television series about lesbians, has had heavy expectations from its anticipatory lesbian audience. Sexually, though, the first season starts out conservatively, pantomiming stereotypes and making sure that nothing shown would set off a 'Code Red' in the Political Correctness Police headquarters. Vertical sexual positions and exotic locations provide titillation. But ultimately the image of lesbian sex is vague and circumscribed. Season one depicts lesbians as people with a disdain for dominant culture's moral order, but let's face it – television adultery has not been transgressive since the days of *Dallas*. Then, at the end of the first season and with the launch of the second, sexual audacity and daringly queer sex explode onto the scene. It is as if the entire first season tests audience reception to merely seeing women naked together, and then the polls come in: Queer it up! Indeed, the second season of *The L Word* dances between many different versions of lesbian sexuality, from exhibitionist to playful, from romantic to sadist. However, while the plot is queered in the second season, there are still some moments of conservatism and avoidance of a prickly subject matter.

Caught between a 1980s feminist urge to paint lesbian sex as benign, and the queer impulse to set lesbian sexual culture against the norm, *The L Word* spans two generations of lesbian history in its first two seasons. Unfortunately, sexually conservative 1980s lesbians and Generation Q queer lesbians make strange bedfellows. To hold its politically astute audience, *The L Word* needs to embrace the full diversity of sexuality and not just pay lip service to the fringe. But for all season two's queer moments, for all its raciness, what we appreciate most about sex on *The L Word* are the flashes of sincerity where the queer viewer, no matter what his or her preferred sex practices, has a sense of recognition: *'Yes. I've felt that.'* Lesbians and queers are a population deprived of anything more than the occasional morsel from purveyors of pop culture. While critics may fear backlash for such a brassy, unapologetic portrayal of dykedom, and while the series still struggles with the conservatism betrayed by its oh-so-discreet title, still we applaud The L Word's chutzpah in traversing unmapped territory. Television fare has never tasted better.

10 The chart

Kim Ficera

In their extremely successful re-creation of all things lesbian in LA-LA Land, the writers of *The L Word* excel at evidencing two very distinct aspects of dyke culture – one mysterious, the other not so much: bad hair and our inter-relatedness.

Bad lesbian hair – inexplicable in its timelessness and universality – is an enigma off and on TV, a puzzle right up there with the mystery of faith. Does God exist? Is there a decent stylist in Hollywood?

I don't know why, when given the unprecedented opportunity to sentence the bad lesbian hair stereotype to a very public death, the decision-makers at *The L Word* would choose to grant it a stay of execution and allow it to live on not on the head of one character, but on a number of characters. But so be it. A bad hair gene or a cosmic follicle force, strong and far beyond mortal control, must be at work.

What's far less cryptic in the lesbian world, and completely within our control, is the company we keep under the sheets. And to that point *The L Word* folks not only get it right, but also provide us with a fun visual that in two short years has earned a top spot in lesbian pop culture: Alice Pieszecki's Chart.

The Chart was introduced by Alice in the pilot episode and served to provide viewers with a not so subtle representation of the characters' sexual ties to one another. Through an excellent example of art imitating life, Alice used the Chart to explain to her naive and then-closeted best friend Dana the seemingly indigenous habits of lesbians and the human highways and byways they and their mutual friends have navigated for sex.

Lesbian viewers understood. We laughed out loud. We've all taken similar paths, after all; only the names of our pit stops were different. Regardless of our ages or accents we saw ourselves in the Chart and we each reacted similarly, as if a long-lost friend had finally gotten the huge break she was waiting for in Hollywood. Dyke viewers in Mississippi smiled knowingly, as did lesbian viewers in San Francisco. We toasted the Chart, ourselves, our partners, and our exes with martinis and beers, over bowls of popcorn and Pier One coffee tables.

Alice's Chart is true to form for her personality. It, like her, is amusing. Together they make a great pair. Unlike the somewhat sexually deprived single girl who befriends a jigsaw puzzle on a Saturday night, Alice manages the Chart. Eventually, the comedian of The L Word bunch makes sport of it – Alice becomes the 'score' keeper of the sex games her friends play. As a result, the Chart rises in status from agitprop to character. And the upgrade is well deserved, because what it represents is as intrinsic to dyke culture as sports and, well, bad hair. But as entertaining as the Chart is, is it as innocuous as The L Word writers lead us to believe?

If we were to be completely honest, some of us – the more sexually active, specifically – might admit that a bit of nervous laughter accompanied the genuine guffaws that followed the Chart's introduction. Guided by the lines shooting out like long, proud notches from Shane's place in the centre of the Chart, we saw all the names that orbit Shane's as if it were the last bottle of tequila on a booze cruise. In an instant, we were all Shane and we were reminded of exactly how 'incestuous' our sexual behaviours are.

Even those of us who aren't very good with numbers were able to do the maths and conclude that the sum of our sex partners, times the sum of our partners' partners, equals a big, fat X – an unknown that's creepy to the power of infinity.

Alice's Chart has helped us all relearn how in a Kevin Bacon-esque way, our exes – four, five or sixty times removed – aren't really removed at all, but rather re-posited into a familiar lesbian landscape and, yes, frequently regurgitated. In a 'Holy Shit!' moment of truth packed with the force of all our orgasms combined, we were reminded that not only do we have exes with exes, but also that we *are* exes.

Reality check, indeed.

In terms of L words, one thing the lesbian world isn't is *Large*. Lesbians, in LA and everywhere else, 'live and love' in ladles – tight, often wet, little circles that ensure our social survival. We depend on one another for everything from softball to sex and, as a result, we tend to guard our social walls with our lives – literally. Our cliques are as essential as air. We're a culture of clusters, devoted to our tight-knit circle of friends at best, suspicious of those who attempt to infringe, at worst. Curiously, our pocketed yet tangled lives are very Roach Motel-ish: Lesbians check in, but they don't check out!

But while most of us play closer to the centre of our social rings, in fixed zones of lesbian comfort and familiarity, there are others who now and then dare to love on the edge. These daring 'fringe' women exhibit independence, a desire to experiment, wander and move beyond the snugness of their environments. And travel they do.

Some manage to escape one circle only to slide into another close by. But others move to different parts of their countries and distant parts of the world, where they make friends, but don't necessarily feel a need to cluster. These autonomous women have sex with other lesbians, bisexuals, and, yes, even men. And that's where this chart business proves, beyond doubt, to be completely unmanageable and, more importantly, unmerciful – as attractive as Chlamydia. When Alice said, 'We're all connected, see? Through love, through loneliness, through one tiny lamentable lapse in judgment,' in episode two, I winced.

The truth hurt.

Nobody's perfect – we all make bad choices now and then, and many of us have regrets when it comes to past sex partners. At one time or another, we've all said something like, 'I can't believe I slept with her!' But the Chart takes our regrets one step further and forces us to think about *all* the things we'd rather not believe or think about when it comes to our sex partners.

I can blame quite a few one-night stands on good tequila and bad judgement. But, more importantly, I'd prefer not to revisit them with the help of a sex map from Hell. I don't want to discover that I'm sexually connected to my second cousin on my mother's side through a woman I slept with after a Police concert in 1982.

Can't. Go. There.

No one should go there.

Uncomfortable sexual connections are made every day – that's life. But we really don't need to keep a record of them. For that reason, I think that every time the Chart appears in *The L Word*, a disclaimer should precede it. Maybe this:

> Do not attempt this at home! These 'lesbians' are professional actresses. They *pretend* to have sex with one another and therefore *pretend* to chart their sex lives. Unless you've only slept with virgins who are programmed by a higher power to self-destruct if they lie about their sexual history, you will *not* be able to chart your sex life.

As an essayist who has more than once drawn on my own sexual experiences for material, I can honestly say that one aspect of my life that I would not present to my friends and family in multicolour, Power Point fashion is a detailed graph of my sexual history. While I can probably count and still remember the names of most of the people I've been with, I'm very, very sure I don't want to know who I'm sexually connected to beyond those people. My chart, my extended lesbian tree, reaches from California to Israel. I don't want to think about the bushes that have sprouted in between as a result.

I did the vast majority of my romping in the 1970s, when bad hair was a less-unfortunate badge of recognition and when love really was free, in the sense that unprotected sex didn't cost me my life. I had a helluva time and make no apologies for having behaved in a Shane-like manner when Shane couldn't say orgasm, never mind have one. I have strange and fabulous stories, but no receipts.

And I like it that way.

L is for 'long term'

Compulsory monogamy on the L word

Merri Lisa Johnson

I think that during many long-term relationships, couples hit some challenging moments. Infidelity is a fact of life and a factor in many relationships, gay and straight. I wanted to see Bette and Tina navigate through these challenges. There is much to be learned from seeing how two people who truly love one another face a challenge like this.

Ilene Chaiken, executive producer of The L Word

I am appalled by the *compulsion* toward monogamy, its cultivated hypocrisy and its violently punitive as well as subtle enforcements.

Celeste West, Lesbian Polyfidelity (1996)

Kissing Time

Marianne Faithfull's sensual and throaty ode to free love, 'The Pleasure Song', sets the pilot episode of The L Word in motion:

I got so much love
So much more
So much more love to give.

A pulsing beat pushes the proclamations of abundance forward: 'So much pleasure draws me like I never saw.' From the 2002 CD, *Kissin' Time*, this single drips with hedonism, the word 'pleasure' drawn out long by Faithfull's tongue. The refrain – 'so much more,/so much more love to give' – seduces the viewer with its promise of an alternative value system, a Marcusian recasting of eros as expansive and limitless rather than restricted and repressed. Indeed, the 'L' in 'L Word' seems at this point to stand for *lots* of love, *lots* of pleasure, *lots* of sex.

As the music fades, Tina Kennard, the earth mother figure of the series, stands in the bathroom beatifically gazing down at a white plastic stick. She calls her domestic partner, Bette Porter, to come see, and they share an EPT moment over the fact that Tina is ovulating. 'Let's make a baby,' Bette murmurs into Tina's mouth. The heterosexual script of making a baby is here appropriated by lesbian media culture in order to queer the reproductive moment, yet its normative effects undercut the initial tone of an alternative erotic system. What first appears as 'so much love', 'so much pleasure', 'so many more lives to live', and 'so much more to know' is transformed back into precisely what we already know and live: a vision of love as limited to heterosexual patriarchal monogamous reproductive models. *The L Word* is punctuated regularly by such jarring juxtapositions of queer and heteronormative relationship imagery. As the two women pledge to propagate the lesbian species, Bette's hand reaches between Tina's legs for a bit of off-screen digital stimulation, holding the straight and lesbian content of the scene tightly together in the same frame.

As is the case with many contemporary media texts, conservative and progressive ideologies intertwine and counterbalance each other on *The L Word*. This dialogic structure can be clearly mapped through its representations of monogamy, as mainstream and counter-cultural perspectives on fidelity contest and interpenetrate one another. Taboo desire, thrilling illicit sex, instant body-rocking regret and absolute renunciation structure the 'cheater' plot, forming a pattern that recurs in several characters' storylines. Following Tony Tanner's classic study of adultery in the nineteenth-century novel, one might suggest that the cable television serial drama depends for its narrative urgency on the unstable triangle of adultery, and that the Showtime channel in particular has engaged in a sustained and deliberate reflection on 'the problem of transgressing the marriage contract' (1981: 12) over the last few years.[1] The L Word likewise takes up the monogamy question, revising adultery into cheating for a community that is not legally allowed to marry and asking whether infidelity can be avoided or overcome by the long-term committed couple.

A sequence of scenes at the end of the pilot episode explores this question by crosscutting emblems of lesbian polyamory, lesbian monogamy, heterosexual marriage and adultery. Two neighbouring couples anchor the series in season one: Bette/Tina and Tim/Jenny. Jenny Schecter has moved cross-country to live with her boyfriend, Tim Haspel, but she is instantly, if ambivalently, drawn to the lesbian community in LA. At a party at Bette and Tina's house, Jenny meets Marina Ferrer, a confident and exotic woman with whom she shares many intellectual interests. Marina follows Jenny into the bathroom for a trademark L Word make-out session. Jenny at first resists, but then melts into Marina's advances, finally backing away in horror. Jenny later seeks Marina out at the Planet, a coffee shop owned by Marina in West Hollywood, to explain that she's not – she can't quite utter the word – gay. After several near-connections with Marina (lesbian night at the Planet, Marina's reading group, a brief kiss in a restaurant bathroom), Jenny and Marina plan a 'proper' Saturday night date at Marina's house that concludes with a steamy sex scene, initiating a pattern of cheater plots on the series. She then returns home and crawls into bed with Tim – Marina's scent still on her body – and sobs silently in his arms. Her struggle between loyalty to Tim and a 'completely dismantl[ing]' attraction to Marina provides much of the drama for season one.

This morose pseudo-monogamous bed scene then cuts to Alice Pieszecki's living room, where she and 'best friend' Dana Fairbanks work on constructing a chart to demonstrate the wide-reaching interconnectedness of lesbian sex partners. Borrowing the premise of promiscuity from gay male culture, Alice asserts that she can connect any two lesbians in six steps or less. The chart covers a whole wall. Dana, who has only slept with two women, is bemused: 'It's like this whole crazy tiny little world.' Alice corrects her: 'Crazy yes, but not tiny.' As the camera moves in on the chart for a close-up of this 'crazy' world, the song 'Up in Your Room', by Mr. Airplane Man, provides a connecting element between the chart and Bette and Tina's bed, as if the camera moves through polyamory and comes out on its flipside, lesbian monogamy. The sex in this scene contains some of the hottest action of the first two seasons. The arching tongues, sweaty brows, panting breath and driving beat combine for a thrilling, carefree visual of monogamous sex. Their fast-paced push towards mutual orgasm pauses only long enough for Tina to stare into Bette's eyes, mooning, 'I am so lucky to have you.' This visual narrative conflicts with the script itself on the heat of monogamous sex. An earlier scene in a therapist's office reveals that Bette and Tina's sexual relationship has been 'pretty shitty for going on three years', in self-improvement guru Dan Foxworthy's (played by Daryl Shuttleworth) words. He attributes their waning attraction to the symbiosis that commonly occurs between 'two women who are doing the work of making a serious commitment to each other', calling to mind Laura Kipnis's imagery of domestic gulags and love's labour in her defence of adultery as a legitimate sit-down strike in the American marriage factory, *Against Love: A Polemic* (2003). 'When monogamy becomes labor,' asserts Kipnis:

> when desire is organised contractually, with accounts
> kept and fidelity extracted like labor from employees, with
> marriage a domestic factory policed by means of rigid shop-
> floor discipline designed to keep the wives and husbands
> and domestic partners of the world choke-chained to the
> status quo machinery – is this really what we mean by a "good
> relationship"? (19)

Her answer, in short, is surely not.

The first episode of the series ends with that ultimate emblem of lifelong monogamy: the engagement ring. Jenny wakes up the morning after her first sexual encounter with Marina – her first lesbian sexual experience – and sits up in bed with a look of overwhelming dread. Beaming with anticipation, Tim calls her to the breakfast table where he has prepared a lovely early morning spread, garnished with diamond solitaire. Her eyes welling with tears, Jenny stares at the gift through a haze of mixed feelings. Her speechlessness and strong emotion fit all too well with the standard media imagery of the proposal scene, but in this case the obligatory tears contain an anti-marriage subtext.[2] The thrill of finally being asked to be Tim's wife is literally adulterated by Jenny's memories of the previous evening. These tears, prompted partly by guilt and uncertainty about the future, also express resistance to the marriage plot as a satisfactory conclusion for our newly lesbian heroine. Jenny longs for something else but is trapped in very specific frames of reference that limit what she perceives as possible. One of these frames is what Dossie Easton and Catherine A. Liszt call 'monogamy-centrist thinking', in their polyamory guide, The Ethical Slut (1997). Against the monogamist tenet 'that the purpose and ultimate goal of all relationships – and, for that matter, all sex – is lifetime pair-bonding' (23), Easton and Liszt propose a non-binary model of desire, dismantling the distinction between love of my life and everyone else (222). Furthermore, they resist 'the belief, so often promulgated in Hollywood films and popular literature, that fucking someone else is something you do to your partner, not for yourself – and is, moreover, the very worst thing you can do to someone' (32). Despite their argument that 'younger lesbians are questioning these traditions' by 'investigating nonmonogamy as a way to form less insular relationships' (48), these alternatives are not fully realised on The L Word. Jenny's tears and Alice's chart do, however, gesture clumsily towards them. When Laura Kipnis proposes that 'it becomes hard to refute the idea that something's missing, something that adultery in its fumbling way attempts to palliate' (2003: 196), one wonders, given the conflicting images that structure the series, whether that 'something' pulsing beneath the surface of The L Word is lesbian polyamory.

Tim's impotence

As Mark Wayland, the resident straight guy of season two, demonstrates, most heterosexual men react to lesbian sex scenes with a raging erection – even, or especially, when it includes their girlfriend. Tim, however, has quite the opposite reaction to walking in on Jenny with Marina's face between her legs ('Lawfully', 1:5). He loses his hard-on. After demanding his ring back in front of a busload of Tim's swimming team members, then force-marching Jenny through a break-up scene with Marina, Tim elopes to Tahoe with Jenny in a desperate attempt to close the distance widening between them. Hardly the picture of happily ever after, they attempt to reassure the presiding minister with a stilted kiss. In the hotel after their makeshift ceremony, the newlyweds open a bottle of cheap champagne and Jenny jumps on the bed like a child. Still wearing the torn black pantyhose that she pulled on with chagrin when Tim caught her with Marina earlier that day – not, in other words, having bathed or changed her clothes since having sex with her lesbian lover – Jenny feigns the appropriate wedding night exuberance of a devoted wife, sticking her hand underneath his clothes and biting his nipple through his T-shirt. Less comfortable with their charade, Tim struggles with his emotions, turning away from Jenny's proffered kiss and asking her to 'take a shower or something' first. Soon squeaky clean, Jenny lies naked in bed, still hoping to consummate their marriage like a normal couple. Tim lies down next to her but faces the ceiling. Jenny reaches beneath the covers and rocks her hand up and down his presumably flaccid penis. She looks worried when he doesn't respond, and in a moment almost too excruciating to watch, she pulls her hand out, puts four fingers in her mouth and slathers them with saliva, then returns her moistened hand to work on Tim's erection. The camera zooms in on Tim's genital area, covered, corpse-like, by a white sheet. Jenny stops trying to stimulate him, and her eyes turn also toward the ceiling in a moment of pause, their wedding rites having turned funereal.

Whereas the stereotypical heterosexual man would not perceive a lesbian lover as a threat, or a lesbian tryst as a serious instance of infidelity, Tim does not underestimate the significance of Jenny's attraction to Marina. Although he does entertain a brief flash of jealousy and anger towards Marina that leads him to belittle their affair – 'What do you even do? You girls? Should I even care? Does it even count?' – Tim does not stay with this normative perspective for long. Instead, he represents a more sensitive de-centred hetero masculinity. He does not discriminate in his jealousy on the basis of sexual orientation, feeling just as disturbed by Jenny's sexual relationship with Marina as he is by his fear that Jenny might cheat with her old college professor, a smarmy creative writing teacher she fellated as an undergraduate. Tim's soft masculinity – a trait that makes him a character with whom many viewers sympathise and identify – is literalised in the petulant flesh of his impotent penis. It refuses to cooperate with the traditional pornographic content of the scene he stumbled into. Instead, his ironically lesbian-friendly lens interprets the scene as a comment on his irrelevance. Like the self-loathing homosexual cop who pulls him over for speeding at the end of this elopement episode, Tim realises that Jenny and Marina were hardly waiting around for an erect penis to complete the scene of coitus. In place of this erection, Tim leaves his wedding band on the nightstand, encircling a sheet of hotel stationary, rolled into a blank column.

While Tim's open-minded acceptance of Marina as a legitimate competing suitor amounts to a progressive reading of lesbian sex as equally real, equally meaningful, his overreaction – his unchecked jealousy, his limp dick – points to a conservative message about monogamy. Their broken agreement literally disables him, demonstrating the 'rampant emotional illiteracy' described by psychologist Deborah Anapol, in *Polyamory, the New Love without Limits: Secrets of Sustainable Intimate Relationships* (1997: 132). Anapol sketches a relevant hierarchy of sexual minorities in which 'variations in relationship orientation are perceived as even more of a threat to the established social order than variations in sexual orientation' (80). In his ideological rigidity and erectile dysfunction, Tim embodies 'old paradigm relating', defined by Anapol as 'a philosophy of relationship which emphasises well defined rules, extensive agreements, ironclad conditions, and the importance of the group over the individual' (178). Anapol contrasts this common approach to couplehood with 'new paradigm relating', in which partners '[use] the relationship to consciously enhance the psychological and spiritual development of the partners', a style of relating 'characterized by responding authentically in the present moment, honoring individual autonomy, equality, total honesty, and self responsibility' (178). Tim's character is deployed in this scene as a familiar image of culturally justified emotional withholding, a product of old paradigm relating. 'Our exclusively monogamous culture enshrines jealousy and possessiveness' (152), as Anapol asserts, and Tim holds tightly to this oversimplification of what is sacred in a romantic partnership. In lying silently next to Jenny, Tim occupies a punitive proximity that functions to remind her of her crime instead of talking with her, making love with her, or taking some healthy time apart from her. He indulges in self-righteous indignation, allowing it to harden between them.

Several episodes later ('Luck, Next Time', 1:9), Tim and Jenny lapse into a night of break-up sex, as Jenny bucks up and down on Tim's lap with more frenzy than solace. The next morning, Tim rejects Jenny once more, telling her he does not want to be back together and calling her phoney and manipulative. 'It's like you've done this thing,' he shivers, 'and you can't wash it off. It's in you. And I don't want it in me.' Tim's vagueness about 'this thing' of which he accuses Jenny collapses her infidelity and her emerging lesbian identity into one image of contagion. Through a strange gender inversion, Tim positions Jenny's lesbian infidelity as a phallic tool of violation that threatens to turn him gay, to penetrate and emasculate him. He is not 'man enough' to countenance being cuckolded by a woman. His pledge of monogamy – what most heterosexual women seek urgently from men – is found wanting. After a few glancing moments of flirtation with Trish Peverell (Nicole McKay), a member of the swimming team Tim coaches, Tim's potential as a player is usurped by Jenny, and her facility in strapping on this traditionally masculine entitlement leaves him queasy. In addition to his discomfort with this gender and sexual fluidity, Tim turns away from the possibility of interpreting Jenny's cheating and lying as symptomatic of a relationship that needs to be redesigned to make room for multiple mates. This 'thing' that Jenny can't wash off, this 'thing' in Jenny that Tim does not want in him, is cast by his language in viral terms – like a sexually transmitted disease – but because many progressive ideas are met with conservative descriptions of them as filth, as agents of social deterioration, it is imperative to separate his metaphorical evocations from the facts he seeks to describe, and to recognise that what Tim rejects is the invitation to queer his understanding of fidelity and orientation. He opts instead for the prison of old paradigms, and by the first episode of season two, Tim heads back to the Midwest where he can pursue serial monogamy in relative peace.

Bette's regret

The L Word uses the common metaphor of long-term monogamous couplehood as a prison to structure the episode, 'Locked Up' (1:12), when Bette is arrested after a scuffle with the bible-thumping protestors who try to block the arrival of a controversial show at the art gallery where she serves as director. Aptly titled *Provocations*, the installation functions as a play within the play that reproduces *The L Word*'s themes of taboo imagery and cultural censorship in microcosm. Bette and Candace Jewell, a carpenter for whom she has sexually charged feelings, protect the provocative art pieces against the encroaching moral majority, forming a human tunnel of linked lesbian arms through which the art movers can safely transport the paintings and videos. In a stretch of plausibility, Bette is placed alone in a cell with Candace because they have been identified by the police as the ringleaders of the riot and are considered more 'dangerous' than the other protesters. Now forced into close proximity, Bette goes to unusual lengths to diminish their erotic connection. First she refuses to sit next to Candace, and then she plays ridiculous word games and proposes childish maths 'problems' to distract her rational mind from her aroused body. Bette has internalised the rules of compulsory monogamy to such an extent that she does not consider simply following her erotic longings.[3] The jail cell thus externalises the prison that her relationship to Tina creates in her mind. 'I am in so much trouble,' she breathes. Bette has penned in her errant desires, refusing to acknowledge her feelings for Candace as legitimate. She is not free to explore them, as monogamy forms a limiting structure within which she must move.

Bette and Candace's apprehension of desire as a freedom that must be managed and curtailed reverberates throughout *The L Word*. In the pilot episode, for instance, Marina mounts a seduction of the presumably straight and spoken-for Jenny by referencing Anne Carson's *Eros the Bittersweet*, a book that 'practically changed [Jenny's] whole life.' Its focus on love as exquisite pain infuses the series. In a later episode ('Locked Up'), Marina quotes Anne Carson in hopes of luring Jenny's new girlfriend, Robin (Anne Ramsay), into a sadistic new triangle: 'The Greek word, *eros*, denotes want, lack. The desire for that which is missing. The lover wants what it does not have. It is by definition impossible for him to have what he wants, if, as soon as it is had, it is no longer wanted.' This construction of desire as lack disappoints with its masculinist perspective. One wonders why these lesbian love pairs – Jenny/Marina and Bette/Candace – reproduce such a negative vision of desire instead of gravitating towards the images of excess and hedonism that define much lesbian sexual philosophy.[4]

Back in the prison cell, Bette laments, 'I can't stand it,' and when Candace responds, 'I'm sorry it's so painful,' Bette repeats, 'It's so painful.' In this incantation of discomfort, Bette and Candace reinforce an interpretation of certain physical longings as socially undesirable. Without considering their alternatives, the two would-be lovers proceed to engage in long-distance lovemaking, as Bette masturbates against the cellblock wall and Candace brings herself to orgasm on a narrow cot.

'I'm lying on top of you,' Bette spins in fantasy. 'You know what I'm doing right now?'

Candace goes along: 'I think so … [heavy breathing] … God, this is fucking insane! What are you doing to me?'

Bette (pained expression, face pressed against concrete): 'Fucking you.'

'Come over here,' Candace reasonably requests.

Bette: 'I am there, you know I am.'

In this sleight of hand, Bette elides the rules of monogamy to which she adheres, eroticising the distance between them instead of acknowledging that she is *not* really there, *not* actually fucking her. Fantasising together can be fun – as anyone who has ever tried phone sex can attest – but when it functions as a cover for a fundamentally patriarchal cultural rule, it seems less like lesbian erotica than monogamy propaganda. While I enjoy a lesbian masturbation scene as much as the next girl, the steamy longing between these two inmates depends problematically on prohibition for its heat. Their disembodied intercourse may seem to transgress Bette's monogamous obligation, but ultimately the mutual agreement not to touch each other prioritises sexual exclusivity. Bette may have lusted in her heart, but carnal sex with Candace is, at least in this episode, unthinkable. In this assumption, The L Word clearly celebrates the heteronormative family values it seems to subvert.[5]

In the season one finale, Bette and Candace uneasily give in to their uncontainable desires. Bette initiates their rendezvous when she slips into the passenger side of Candace's car with a pained look on her face and asks Candace to 'take [her] somewhere'. Like Jenny, Bette feels powerless against her desire and is soon filled with self-loathing, collapsing in her shower at home in tears. When Bette and Tina return home after the opening of *Provocations* at the art gallery, Tina confronts Bette about her affair with Candace. The hysteria of the scene, the intensity of Bette's regret, and the lengthy process of winning Tina back over the entire second season demonstrate catastrophic thinking about infidelity. Exhausted from the grief of their break-up, Bette tries to pinpoint 'the exact moment when [she] could have stopped [her]self', language that once again positions non-monogamous desire as a threat to be contained. Tim uses similar language to indict Jenny for her affair with Marina, his voice breaking as he yells, 'Why couldn't you stop?' Not being able to 'stop' oneself is seen here as a symptom of moral deficiency, a force of social destruction. Gratification is, in Marcusian terms, 'tabooed as perversion' (1974: 37). After getting into a car accident because she is distracted by thoughts of Tina, Bette is confronted by the driver she ran into. He threatens a lawsuit and shouts, 'You'll be one sorry bitch.' Bette grabs him by the collar and screams in his face, 'What makes you think I'm not already? What makes you think I'm not already!' Bette is indeed one sorry bitch after her brief affair with Candace, and her acceptance of 'cheating' as an unquestioned deal-breaker in serious relationships reproduces a common representation of long-term monogamous commitment as claustrophobic as well as fragile and at risk.

While Bette's affair with Candace may seem to stem from what her sister, Kit Porter, calls 'the daddy blues' – a response to the pressure of being her family's sole provider – a careful review of season one reveals a deeper well of dissatisfaction within her relationship to Tina. In a group therapy session before the affair begins, for instance, the audience is made privy to the participants' inner thoughts. Bette, a reluctant therapy participant, never speaks her most private worries out loud, but here she worries silently, 'What's happening to me? Am I just panicking? Is this about the baby? ... Or am I falling out of love?' The episode's title, 'Listen Up' (1:8), invites the audience to pay attention to all of what is going on between Bette and Tina, but the structure of this scene averts focus from Bette's fretting thoughts by framing them with Tina's words. Before Bette's revelation, Tina says, out loud, 'I know group was hard today, but I think we got to talk about some really important things. I think too often people are afraid to say what they really feel. Um, they're afraid they might be rejected.' After Bette's musings, Tina says, also out loud, 'It's hard to be honest because people don't really want to hear the truth.' Tina's words, awkward and ironic, highlight her obliviousness to Bette's unhappiness, rather than Bette's unhappiness itself. In the background, Rufus Wainwright's 'Foolish Love' provides an additional dimension of commentary, as he croons, 'Why won't you last? Why can't you last?' The pressure to be an adequate 'daddy' to Tina's baby, the only fear she is willing to share in therapy, is presented as mere artifice, a more acceptable anxiety than Bette's root concern that love cannot last and that desire inevitably strays.

Throughout season two, narrative and audience desire become fixated on a reunion between Bette and Tina, and this desire eclipses the subtle story line in which Bette had been falling out of love with Tina throughout season one. The audience and writers seem all too willing to forget Tina's words in episode ten: 'I get this feeling from you that you're so proud to be with me, and it makes me feel really safe and loved. It's great. ... But lately I haven't been feeling it. ... So I've just been trying to concentrate on myself and trying not to get scared about it.' At the Dinah Shore Golf Classic in episode eleven, Jenny asks, 'Why is it so difficult to meet the right person? You know? All of your [coming-out] stories are about confusion and unfulfilled desire and disappointment.' In response, Tina offers the story of meeting Bette as a counter-narrative characterised by certainty, fulfilment and ecstatic long-term commitment, but even in the midst of this intention, Tina admits that she sometimes thinks, 'God, am I going to go to my grave and Bette will be the only woman I've ever slept with?' She quickly retracts this worry by explaining, 'Then I look at her and think, "What more could I want?"' Clearly, Bette is not the only one experiencing their relationship as a limiting structure. Bette's affair with Candace thus becomes a convenient focal point as *the* problem that needs to be worked out, through recommitment and forgiveness, rather than being acknowledged as part of a larger pattern of separateness and dying desires. Yet what Bette regrets may be something more complex than fucking Candace.

Alice and Dana's rules

Season two begins with a barrier that parallels the jail cell for Bette and Candace. Dana and Alice finally acknowledge their mutual attraction after several years of friendship, but Dana is engaged to Tonya (Meredith McGeachie), an objectionable star-fucker who glommed onto Dana at a tennis tournament. In a half-hearted effort to contain their desire, Dana and Alice generate a list of rules. These rules function as prophylactics between the two women's bodies in order to reduce the effects of temptation. They are the 'rules of un-attraction', in Alice's words. As they jog together in a remote canyon, Alice proclaims, 'It doesn't have to mean anything. I mean being attracted to someone's no big deal.' Alice's effort to curb their attraction is another measure of compulsory monogamy. Dana's investment in these rules is easier to apprehend, as her pending marriage to Tonya is at stake. Alice has no such investment, particularly since she finds Tonya objectionable, other than the cultural imperative to support monogamy – one's own as well as others'. Her statements – 'We have to agree not to act on it' and 'We need to counteract it' – presume this imperative. Once this decision has been made, Alice and Dana take turns offering rules:

Dana: Okay, like never be alone together, places like the bathroom at the Planet.
Alice: Right. Never be alone together.
Dana: Especially never be alone together in places where there's like a bed or a couch.
Alice: Right, or a table. Or a floor. Or the backseat of a car.
Dana: Ooh, that'd be good. That *wouldn't* be good!
Alice: Okay, you need to stop showing up at the Planet after you've worked out, when you're all sweaty and your veins are all popping all over the place.

Dana: You like that? Tonya hates that. Alright, well then you
        can't wear those shirts any more.
Alice: What shirts?
Dana: You know, the ones where they cling to you in some
        places and fall off you in others.
Alice: ... [big grin] ...
Dana: Fuck you.
Alice: Okay, that's *totally* against the rules.[6]

Their playful repartee takes for granted the necessity of not doing what
they want. Desire outside the assigned couple is 'totally against the
rules'.[6]

A clip from Jenny's tortured writing earlier in the episode describes
her protagonist, Sara Schuster, in terms of this rejection of desire: 'And
now she reviles you, like you revile your own craving.' Jenny's words
(read aloud by Tim) are intercut with scenes of struggle between Bette
and Tina, who argue over potential sperm donors and participate
in tension-filled therapy sessions over their sex life and relatively
traditional 'husband' and 'wife' roles in their relationship, as familiarity
once again breeds contempt and children. Through this juxtaposition,
the phrase 'reviling your own craving' conveys two meanings, including
the truism that we treat our loved ones the most poorly (picture Jenny
scowling at Tim when he reads her writing over her shoulder) and the
Freudian rejection of craving as the enemy of civilisation (why does Tim
overreact so intensely to Jenny's affair with Marina? Must their world
completely unravel as a result?) Reviling one's own craving may indeed
be the troubling subtext of the episode and series. Surprisingly, The
L Word openly promotes what Herbert Marcuse (1974) calls surplus-
repression, and Laura Kipnis cleverly revises into surplus-monogamy.
'[Renunciation] chafes,' explains Kipnis, 'particularly when the
quantities demanded begin to exceed the amount of gratification
achieved, for instance when basic monogamy evolves, as it inevitably
does under such conditions, into *surplus monogamy*: enforced compliance
rather than a free expression of desire' (2003: 44).

At the end of season one, the viewer glimpses an alternative
arrangement of desire in a momentary embrace of abundance. Jenny,

having married and divorced Tim, then loved and lost Marina, has begun to date. She is seeing Gene Feinberg (Tygh Runyan), a girlish boy who curates fish at a local aquarium, and Robin, a woman she met at the Dinah Shore Golf Classic in Palm Springs (aka 'spring break for lesbians'). After a hurtful encounter with Marina, Jenny returns home with Gene and finds Robin already there. Marina has left a plaintive message on Jenny's answering machine saying she is in love with her and would give anything for another chance. Robin and Gene both offer to leave, but Jenny pauses, looks at each of them, and says, 'I don't want either of you to leave.' Jenny reaches after the possibility of spending time with multiple lovers without it feeling like a competition or a threat to anyone. She takes a chance on cultivating a less confining version of love and attraction in which abundance is a good thing, not a catastrophe. Jenny, a character who starts the series as the token straight girl, interestingly morphs here into the most fluid sexual identity on the show, demonstrating that, 'for the polyamorous woman, it is not assumed that because a lover sleeps with someone else, she is no longer available in the original relationship,' as one contributor to The Lesbian Polyamory Reader puts it (Munson and Stelboum 1999: 20). In such a configuration, 'everyone is asked to stretch in communication and self-knowledge' (ibid). The scene of Jenny's possible polyamory in season one is intercut significantly with the final scene of the season's finale – an enactment of monogamy panic in the violently titled, 'Limb from Limb' – in which Bette and Tina not only break up over Bette's affair with Candace but attack each other physically. This moment of possibility is not explored further, as Jenny breaks up with both lovers in the first two episodes of season two, opting instead for lesbian monogamy with a new character named Carmen de la Pica Morales, even though Carmen actually loves Jenny's roommate, Shane McCutcheon.

Shane's longings

Shane, as representative of casual sex, is frequently pitted against Bette and Tina, the show's spokeswomen for monogamy. In the pilot episode, Shane emerges from the bushes after a night of debauchery to find Bette and Tina sitting on their front steps in a rare moment of pseudo-married post-coital glow. A leather halter top strapped around her boy-flat torso, Shane stands there, an image of uncontainable queer desire, ducking her chin in mock humility as she admits to not having gone home yet, implying that she bedded down a neighbour and kept her up all night in the throes of hard no-strings sex.[7] Offering an uncharacteristic homage to long-term commitment despite her repeated assertion that she does not do relationships, Shane looks wistfully at Bette and Tina and says: 'You two totally just got laid. That gives me hope. Because I love knowing that two people who've been together that long can still make each other that happy.' In this expression of hope for contented monogamous sex, Shane betrays her espoused beliefs and longings, along with her supposed super-queer role in the show, as the script harnesses her rogue character to the monogamy imperative. Because her statement does not match her behaviour and proclamations in other scenes, her words must serve some other function besides fleshing out her character, such as reining in the queerness of lesbian desire. This concession to widespread ideological investments in compulsory monogamy renders the series safe for liberal Middle America in its opening episode.

Shane's professed beliefs about relationships are showcased in the episode 'Longing' (1:4), through a confrontation with her disgruntled former lover turned stalker, Lacey (Tammy Lynn Michaels). Lacey feels slighted by Shane's lack of interest in an ongoing romance and distributes fliers calling Shane a 'user'. Their dialogue about this 'big misunderstanding' illustrates a complex debate within the series and the lesbian community over sexual commitment. Lacey says, 'I don't understand what happened,' and Shane counters, 'Babe, nothing happened, okay? It's just about having a good time and enjoying each other's company.' While Shane could be perceived here as articulating a stereotypically masculine view of sex as fleeting fun, a shift in frames of reference reveals that she is more significantly articulating the marginalised philosophy of lesbian polyamory. In her 'pleasure guide' on this subject, Celeste West asks, 'what if extra lovers were considered harmless fun, not framed as threatening?' (1996: 11), a question Shane also raises through her lifestyle. Like West, Shane might well consider compulsory monogamy a form of 'relationship bigotry' that ought to 'be challenged, rather than aped' (39). Shane's character seems to dramatise an alternative perspective on sexual commitment similar to that of West. Lacey, conversely, voices the more familiar 'body-ownership ideologies' that West presents as a 'copycat portrayal of het-conditioned sexual responses like rote jealousy' (128). With her face pulled tight in a pout, Lacey says, 'I know, but then you went off with that other girl,' invoking the hetero imagery of competition within an economy of scarcity, a framework that triggers panic about sharing sexual affection with additional lovers. Shane resists this model: 'Yeah, I don't see what the problem is with that.'

Despite the fact that the show's writers give Shane a dysfunctional childhood in season two to explain her resistance to monogamy – in yet another concession to compulsory monogamy – her dialogue with Lacey interjects a sensible counter-discourse about dispensing with rote jealousy, dramatising key tenets of lesbian polyfidelity. These include its appeal to human rights, according to West, who pointedly asks, 'Can we freely express the sexual energy that naturally exists between people and maintain the historic hierarchy of relationship/ownership?' (40) Furthermore, lesbian polyfidelity in West's formulation intervenes in dominant ideologies of capitalist individualism, as it resists 'the constant propaganda upholding belief in an economy of scarcity and of possessiveness', and recognises the disastrous emotional consequences of a relationship system in which 'privatization of resources becomes a form of security and pride' (128). Shane later accepts the negative interpretation of her non-monogamy, in the heartache of losing her married lover, Cherie Jaffe (Roseanna Arquette). She says, 'All my life people have said I would become a psychopath if I didn't learn how to feel. But I want to know what the fuck is so great about feeling. Because I finally let myself and I feel like my heart's been completely ripped out.' These limited options – monogamous lover or polyamorous psychopath – place in stark terms the cultural pressure to renounce wide-ranging desire in favour of privatised sexual and emotional resources. Non-monogamy is treated here like a vice or crime – the unacceptable – even though a significant community of lesbians has been devoted to polyfidelity for many years, along with remaining committed to carrying on a history of lesbian-feminist critiques of marriage and monogamy.

Lacey's stubborn voice drowns out this history, as she announces to Jenny about Shane's behaviour: 'That's just wrong. You just can't treat people like that. You have to tell Shane that that's just not right.'

The debate between Shane and Lacey is duplicated within Shane herself. There seem in fact to be two versions of Shane in this episode, perhaps reflecting conflicting views of monogamy within contemporary American culture. One 'Shane' is deferent to Bette and Tina's monogamy, actually offering a small bow to them on the stoop, while the other 'Shane' kindly but firmly refuses to indulge Lacey's jealousy, possessiveness, and reductive evaluation of their sexual experience according to an exclusivity model. The tension housed within her character between glorifying and undermining monogamy reflects a central tension within the series as a whole. Two utopian visions battle each other for primacy: the slut utopia of promiscuity and the domestic utopia of nesting lesbians. Abundance and security compete with each other as equally compelling life experiences in Shane's mind. One can have both, according to The Ethical Slut, if one is willing and able to do the work of cultivating an 'internal security that is not dependent on sexual exclusivity' (Easton and Listz 1997: 136).

Miserable as the rest of us

Within the gay and lesbian community, two groups compete to represent homosexuality: the assimilationists, well represented by Andrew Sullivan's 1995 manifesto, Virtually Normal, and the sex radicals, who find a powerful voice in Michael Warner's 1999 response, The Trouble with Normal, a defence of non-normativity in queer ethics. The L Word, in its representations of monogamy, falls decidedly in the 'virtually normal' camp, and in its uncritical allegiance to cultural norms of couplehood, the show does minimal work in queering representations of desire, often reiterating scripts of possession and betrayal from the hetero world. Yet it is too easy in feminist media studies to lapse into tedious analyses of television shows and characters as not feminist enough or not radical enough or not queer enough. Admittedly, my reading of cheater plots on The L Word threatens to devolve into precisely this sort of analysis. However, my interest is not directed primarily at The L Word.

Rather, I am concerned that the presumption of monogamy – the monogamy imperative – pervades, one might even say plagues, the whole of western culture, up to and including lesbian media imagery. The motivation for this chapter lies therefore in examining the cultural scripts that lead media culture to take up the question of monogamy again and again, staging debates between characters over its values, its difficulties, as well as its place within and implications for queer communities. That these media texts – from *The L Word* to *Queer as Folk* to *Out of Order* to *Huff*, just on the most recent seasons of Showtime alone – resolve the question in familiar and often conservative ways is perhaps less important than the fact that they keep posing the question anew.

Why, then, does the cheater plot dominate contemporary gay and lesbian media culture? And what does it mean to import an adulterous dynamic from straight media culture in the context of a community that is not legally allowed to marry in most states? A heteronormative world-view scripts these shows as if gay and lesbian partnerships will necessarily and ideally reproduce the same pleasures and, to the delight of many pundits, the same disasters as their straight counterparts. To be 'virtually normal' is to be trapped, it seems, in a jealous triangle, one's emotional well-being at the mercy of adultery's instability. The new cliché argument – for? against? – gay marriage comes in the form of backhanded support: 'Sure, gays should be allowed to marry. Let them be as miserable as the rest of us.'[8] This assumption that gay and lesbian partnerships, if legally sanctioned, would be as unhappy as heterosexual marriages seems to have influenced gay and lesbian media texts to reproduce the adultery plot. The cynical pleasure of the gay divorce storyline is at once a progressive critique of marriage as unfulfilling for many people – straight and gay, male and female – as well as a conservative critique of gay and lesbian relationships as locked into doomed hetero models.

This opposition of casual sex and romantic love, or of multiple lovers and long-term commitment, may make a certain limited sense in gay contexts, but it is not queer. 'One of [queer culture's] greatest contributions to modern life,' as Michael Warner asserts in *The Trouble with Normal*, 'is the discovery that you can have both: intimacy and casualness; long-term commitment and sex with strangers; romantic love and perverse pleasure. To cast the conflict as one between sex and love is to deny the best insights and lived experience of queers' (1999: 73). In the same way that Warner proposes to consider marriage 'as an ethical problem' for queers (107), I would likewise suggest that the adultery or cheater plot poses an ethical problem for queer culture, in that the taken-for-grantedness of state sanction bolsters the drama of cheating. Our media images, like our political debates, need to 'dramatize independence from state-regulated sexuality' (134). Towards the end of season two, Kit and her transman suitor, Ivan Aycock (Kelly Lynch), argue over the difference between his non-monogamy and her adultery with Benjamin Bradshaw, a married man ('Late, Later, Latent', 2:9). This important distinction warrants more airtime and more careful debate.

It would in fact be quite thrilling to see Showtime explore more thoroughly the question of whether every long-term gay or lesbian relationship must be marred by what Brian Kinney, of Queer as Folk, calls the 'Stepford Fag' syndrome. Perhaps season three of The L Word will consider in more detail a vision of 'long-term' that is not synonymous with stifling monogamous arrangements. Executive producer Ilene Chaiken expresses her interest in seeing Bette and Tina work through the difficult circumstances of an affair. I believe, like Chaiken, 'There is much to be learned from seeing how two people who truly love one another face a challenge like this,' but I am not sure that The L Word has yet offered a sophisticated or varied range of tactics for navigating this emotional challenge. The 'violently punitive as well as subtle enforcements' of compulsory monogamy (in Celeste West's words) continue to fascinate, but they reflect a paucity of queer answers to the complex mix of desire and commitment in long-term lesbian relationships. To reiterate, the show is not the problem: it is the culture itself which is not feminist enough, not radical enough, not queer enough to come up with something new to say about non-monogamy, and even our most progressive media images struggle to break through these ideological barriers. The focus on monogamy demonstrated by The L Word and its Showtime network peers at least suggests an ongoing inquiry into the pitfalls of this model. Even though its imagery is somewhat predictable and at times implausible – Bette and Tina slap each other and then fuck?! – *The* L *Word's* persistent focus on this topic speaks to latent desires among writers and readers alike for new configurations of erotic partnership.[9]

Notes

1. For instance, in the summer of 2003, the five-episode series *Out of Order*, starring Eric Stoltz and Felicity Huffman, dramatised contemporary debates over marriage and postmodern morality, as the main character rationalised an affair for several episodes and then retreated into what can only be called marriage propaganda to reaffirm his commitment to his wife. Season four of *Queer as Folk*, another hit series on Showtime, spiced up its marginal lesbian couple narrative thread with an adultery plot. Lindsay Peterson (Thea Gill) cheats on her domestic partner, Melanie Marcus (Michelle Clunie), with a man, and the brief dalliance ends their long-term relationship. Throughout its five seasons, *Queer as Folk* has featured regular debates over the relationship between queer life and hetero models of marriage, domesticity, and monogamy. Brian Kinney (Gale Harold), who moves from club boy to club owner over the course of the series, insists on the centrality of non-monogamy to queer identity, proclaiming in the episode where Michael (Hal Sparks) and Ben get married in Canada, 'We're queer – we don't get married.' Brian refuses to settle down into what he sees as the 'Stepford Fag' life even though it means losing lovers he cares deeply about.

2. In *Here Comes the Bride: Women, Weddings, and the Marriage Mystique*, Jaclyn Geller devotes a complete chapter to the proposal scene in the contemporary imagination. In this scene, the woman 'must appear disoriented, overwhelmed by shock and delight. Despite the hard work and perseverance that may have actually brought her to the moment of securing male commitment, she must seem to be caught off guard' (2001: 90). Furthermore, 'the modern bride-to-be's amazement must in fact appear so intense that in the standard proposal scenario she loses her capacity for speech. In today's commercialized romantic ethos, incoherence is a sign of true love' (91). Jenny's speechlessness at the moment of Tim's proposal indeed

expresses the incoherence of her identity, as she tenses beneath competing desires and sexual identities.

3. I am using 'compulsory monogamy' here as a parallel to Adrienne Rich's famous formulation of 'compulsory heterosexuality', an exposé of a relationship configuration as socially constructed rather than natural. Borrowing from Chrys Ingraham's more recent work on compulsory heterosexuality, *Thinking Straight: The Power, the Promise, and the Paradox of Heterosexuality*, I propose a paradigm of *thinking monogamously*, which involves 'an understanding of [monogamy] as naturally occurring and not as an extensively organized social arrangement or means for distributing power and wealth for male to female behavior' (2005: 3). With Ingraham, I would suggest that thinking monogamously, as a subcategory of thinking straight, is an investment in 'the illusion of well-being that institutionalized heterosexuality [and/or monogamy] promises, not in its realities' (4).

4. Luce Irigaray's formulation of female sexuality as multiple and autoerotic in *This Sex Which Is Not One* (1985) is among the most well-known theoretical versions of alternative sexual philosophy. Dossie Easton and Catherine A. Liszt provide a more commonsense guide to sexual abundance in *The Ethical Slut* (1997).

5. This statement inverts Tony Tanner's analysis of the 'adultery plot' in the novel. Tanner argues that the novel is 'a paradoxical object in society', in that it seems 'to move towards marriage and the securing of genealogical continuity', yet it depends on 'an energy that threatens to contravene that stability of the family on which society depends' (1981: 4). The novel is, in his view, 'a text that may work to subvert what it seems to celebrate' (ibid). In other words, while the novel seems to move towards a conservative agenda of reinforcing the marriage plot as a natural resolution in the individual's life, its constant attention to adultery betrays an ulterior interest in inevitable transgression. Contemporary television, in contrast, is often considered a medium that depends on taboo topics, trades in improper images, and pulls the family apart with its salacious array of sex scenes. Certainly, Showtime's original series are known for their near-pornographic content and PFLAG (Parents, Families, and Friends of Gays) pride in non-normative sexualities.

The generous imagery of queer sex is, in fact, a welcome departure from the heteronormative soft porn of most soap operas and prime-time dramas. However, in its focus on adultery and its consistent conclusion that infidelity ends long-term relationships – lesbian and straight – The L Word is perhaps more interested in the consequences of transgression than in transgression itself.

6. The transcripts of certain scenes cited in this chapter come from The L Word Fan Site, an incredibly useful Internet source for close readings of individual episodes.

7. If The L Word is Queer as Folk for lesbians, as some advertising copy proposed, Shane plays Brian. These characters act as foils for the rest of the cast, refusing to accept the assimilationist tactics and identities crafted by their friends. They are lone voices in the wilderness of compulsory social graces and contracts. However, whereas Brian consistently preaches against normativity to his married friends, asserting, 'We're queer, we don't get married' and insisting throughout the five seasons of Queer as Folk on the validity of a life filled with poppers and anonymous blowjobs, Shane caves on this point as early as the pilot episode of The L Word.

8. This line was made popular by Det. Lenny Briscoe (Joe Orbach) on NBC's Law and Order and is bandied about regularly by comedians and everyday Joes. A Google search of the phrase, 'Let them be as miserable as the rest of us,' currently turns up over a hundred hits.

9. For her keen insights, careful readings, viewing companionship, and stimulating conversations on all things L Word, I am indebted to Maria Bachman.

L12 Why is the **L** word sexy?

Kathy Belge

'Why did we invite all these people over?' my girlfriend asked as I shut the door and she slammed me against it, kissing me hard. Like most of the lesbian nation, we anxiously awaited the start of *The L Word*. We made a party out of première night and invited a bunch of friends over. I don't know what I was expecting, except to finally see some portrayal of lesbians on TV. One thing I was not expecting was how damp my boxers would be by the end of the evening.

I've heard a lot of criticism of *The L Word*, but one thing I have not heard is that it's not sexy enough. My friend Miriam said she wouldn't watch. She refused 'to support some pseudo lesbian drama whose sole purpose was to titillate straight men'. Whatever, Miriam! I heard her girlfriend was plenty titillated and she didn't refuse the lust she brought to their bedroom after watching at my house.

I wondered if other lesbians around the world were also hopping into bed for post-*L Word* coitus. (I guess the ones who weren't hopping online to chat about it were.) What is it that makes *The L Word* sexy? Sure, there's a lot of sex in *The L Word*, but this is not what makes it sexy. What makes *The L Word* sexy is its accurate portrayal of sexual and sensual situations that lesbians find themselves in.

The character who engages in the most sex is Jenny, the newly out bisexual girl. Although she hops into bed with just about anyone, she appeals least to lesbians, according to many Internet polls. Awkward Jenny lacks the subtlety required to turn most lesbians on. It seems she thought the way to seduce a woman was to take her shirt off and stand there. Most of us have been in a locker room. The simple sight of a woman's breasts isn't going to do much for us. Maybe Jenny is the one Miriam feared is planted to attract straight guys.

So, it's not simply sex, but sex appeal that turn us on about The L Word. While what is sexy to one woman may not be to another, I think there is a lesbian sensibility, some universals, that The L Word writers have mastered. They've created a drama that keeps us tuning in week after week, the drama of subtle seduction, and the surprise hit of forbidden love.

Subtle seduction

The L Word masterminds have done a good job of creating believable characters. As someone in a long-term partnership, I find many parts of the relationship between Bette and Tina to be true to life. There's a scene in the first episode where Bette and Tina get it on after quite a drought. (Okay, that same night they almost got it on with a GUY. I didn't say The L Word was perfect.) But, after the guy leaves, Bette and Tina have one of the most honest sex scenes I've seen portrayed. There's passion, there's love and there's even orgasm. (Which, by the way, Jennifer Beals mastered. Go Jennifer!)

Even sexier is the next morning, when Bette and Tina are leaning up against each other on the porch drinking morning coffee. Their friend, playgirl Shane, walks by and comments on their 'just got laid' look. That moment is so intimate, so real and so lesbian. It's one reason I think The L Word is sexy.

Sexiness is all about subtleties: the kind of killer glance your lover shoots you from across a crowded room that says, 'I want you and I want you now.' There's something about the fact that you can't have her now that makes her even more desirable. It's a word said in just the right way, the brush of a hand under the table, a glance back as she walks to the bathroom, motioning for you to follow. These are the types of situations The L Word creators have mastered.

The surprise hit

The L Word is a fantasy. Marina, the queen seductress in season one wound up in many lesbian fantasies after she seduced Jenny. The first-episode scene, when Marina follows Jenny into the bathroom and kisses her, is the sexiest moment of the series for many of my friends. It's the fantasy of a beautiful stranger hitting on you in a completely unexpected way.

That kind of surprise seduction also makes for good drama. When sous-chef Lara Perkins (Lauren Lee Smith) kisses tennis pro, Dana, in the locker room, not only were our gym teacher fantasies fulfilled, we were all pleasantly shocked by the advance ('Let's Do It', 1:2). Finally, some action for cute Dana!

In the ending to season one ('Limb from Limb', 1:13), another moment of surprising seduction: Alice, Dana's confidante and best friend, shows up in the middle of the night to unexpectedly plant one on her and declare her love. What else is worth getting pulled out of bed in the middle of the night? It's moments like these that leave us longing for more, that play out the fantasies we may silently harbour. It's moments like these that send us to the chat rooms to ponder what's next or propel us to bed with a lustful look in our eye.

Forbidden lust

For all her lack of finesse, troubled writer Jenny nails it on the head when she says to Marina, 'Every time I look at you I feel so completely dismantled' ('Longing', 1:3). She's fighting her attraction for Marina because she's engaged to Tim, who she thinks she loves. Even though their situation is tortuous, part of the allure is the chaos, the sense of feeling alive. We may not wish for that kind of an attraction in our own lives, understanding its ultimate destruction, but the overpowering energy is so appealing: the raw lust, the unknown possibilities, the danger of getting caught...

Although many long-term coupled lesbians complained about Bette's affair with Candace Jewell, my guess is most were secretly turned on by it. Who hasn't been attracted to someone who is off limits? Whether it be a straight woman, our boss or someone else's lover? Who doesn't long for the kind of jolt from someone whose very presence in the room rattles her foundation to the core? Who doesn't long for the touch of someone whose little pinkie can send shivers through every pore of your body? Is there anything more sweetly torturous than forbidden love?

When Bette and Candace, locked in jail together, can't touch each other and so grope at themselves ('Locked Up', 1:12), not only was their masturbation scene underwear sweat inducing, it caused lesbians to race to the Internet forums to debate what constitutes cheating. The appeal is not only to pleasure the body, but to masturbate the mind. To talk about what turns us on, what is sex, what is unfaithful, what is lesbian? Lesbians love to debate and The L Word gave us plenty to debate about.

I love lesbians. I love how we rant and rave and bitch about things. But most of all, I love how we love each other, how we seduce each other, how we fuck each other. Nothing makes me hotter than seeing all those things together. That is why The L Word turns me on.

13 What is a straight girl to do?

Ivan's serenade, Kit's dilemma

Janet McCabe and Kim Akass

We could not quite agree on how we wanted to approach this topic when we began. Endless days followed spent in animated discussion and intense debate. Starting from the same place, diverging in opinion, asking separate questions, coming to different conclusions, found us deciding to use our conversation as the way forward for presenting our thinking on Kit Porter's heterosexual confusion when Ivan Aycock comes a-courting. Our dialogue covers various subjects like the heterosexual romance, race, cross-dressing and the performativity of gender, desire, phallocentric thinking, feminism's sex wars and third-wave feminism. What follows is a knowing transgression of academic writing protocol. But we propose that this exchange between two straight women with decidedly queer sensibilities will somehow capture the energy of the daring challenge that Ivan's serenading of Kit seems to pose for the sexual politics of television representation concerned with romantic (heterosexual) love and female (erotic) desire. If only momentarily.

Janet McCabe: Kit Porter is looking for love. The romantic, passionate, all-consuming type that women continue to believe will *complete* them.

But seeking out true love finds Kit searching in all the wrong places. Years of living on the road and struggling with alcoholism have long meant finding romance often involved a quick fuck in a hotel room with a bloke she had just met in the bar. Thrill mixed with mortification. Confusion. Pleasure. Living with mistakes. There is little anyone can tell this sassy (if somewhat damaged) lady about one-night stands, infidelity, and the pulsating pain of a broken heart. Satisfying libidinal drives, feeling lonely, regret and remorse for 'going all the way'.

Somewhere between her desire for love and the lived messiness of her sex life, Kit does not have much luck with men. Even in her second-season relationship with married business guru Benjamin Bradshaw (Charles S. Dutton), she seems a little too eager to give herself – and her business – over to him. Her attraction to his patriarchal macho image finds this black woman smitten. Wanting him just a little too much. Falling hard for a powerful phallic male who is smart and financially successful, assertive and self-confident, able to take charge (and teaches others to do the same) should not be too surprising for a woman like Kit. Her desire to be adored, her wish for someone to watch out for her, her hankering to be swept up in his strong male arms, sees her seduced by this stereotype of male dominance. Jeez. Is it any wonder that she ends up in a passionate clinch with him in a hotel room?

Good grief. Has the woman learnt nothing from past experience? I find the politics of her erotic desire arousing and perplexing in equal measure. Never one to shirk from telling it like it is, bell hooks alerts us to the 'major obstacle preventing us from transforming rape culture is that heterosexual women have not unlearned a heterosexist-based "eroticism" that constructs desire in such a way that many of us can only respond erotically to male behaviour that has already been coded as masculine within the sexist framework' (1994: 111). Race, age, class, sexual and cultural hierarchies may condition attitudes to erotic desire in specific ways. But feminism has long reminded us that women remain imbibed into accepting heterosexual-based fantasies of dominance and submission as the norm. However we may resist, transgress the rules, provoke and challenge, dominant patriarchal culture powerfully shapes our fantasies into 'scenes of dominating women'. The continuity of such a discourse is accompanied actively by television's heteronormative depiction of single heroines with a yen to be dismantled by love, as evidenced by shows like *Sex and the City*,

Charmed and *Friends*. Such pop culture representation functions not to ask serious questions about traditional dating rituals, the phallocentricism of desire or (hetero)sexual hierarchies, but to keep these ideals more or less in place.

But as a pop-cultural babe, I know who Kit *really* is.

She is played by none other than Pam Grier. Pam Grier. The *Queen* of Blaxploitation. Few men ever got the better of her. An actress who gave as good as she got in the misogynistic, uncompromising, testosterone-fuelled patriarchal world of black male urban culture. Anyone who can dispense vigilante justice like Coffy (1973) or talk as tough as Foxy Brown (1974) is OK with me. For pity's sake, this is the woman who pulled a gun from her Afro to waste some dude from the mean streets. What's not to like? She is an icon on the border, someone who defies limits and challenges representational certainties. She is someone I associate with disruption – disrupting mindsets, upsetting expectations. A girl like me loves her for being the ultimate radical outlaw – her iconic status confirming what hooks says as 'defined as on the edge, as pushing the limits, disturbing the conventional, acceptable politics of representation' (1994: 5).

But I remain troubled.

There is no getting away from the fact that on the surface at least Kit appears an old-fashioned stereotype. Ticking off the boxes: Bette's African-American half-sister, who comes from a broken home; she is a black single mother who proved incapable of raising her son, David (Colin Lawrence); an R&B crooner who made it big in the 1980s before addiction got the better of her. Someone much older than the other girls, who has seen a bit more of the world. Claiming to be a feminist ('Lacuna', 2:13), she does not seem to have had the luxury of defining her sexual freedom in quite the same way as white, economically privileged women have done. And besides, she contradicts her feminist self by making it clear that she is looking for a macho man who will make her feel *necessary*. But nothing is ever quite what it seems in The *L Word*. With its shifting centre of gravity where 'we live in an advanced state of sexual identity blur' (D'Erasmo 2004: 1) there is something decidedly over-determined about scenarios of (erotic) desire involving this self-proclaimed heterosexual woman. And let us not forget the presence of

Grier, 'adding some heavy-duty coolness' (Polly 2004: 20), a cultural icon who evokes a sense of radical possibilities and someone strongly associated with challenging assumptions around sexuality, race, class and gender performance.

Nowhere is the intervention, the challenge and provocation, more evident than when Ivan serenades Kit in an underground car park. Ah, the romance of it all. But where did it all begin?

Kim Akass: In 'Locked Up' (1:12), Ivan stars in the Planet's 'Kings of the Night' drag-king show. Kit is entranced by his rendition of 'Savoir Faire' and, serenaded by Ivan, she is tempted onto the stage signalling the beginning of a flirtatious relationship between the heterosexual woman of colour and the male impersonator. The next day Kit has trouble recognising Ivan out of her drag-king stage gear but, despite the mix-up, continues her relationship with the female-to-male cross-dresser. At this point it is difficult not to share Kit's disorientation. The cross-dresser typically arouses confusion and sometimes violence; their appearance unable to reconcile what Francette Pacteau calls 'the observation of *threat* with that of desire' (1986: 63, my emphasis). While I am pretty sure that I understand the threat that the image of the cross-dressed body arouses I am not so sure of the desire. Whose desire are we talking about here? The desire of a woman to dress as a man and move with the freedom of a man in a man's world; surely there can be nothing wrong with that particular desire? The same freedoms enjoyed by men are surely now freely available to women – aren't they? And, what's so darned pleasurable about walking around in men's clothes anyway? If Diane Torr, who made her name running drag-king workshops over the past twenty-odd years, is to be believed, women still feel the need to walk in a man's shoes for a day. According to Torr, it is all about power: 'getting it, losing it, being born to it' (Jowitt 1995). It should be little wonder then that the journey traversed by the male-to-female cross-dresser is one that proves attractive.

Surely this is not the end of the question of desire though? I am relatively free (at least compared to my foremothers) to move in the world, participate in it and, if nothing else, I am free to find my own space within my oppression. So, there must be another desire going on here, one that is a mite disconcerting, is it that we – or more particularly I – desire the cross-dressed body? That female/male manifestation of masculinity? Is it possible that I, as a straight(-ish) woman in her late forties, desire a woman dressed as a man? Could it be possible that this is the only way I can reconcile any same-sex desire in my otherwise heterosexual life?

Or, on the other hand (and dare I even voice this?) is it that I desire the image of the emasculated male? The man deprived of the very thing he holds dear, the occlusion of power and its eventual downfall. Surely not – perish the thought.

It is a thought that I have grappled with over the course of a decade or more. Ivan is certainly not the first character we have seen dressed as a man on our screens. Since Marlene Dietrich's same-sex cross-dressed kiss in *Morocco* (1930), and Katharine Hepburn's androgynous Sylvester Scarlett (*Sylvia Scarlett*, 1935) the female-to-male cross-dresser has gradually evolved, through myriad incarnations, into *Virgin Machine's* (1988) Ramona (Shelly Mars) complete with ejaculating beer bottle. We have regularly been privy to the often hostile reactions of friends, family, bystanders and witnesses as the 'transgressor' is unveiled. In contrast to the joyous mocking laugh of the sole female witness, the unveiling of Josephine Monaghan (*The Ballad of Little Jo*, 1993) to the assembled audience of men reveals a variety of horrified and violent reactions to her secret. As if to underscore the uneasiness surrounding female-to-male cross-dressers even Walt Disney's Mulan comes under threat of execution despite having saved Captain Chang's life (1988). Most remarkable is that she actually sports a bloody wound which, psychoanalytically speaking, signifies her castration. I may be reading too much into this but it seems to me that this is an early warning system designed to alert our children to the fate of any girl that impersonates a man and thinks she can get away with it. Deceiving your contemporaries is never a good idea even if it saves your ageing father from having to serve in the military with a gammy leg.

And as if Mulan isn't enough to put us off the practice of female-to-male cross-dressing, the fate of Brandon Teena (Hilary Swank) in *Boys Don't Cry* (1999) graphically demonstrates how two men reconcile their 'observation of threat with that of desire'. Murdering Brandon only after they have viciously raped her both anally and vaginally is a perfect illustration of Pacteau's theory. And it serves as a warning of what happens when girls go off the rails and think they can get away with fooling real men. Don't get me started – I haven't even mentioned Orlando (well – in Sally Potter's film version at least) and how he/she is viciously tricked out of his inheritance just because he changed sex. 'Same person, different sex.' Really, some people are so intolerant. Here I go again, passionately defending the cross-dresser. Sanctioning the idea that it really is OK to deceive everyone around you into thinking that you are one sex when you really are another. Having seen the results of this kind of deception it is obviously *not* OK with everyone else. Particularly men. Which brings me onto *The L Word* and back to Ivan and Kit.

It is obviously not just the heterosexual world that treats characters such as Ivan with thinly veiled hostility. Bette warns her sister, 'Kit – believe me. You may not be able to read the signals, but they're there. I saw the way she looks at you, she is *fully* courting you old school, and you're letting her' ('Limb from Limb', 1:13). The slippage in language here – Bette's insistence on referring to Ivan as 'she' while Kit is willing to accept him as a 'he' not only points to a linguistic tension embodied in the female-to-male cross-dresser but also their awkward status within a world defined by sexual binaries. It would have been nice to think that in the lesbian friendly world of *The L Word* those sexual binaries could be relaxed. After all, Alice was quite happy to have sex with lesbian-identified 'Lisa' (Devon Gummersall, in 'L'Ennui', 1:7) and Jenny seems to be getting the hang of fucking both men and women. But (and why is this not a surprise?) things are never quite that simple in the cross-dressed universe.

Leaving the opening of *Provocations*, Kit and Ivan provide us with, for us, the most haunting scene from the first season of *The L Word*. Brushing aside Kit's unease at their developing relationship, Ivan leans into his Thunderbird, dons a snazzy Fedora and invites Kit to perch on the bonnet of his car. As the music begins, Ivan lip-synchs to Leonard Cohen's 'I'm Your Man,' in full drag-king style, serenading his lady love and seducing her with Cohen's ode to an archetypal and yet potent ideal of masculinity. Kit willingly takes Ivan's hand as he mimes to the words, 'If you want a lover,/I'll do anything you ask me to./And if you want another kind of love,/I'll wear a mask for you,' moving in time with his desire and the music. In a world defined by lesbian sexuality Ivan's performance and Kit's obvious attraction to him problematises the whole notion of heterosexual female desire. Again, we're back to desire, the desire of one late-forties heterosexual woman for a woman dressed as a man (sound familiar?). Animating the song, he leans into Kit and mouths the words, 'If you want a doctor,/I'll examine every inch of you.' The sheer force of raw sexual innuendo emanating from this effeminate he/she brings us up short. Ivan's performance is spot-on. It is sexy and sassy enough to turn any a-maiden's head but still, I wonder, with a confusion obviously shared by Kit – what is it about this scene that is so darned erotic?

The question has haunted me ever since. It compounds my decade-long fascination with cross-dressing. Ever since Robert Stoller (1968: 195) asserted that women do not get erotic arousal out of dressing as a man (I always avoid wearing Levi's when giving that particular lecture), I have been fascinated with the erotic arousal that I get out of imagining having sex with a woman who parades herself as masculine-identified. As Kit tells Ivan: 'You always seem to know what I want before I even know that I want it.' Could this be a clue to the erotic fantasies I weave around the figure of Ivan? Is this as true of Ivan in the sack as it is of his command of the lunch menu and Kit's proclivities?

JM: As if to prelude a night of light queer romance, Bette proclaims to the local media at the opening of the controversial art exhibition she curates: 'Provocations is the edge of our present culture. Where we stand and face ourselves before we jump into an unknown future.' Prevarications over Provocations. Its visions of sex and sexuality adorning the gallery walls at the California Arts Center pick up on contemporary feminist thinking, summarised by Lee Damsky, as about 'the power to seek pleasure, to explore sexuality, express our desires, to find sexual fulfilment – as well as all the ways our power may be constrained' (2000: xx). Opening up new avenues for talking about sexual freedom and repression, pleasure and perversion, and agency and submission, weaving a highly personal confessional style with a critical engagement with theory, the new sexual politics gets down and dirty when talking about our desires – for sex, for being in love (Walker 1995; Bauer Maglin and Perry 1996; Damsky 2000; Johnson 2002; Henry 2004: 88–147). 'Sexuality, in all its guises, has become a kind of lightning rod for this generation's hopes and discontents (and democratic vision) in the same way that civil rights and Vietnam galvanised [a previous] generation in the 1960s' (Bauer Maglin and Perry 1996: xvi). But stepping outside white, patriarchal laws governing sexual norms and hierarchies of erotic desire is a precarious business. Not for the fainthearted.

Out of sight from the protestors denouncing the *Provocations* exhibition as immoral and beyond the patriarchal pale, away from where a new formation of sexual politics and identity is being conceived, Kit finds herself on 'the edge of [her] present culture'. A reluctant pioneer who just cannot help herself. Coy and uneasy but leading him on anyway. 'Everything you need is right here,' Ivan declares. He is very persuasive. And terribly sexy. Penetrating her with his sultry leer. Placing his hand on his heart in a gesture of love and intent. Kit swoons. My knees go weak. There is no going back – we are renegades, heterosexual outlaws, given to moonlight and romance.

> Ah, the moon's too bright
> The chain's too tight
> The beast won't go to sleep.

Ivan's commanding rendition of possibility quite literally sweeps Kit off her kitten heels, and offers a moment of narrative deferment, a suspension of the fictional space. In the sanctuary provided by the performance, where narrative rules are suspended, anatomical certainties collapse and gender protocol queered. In its place a libratory vision of sexual promise and romantic possibility – a sense of coming freedoms, concerned with mandating and cultivating new (erotic) passions that invites the audience to speculate on the prospect for rearranging desire and traditional notions of romance.

> If you want a partner
> Take my hand

Or if you want to strike me down in anger
Here I stand
I'm your man

The camera swirls around the waltzing couple. Moving, swishing. Energy shifts from margins to centres, from patriarchal protest to polymorphous passions, from fairy tales to queer tails, in a finely choreographed dance of courtship, romance and fulfilment. Ivan is pitch perfect. Is this not where the pleasure lies, in the process of performing heterosexual romance, in our (heterosexual) curiosity of what will happen next before we even know what we want, of playing with stories that we know are oh-so bad for us but find nonetheless oh-so hard to abandon.

What takes Kit (or am I talking about me) by erotic surprise is Ivan's theatrical self-awareness as he performs romance and seduction. Here I am reminded of Marjorie Garber's 'transvestite continuum', her contention that the performance of transvestism 'is not – or not only – a recuperative structure for the social control of sexual behaviour, but also a critique of the possibility of "representation" itself' (1993: 353). What strikes me is the sheer physical sexual prowess of his visual image – the delicacy of his chiselled features, the black-conked pompadour wig, the sideburns, the suave pencil-thin moustache, the mascara-defined sultry eyes, the wry smile, the ill-fitting male attire, the sassy shuffle. Swashbuckling pirate, rockabilly Elvis, exotic gigolo. Impersonation here is about crossing borders, 'a living category crisis' (367), whereby Ivan deliberately disrupts and violates gender, racial and class boundaries in his construction of the ideal male phallic lover in his wooing of Kit. Replicating, duplicating, male attributes, as if one image would never be enough, points to an insatiable female desire never satisfied. But the female impersonation of culturally sanctioned ideas of the male sex symbol makes strange, foregrounding illusion (however convincing), and revealing that desire exists *only* as representation – and an inherently *feminine* one at that. Transvestism as performed by Ivan confirms what Garber says as 'a mechanism that functions *by displacement* and *through fantasy* to enact a scenario of desire' (366).

Adapting Ruth L. Schwartz's thinking here on lesbians joining forces with gay men during the AIDS crisis, Ivan offers Kit – the lesbian drag king and the black, straight, middle-aged woman – 'the ability not to hesitate, not to wonder whether you could get what you wanted or whether you deserved it, but just to go for it, whatever it was. There was something in that arrogant energy ...' (1993: 235). Yes, that's it. 'Arrogant energy'. He has something she badly wants, something our heterosexual prohibitive culture cannot give her – something out of bounds, forbidden. The hybridity of language she is searching for proves more elusive than I had imagined. It is a desire that dare not speak its name. Not because it cannot. But because it has no adequate language of expression. Yet is this not where the true power lies – a messy, hybrid, contradictory desire that refuses easy definition, repudiating any language that runs the risk of making it vulnerable? Silence must shroud it. Tears well up in Kit's eyes. She is speechless.

The L Word delights in the frisson of possibility here. But the difficulty in articulating her desire-with-no-name reveals how Kit remains mired in a media representational form that continues to have difficulty conceiving of female sexual agency beyond a deeply engrained phallocentric thinking. However hard she tries. Damn it. Pointing to the continued difficulties in crossing boundaries – of gender, of sexualities, of sexual preference, of object choice – she will not, shall not, can not, go all the way.

KA: There comes a point when you just have to talk about the real issue here. Which is, for me, the dildo, the strap-on, the vibrator. It is obvious that as a female-to-male cross-dresser Ivan does not sport the 'real' thing – maybe this is the basis of my erotic imaginings about him. The idea that a relationship with Ivan will reveal exactly what is in his trousers. How rude. Bette obviously does not share my fascination – she is openly hostile and suspicious towards him. It is easy to see how Ivan's affected old-style 'masculinity' would grate on her nerves. He tells Bette to get home to her 'little lady'; he opens doors for her half-sister, brings her flowers, flatters her, orders lunch for her and generally worships her through the masculine archetype celebrated in Cohen's lyrics. It could be that Bette's knowledge of his artifice is further compounded by a hangover from feminism's sex wars where, at least for Andrea Dworkin, '[the] normal fuck by a normal man is taken to be an act of invasion and ownership undertaken in a mode of predation' (1987: 63). Whether it is OK to penetrate or be penetrated. Sarah Smith tells us: 'The pleasure of vaginal penetration was revealed as myth. This discovery was hard for me to accept because the entire time I was male partnered, I played with vibrators and dildos during sex play' (2002: 295). Lucky Sarah. But, the point is she tells us that as a 'heterosexual' woman it was considered OK to embrace the dildo but as a lesbian it was not. She goes on to talk about her experience of running a sex-positive sex toy business telling us that 'the dildo's potential as a feminist tool is sometimes belittled because of the stereotype that only lesbians use dildos' (305). But whereas her experience tells her that the lesbian community seemed 'so hung up on the political meaning of buying a sex toy and how the purchase would look in the eyes of their peers' (ibid.) heterosexual women cannot wait to get their hands on the power tools on offer.

Season two's opener finds mechanic Ivan with his head under a car bonnet (how macho) sporting facial hair and ever more masculine. Things are going well until Kit uses the keys that Ivan has previously pressed upon her. Walking into a seemingly empty apartment, Kit comes across Ivan's strap-on. We see the look on her face as she runs her hand across it, her confused stroke, her curious caress, just as Ivan emerges from the bathroom, breasts unbound, all nude femininity, shouting at Kit to leave. In contrast to most unveiling narratives, it is Ivan that is freaked by the disrobing, not Kit. After all, sassy lady that she is, she knew all along that Ivan was not a real dude; his whole gender performance a come-on, from old style courting to permanent hard-on.

Could this be a clue to what lies at the bottom of my uneasy attraction to Ivan? Eroticism and desire have to be woven around the prohibitions that inhibit our own fantasies. One woman's de rigeur sexual behaviour is the other's pornographic imaginings. Shock and shame intermingle until they become erotic. The truth is I feel ashamed of my fascination with and desire for the erection that the dildo represents. Whether real or synthetic, male or not, the thought of Ivan sporting a strap-on offers me a modern (if a little queer) version of a simple fantasy I enjoyed before it all got complicated: the rescue fantasy of somebody who will look after, worship and pleasure me rather than the 'exploitive, male-identified, sexual behaviour' (Smith 2002: 296) that penetrative sex is thought to represent. Through the body and performance of Ivan I can relive more innocent times – before the fantasy of penetrative heterosexual sex became politically incorrect. The contrariness of the cross-dresser becomes ever clearer here as Ivan clearly embodies a contradictory fantasy: one that animates a standard heterosexual rescue fantasy while simultaneously offering a theoretically challenging and potentially revolutionary representation. Chris Straayer suggests that 'the dildoed body contains radical potential, especially as a deconstruction of masculinity' (1996: 282). Smith expands on this when she argues that 'dildos represent increasing complexity in female sexuality. Strapping one on permits women to embody phallic power, weakening the myth that the phallus can only be represented by the male sex organ' (2002: 298).

Some nine episodes pass before Kit seeks out Ivan after being let down by her new alpha male paramour, Benjamin Bradshaw ('Late, Later, Latent', 2:9). Attending the AA meeting that her erstwhile suitor is running Kit tells the story of being stood up, how she was tempted by alcohol and, actually, how she just wanted someone to listen. After the meeting, Ivan takes Kit to a club where she is introduced to his long-time partner, a seemingly heterosexual dancer who never hangs out with lesbians because 'it's too much drama'. Kit is floored. So am I. The fantasy is over along with my infatuation. I feel like I've been slapped in the face. It also makes me wonder: does strapping on a dildo and embodying phallic power mean that you necessarily turn into a two-timing rat? It seems so. Ivan may tell Kit that they never discussed monogamy and that 'if we had, I would've explained to you that it just doesn't work for me.' But you have to ask yourself, how many times have you heard that? Compared to Bette's guilt-stricken philandering with Candace, followed by nearly a whole season's pleading to be forgiven, Ivan's explanation is, dare I say it – offhand and stereotypically male. Ivan seems to be a good example of 'the disobeying, lying nouveau lesbian butch [who] creates new meanings with her body. Intruding upon *male action* as well as image, she challenges conventional notions of sex, gender, sexuality and physicality' (Straayer 1996: 287, my emphasis).

JM/KA: And so the dream ends. Or does it?

Does not, in the words of Astrid Henry, '[heterosex] become transgressive sex when lesbian sex becomes routine' (2004: 138)? How weird is it watching a show like *The L Word* in which heterosexual sex is not the norm (despite what the pilot episode would have us believe) so that our attention turns back to the phallus and penetrative power tools? Our curiosity and arousal at what seems like the final frontier of heterosexual desire displays 'an often conscious knowledge of the ways in which we are compelled and constructed by the very things that undermine us' (Heywood and Drake 2003: 11). Despite championing (however precariously) an empowered vision of female sexuality and desire, women of our generation – and here we agree with Merri Lisa Johnson – 'hesitate to own up to the romantic binds we find ourselves in, the emotional entanglements that compromise our principles' (2002: 14). What lies not too far beneath the surface of hard-won rights and progress for women is our continued struggle to theorise heterosexual desire and being aroused by romantic possibilities that walk a fine line between erotic indulgence and our (cultural) humiliation.

Still. Kit needs to stop being duped into taking all kinds of shit that hurt and humiliate her just to get a date with a man on Saturday night. Even so her dalliance with Ivan leads to a strange encounter with what looks suspiciously like heterosexual power games. But her outlaw status does not quite prepare us for the possibility of re-evaluating female heterosexuality – erotic desire, agency, pleasure – that a relationship with Ivan promises. A phallic female as adept at performing 'macho' masculinity as s/he is at fiddling under the bonnet of a vintage convertible arouses unexpected passions and pushes us in unforeseen directions, leading us, in turn, to question the very nature of what we mean by heterosexual female desire. Lifting the phallic mask worn by Ivan to reveal, well, an anatomical woman further weakens normative boundaries and hierarchical relationships between straight and gay cultures. It is arousing, scandalous and shocking all at once. Just as Kit is uneasy with her desire, unsure of where it is all going, so are we. It leaves us on the brink. Uneasy with desire, unsure of how to utter it.

As a woman it should be no surprise that Ivan always seems to know what Kit wants before *she* even knows she wants it. But it is an even bigger blow when Ivan behaves just as badly as Benjamin Bradshaw by leaving her in the lurch. We may be able to forgive Benjamin (and so does Kit), but not Ivan. Never. Excited by the revolutionary possibility offered by him, the tantalising promise of that 'arrogant energy', our disappointment is far greater and more keenly felt. It is not long before the representation that Ivan performs so well to impress the ladies reveals its true heterosexual colours. Has *The L Word*, like Ivan, led us on just a little too much, treated us just a little bit shabbily? It tickles our fancy with the promise of queer desire. Only to make us feel tricked and slightly ashamed.

But, whatever else Ivan does, could his performance of possibility 'somehow anticipate the coming freedom' (Foucault 1998: 6).

Part 4 **L**abels

14 Is she man enough?

Female masculinities on the L word

Candace Moore and Kristen Schilt

Showtime's *The L Word* is breaking new ground as the first series written and directed primarily by queer women. A portrayal of a lesbian community, rather than one lone lesbian character amid a sea of heterosexuals, the serial drama has the unprecedented opportunity to offer diverse visions of alternative identity expressions, love relationships, friendships, spaces and 'family' formations. *The L Word* increases lesbian visibility on television exponentially, a gesture that arguably has revolutionary cultural repercussions. As Michel Foucault has suggested, it is queer life, rather than queer sex, that provides genuine menace to those who wish to, and fight to, uphold heteronormativity: 'What bothers those who are not gay about gayness is the gay life-style, not sex acts themselves' (1988: 301). The show also goes beyond the stereotypes of lesbians as either unattractive, fashion-backward man haters or commitment-focused women who 'bring a U-haul' on the first date. However, with its emphasis on generating positive images of lesbians, representations of female masculinity that might be unpalatable to both lesbian and straight viewers fall to the wayside – especially in *The L Word*'s femme-centric first incarnation. Deficient in definitive butch representations, *The L Word*'s first season also initially lacks representations of other expressions of gender variance that have become not merely resident, but increasingly welcome, in queer culture, such as drag kinging, genderqueering and transgenderism

(Halberstam 1998; Rubin 1992: 466–82). While the short shrift given to representations of female masculinity are nominally addressed in season two through the introduction of a slew of butch extras, the show remains centred on the experience of gender conforming lesbians.

Plenty of criticism has been dealt The L Word's producers for depicting an unrealistic, über-feminised lesbian scene, even within the context of generally femme-filled West Hollywood. Yet, little effort has been made to explore the few portrayals of female masculinity that the show does represent, and how they dialogue with current theories of gender identity and expression. Rather than critique the lack of strongly identified butch and transgender characters, we will consider how The L Word has treated the representations of gender variance that have trickled into the show, through an examination of the characters Shane, a soft butch/inbetweener, and Ivan (Kelly Lynch), a drag king/ genderqueer.

Hypothetically speaking: scripting masculinity through Shane

Within the WeHo logic of The L Word's fictive, butch-lite universe, the concept of 'butch' is played out through the character of Shane, with her typically male name, androgynous, rail-thin body and husky voice. Her boyish physical gestures, Bowie-esque glam-rock stylings, and predatory womanising seem meant to position Shane as a confident, somewhat masculine-identified dyke, comfortable with her particular brand of boyish sex appeal. The actress who plays Shane, Katherine Moennig, has a history of playing both transgender and cross-dressing characters. Highlighting Moennig's androgynous flexibility was the fact that she was cast as a male-to-female (MTF) transsexual for Law and Order: Special Victims Unit and a cross-dressing teenage girl, Jacqueline 'Jake' Pratt, for the WB's television show, Young Americans. As Shane, Moennig integrates some masculine ways of speaking, gesturing and moving into her portrayal, but ultimately reads visually and contextually – as one of a circle of lesbian friends – as undeniably female.

Despite her female visibility, dialogue in 'Losing It' (1:6), leads us to believe that Shane is easily misidentified by gay men as male, and has

banked on this commonly made mistake to turn tricks as a male pros-
titute in her sordid past. Upon meeting Shane in a gay bar, Harry Sam-
chuk, a minor character, refers to her as a 'him' until corrected. When
corrected, he's genuinely surprised: 'Androgyny confounds, doesn't it?
Well, I suppose it's revolutionary, but I must admit I am disappointed,
because it's always the skinny boys that have the biggest cocks!' Shane
elaborates on this ability to pass as male in 'Looking Back' (1:11), while
describing her unsavoury history of passing as a 'little street fag' to an
unwanted persistent suitor. Although Shane's androgyny is readable in
the script, it lacks full believability on-screen in season one. This allows the show's producers to have their cake and eat it too: they are
able to successfully introduce the notion of a woman unintentionally
being read or intentionally passing as male without visually alienating
squeamish viewers by rendering one of *The L Word*'s permanent characters male in appearance, or worse, gender ambiguous. Relating this
scripted androgyny to butch representations, Shane does not register
explicitly butch signifiers but rather is *implied as contextually butch when
positioned alongside the other characters' femme gender displays.*

While Shane might not make the ideal stand-in for the 'butch'
contingency of lesbian culture, the character does speak to current
ideas about gender fluidity. Considering where Shane falls along a
high femme to stone butch spectrum, it seems reasonable to label
her as a 'soft butch'. The term 'inbetweener' seems suited to Shane's
particular femme-butch slippage. Although Shane leans towards the
masculine, especially in season two, her comfortable inhabitancy of a
grey area is distinct and contemporary. As our only representation of
butch identification, Shane may leave a lot to be desired to members of
the lesbian audience; however, viewed as an inbetweener, Shane does
challenge ideas about what constitutes 'butch' in our new millennium.
It should be noted, though, that it may be misleading to describe femme
and butch identity using this prevalent analogy to varying shades of a
colour continuum, given that there is no *fixed* sense of what makes one
more or less butch, just as there are no true ways of describing what
makes one more or less masculine. These abstract concepts – 'butch'
and 'masculinity', 'femme' and 'femininity' – are *over-determined* and
in constant flux. Therefore, just as 'butch' depends on concepts of

'masculinity' and, by extension, 'femininity' for definition of both *what it is* and *what it is not*, 'soft butch' is a completely dependent term in that it denotes a 'masculine' lesbian who is *more* 'feminine' than what is determined 'butch'. Recognising the problematic elements of attempting to give fixed meaning to socially constructed terms, however, we still must employ and constantly negotiate and reclassify these identity terms to discuss representations, with full knowledge that they will never mean the same things to different individuals, groups or cultures, nor act as stable signifiers over periods of time.

It is in that spirit that we next seek to describe a term used casually in lesbian populations and appearing in print and online with a variety of definitions attached to it: 'inbetweener' (or "tweener' for short). The concept of an 'inbetweener', when used in reference to a lesbian, describes someone who exhibits or adopts a mid-continuum, postmodern dyke identity that takes from both femme and butch styles, presentations and roles at will. This pastiche of gendered signs and activities can be exemplified and joined into one expression, or the same individual can switch between gender presentations in different contexts. It can be an intentional play with gender and rejection of the butch-femme divide while remaining specifically associated with lesbian identification. Or it can arise out of a natural self-expression of a lesbian's sense of inbetween-ness and comfort with inhabiting various points on sexual and gender continuums.

One way in which the character of Shane is not groundbreaking, however, is in the show's seeming conflation between her masculinity and her promiscuity. A 'player' on the lesbian dating scene who seemingly scores women with the ease of a Ginzu knife through butter, Shane is candid and unapologetic about her promiscuity. What does it mean that the *butchest* character on the show is also shamelessly sexually predatory? On Alice Pieszecki's chart of LA's networks of lesbian sex, Shane's name is 'a major hub'. Shane estimates her own sex count at 'somewhere between ... 950 and 1200 since I was 14'. With Shane, *The L Word* seems to make a one-to-one correspondence between more masculine self-expression and unattached sex with multiple partners, a comparison that veers toward pop-psychology-based essentialisms. In the season one finale, when Shane's boss accuses her of sleeping with his daughter (when in fact she has slept with his wife), he even puts his reproach in masculine terms: 'You know, when you're in business with someone, you gotta learn to keep it in your pants when you're around their family.' This is the second time Shane has been given a hypothetical penis in jest (see the 'skinny boys have the biggest cocks' quote), underscoring how Shane's hypersexual drive is equated with an imaginary, male-gendered body. This promiscuity is further associated with a lack of progressive gender politics, as, in a roundtable discussion with Gloria Steinem in the season two finale, Jenny scoffs at the idea that Shane could be a feminist because of her predatory sexuality. While Shane appears to counter this characterisation, as she claims she 'loves women', the viewer recognises the ironic tone of the comment as it positions Shane's love for women as merely sexual. Thus, with Shane's masculinity comes the reproduction of many negative stereotypes of 'bio' men: disregard for women's feelings, a sexually predatory nature and a lack of desire for intimacy or connection.

Shane's inbetweener gender presentation is thrown slightly male of centre in the second season through visual markers, such as her shorter hair and increased preference for thin ties, as well as an opening credit sequence which depicts her entering a men's room for a make-out session with a lady love. Additionally, Shane's form of masculinity becomes more 'male' through her developing relationship with Mark Wayland. Mark, Jenny and Shane's new roommate, was introduced in the second season because, as Greenblatt told *Entertainment Weekly*, the male audience needed 'a guy they could relate to' (Fonseca 2005: 38). His story arc bends throughout the season from creepy and reprehensible – he sets up surveillance cameras in Jenny and Shane's house to videotape their lesbian sexual adventures – to noble and puppy-doggish – he defends Shane in a street fight and performs odd jobs slavishly around the house to win back his roomies' respect after he's betrayed their trust. By the end of season two, Mark has become solidified as Shane's male sidekick, buddy film style – a relationship which enforces Shane's masculinity as she relates to Mark, and as he relates to her, as 'one of the guys'. At the same time, Shane shelves some of her previous stoicism and makes awkward attempts to be emotive while entering a relationship with Carmen de la Pica Morales. This shift represents an interesting twist: as Shane looks and acts masculine in season two, she also becomes more 'in touch with her feelings' and able to cope with intimacy through her realisation that she has formed a deep romantic connection with a woman. While the show can be applauded for working up here to a complex representation of gender identity that refuses to conform to essentialist stereotypes, its overarching message seems to be that masculinity must be tempered by the feminine in order to be transformed into something progressive, rather than illustrating that alternative masculinities can be radical in their own right.

Masculinity-as-performance: Ivan as drag king? ftm? genderqueer?

The last episode of season one makes a sincere and significant attempt to address alternative gender identifications by exploring the realm of transgender and genderqueer identities through the character of Ivan. Ivan first appears performing as a drag king, 'Ivan A. Cock', at a benefit show, A Night of Kings, an event which Kit Porter, Bette's heterosexually identified sister, emcees. Ivan's appearance in typical trappings of kingdom, a kitschy pompadour, painted-on beard and moustache, and a tailored suit blazer, offers a glimpse at a previously unrepresented-on-television expression of female masculinity. In a departure from the typical usage of drag on television, namely humorous or degrading attacks aimed at 'men in dresses' (Mackenzie 1994), Ivan's female-to-male gender-crossing appearance and sexy crooning of 'Savoir Faire' are represented positively to viewers unfamiliar with drag king identities as a type of performance both typical of and well-received by, as evidenced by the uproarious audience, lesbian communities.

Ivan's performance of masculinity becomes more complicated, however, once he leaves the stage. While 'drag king' is a term to be understood nearly entirely in terms of performance, Ivan's masculinity extends into his off-stage persona. Throughout the evening, he caters to Kit, who is drawn to his form of chivalrous masculinity. He abandons the hyper-stylised expression of masculinity for their next meeting, but he retains the name 'Ivan' and appears in masculine dress. While Kit is shocked at first to see him out of his performance gear, possibly because he has traded the pompadour for an extremely unfashionable mullet, she continues to refer to him by masculine pronouns, demonstrating her reading of him as a man. The lesbians around Kit, including her sister Bette, however, read Ivan as an 'old-school' butch lesbian, and continually follow Kit's male pronouns with female ones. Ivan, witnessing the debate, simply states, 'Hey, no worries. I'm happy either way.'

Bette and Kit's pronoun skirmishes speak to an issue in both lesbian and straight communities about how to refer to and receive female-bodied, masculine-identified people. While Ivan is 'happy either way' in regards to pronouns, Bette obviously reads Ivan as a relic of lesbian identities past: an 'old gay' butch. Signifying this, she tells Kit that Ivan is 'courting her old school', adding, 'she wants to be your husband.' Like 'new gay' lesbian feminists in the 1970s charging 'old gay' butches with being 'dinosaurs' who sexually exploit their feminine partners (Hollibaugh and Moraga 1992: 394–405; Stein 1997: 23–46), Bette's dismissal and discomfort surrounding Ivan's courtship of her sister springs from her interpretation of Ivan's masculinity as an outdated, non-progressive gender identity. Bette's positioning of Ivan's behaviour (and by extension her perception of Ivan's identity) as retrograde speaks to the long-standing discomfort about 'butchness' and female masculinity that exists among predominantly middle-class, gender-conforming lesbians (Kennedy and Davis 1997: 27–72; Morgan 1993: 35–46; Rubin 2003; Stein 1997: 23–46). Interestingly, Bette's negativity toward Ivan's gender expression does not extend to her interpretation of Shane's identity, demonstrating she characterises Shane's soft butch, sexually predatory gender expression as somehow more progressive than Ivan's 'old-school' butch identity; or, Shane plays the 'boy' to Ivan's 'man', making her less threatening.

The difference, of course, lies in presentation. Shane's masculinity is talked into being via conversational cues while her appearance, except for the fact that she always wears pants, does not differ radically from her circle of friends. Underscoring the importance of gender presentation, Bette is depicted in season one as the stereotypical domineering husband, the very role she claims Ivan seeks in his courtship of Kit. She makes more money than Tina and is more than willing for Tina to give up her job to have a baby. She controls the household monies, as she controls their sex life. Finally, she has an affair after Tina's miscarriage because of the emotional distance she feels from her depressed partner. However, because Bette is gender conforming, these aspects do not seem to get labelled as 'old school' or position her as a dinosaur. This suggests that what is problematic is not masculinity and 'masculine behaviours', but the overt, visibility of female masculinity (and possibly, in this WeHo landscape, bad fashion).

Kit, on the other hand, reads Ivan as male despite Bette's insistent positioning of him as female, suggesting that being a man is about how one treats 'a lady'. However, her perception of his gender identity seems to be complicated by her knowledge that Ivan is not biologically male. After a night of 'courting', she informs Ivan that he would be 'the perfect man', if only he were 'really' a man, locating him back into a female-bodied category, a tomboy who has pushed the fantasy too far. Rather than being deflated by this rejecting of identity, however, Ivan plays with her reading of him, doing a private lip-synch for her to Leonard Cohen's 'I'm Your Man', a performance that appears to shake Kit's certainty about gender binaries.

These different readings of Ivan are possible, of course, only because of his uncomplicated reaction to the different identities being foisted upon him. On one hand, his acceptance of either pronoun, despite his traditionally masculine appearance and use of a masculine name, demonstrates the type of fluidity that often accompanies a genderqueer identity, an identity that denotes, 'someone who ... views the gender options as more than just male and female or doesn't fit into the binary male-female system' (Marech 2004: A1). While Ivan never specifically names his identity as 'genderqueer', his 'happy with either' attitude at least opens up some dialogue about the fluidity of gender identity. Kit's confused reaction also presents a look at a topical issue: how do heterosexually identified women make sense of their attraction to female masculinity? Thus, at the end of season one, the introduction of Ivan allows for the development of provocative questions about the connection between gender and sexual identities and desire.

This provocative development, however, falls flat in season two. Ivan appears to have moved from fluid and genderqueer to definitively male, as he appears at his body shop job with real-looking facial hair, rather than his drag king eyeliner acting as a five o'clock shadow ('Life, Loss, Leaving', 2:1). This move to using pasted-on facial hair goes un-remarked. However, put in the context of Ivan at work, it seems to suggest that he passes as male at work and the facial hair is a prop that helps in this passing. Signifying the shift away from masculinity-as-performance, Ivan's last name is revealed to the viewer, via a framed newspaper article, to be 'Aycock', rather than the 'A. Cock' of his *Night of Kings* performance, changing it from a campy stage name that sounds like 'I Want a Cock' into an unbelievably coincidental 'real' last name. Ivan's courtship of Kit abruptly ends as well, after she sees him coming out of the shower, naked and female-bodied, his strap-on lying on the counter. Building on Kit's attraction to Ivan, the scene could play out quite differently, with Kit perhaps learning that her sexual attraction is to masculinity rather than to a penis. Instead, Ivan, in shame, leaves town. The source of Ivan's humiliation is never named, though his butch employee, Dax (Luvia Petersen), suggests to Kit that what transpired between them, something that is too horrible to actually verbalise, is beyond repair. The Ivan who is fluid in gender identity disappears, leaving a male-identified Ivan full of shame about his female body.

The last scene in which Ivan appears confuses his identity even further ('Late, Later, Latent', 2:9). His chivalrous behaviour is cast aside, as he takes Kit to a bar to meet his long-term girlfriend who he has kept hidden from her. The girlfriend, an extremely femme waitress, positions Ivan as fully male through her statement that she 'hates lesbians'. Ivan's 'happy with either' identity seems to have been traded for a female-to-male transgender (FTM). While the issue of butch lesbians transitioning to become FTMs is a timely issue in many lesbian communities, Ivan never articulates his identity either way, an omission that makes his transformation appear confusing, abrupt and duplicitous. Kit verbally locates Ivan as living a lie, when she learns of his girlfriend, charging him with 'deceiving people with [his] lifestyle'. This comment is aimed at his confession of polyamory but seems to speak as well to the confusion resulting from the ambiguity of his gender identity. Kit's comments also locate Ivan's identity into a narrative of deceit and deception, tropes usually used with transgender identities on television (Gamson 1998), a sharp departure from the more progressive representations of his identity as fluid in season one. What Ivan carries over from the first season is the charge of out-dated gender politics. What he gains is a masculine identity that is played out via sexually predatory and deceptive tactics. Thus, while Shane is able to become more visibly masculine because she gains a 'feminine heart', Ivan's more fixed masculine identity moves him into unredeemable territory (and pushes him off the show without the need to engage more with his identity transformation).

Implications of ambivalence

The L Word reflects a cultural shift in thinking about queer identities, and should be lauded for the leaps it has made in attempting to showcase some variety in gender expressions. The show playfully establishes a dialogue with theories about the social construction of gender that dismantle the supposedly natural connection between the body one is born with, sexual and gender identities, and gender performance (for example, Butler 1990; Taylor and Rupp 2003). Yet, The L Word doesn't seriously offer a wide range of lesbian representations, as the majority of main characters, except perhaps Shane, are traditionally beautiful feminine women, indistinguishable from the straight women we see portrayed as 'pretty' on television every day. While this may have initially challenged straight viewers' misconceptions that all lesbians are visually identifiable, it neglects to show that butch and masculine-identified lesbians are an equally important part of the culture – and yes, even the WeHO culture too. The show continues to play it safe by not yet providing any examples of lesbian characters that consider themselves expressly (and visually) butch, or who openly struggle with the dilemma of transitioning to male within a lesbian community (Ivan, for instance, never talks about this struggle, he just exits stage left). While The L Word's ambivalence does leave characters open to multiple interpretations, it also allows the show to maintain a crossover audience by avoiding confrontational identities that seriously challenge current ideas about masculinity and what defines being a man.

Looking at the implications of these existing representations, we argue that, despite The L Word's ostensibly third-wave feminist leanings, the show ends up demonising 'masculinity' – in both its female and 'bio' male exhibitions – rather than exploring the potential that exists for both male and female bodied individuals to transform or 'queer' masculinity (Halberstam 1998; Heasley 2005: 310–20). The representations of Shane and Ivan, and indeed the majority of biological men on the show, maintain a fiction of masculinity as somehow inherently anti-feminist. These men on The L Word are represented as deceptive: roommates with hidden cameras, married men having affairs, or sexual predators who demand access, forcibly if necessary, to women's bodies. Even Tim, the representative 'nice guy', is tarnished, exiting the show after what could be read as an attempted rape scene. Female masculinity fares little better, as female-bodied characters engaging in masculine performativity are placed within the same narratives, coming across as gender Neanderthals who deceive women for sexual gain. Masculine people might 'love women' but they act this out in a sexually predatory manner in which sensitive feminine hopes of long-term commitment and romance are shown to be mere pillow-talk. Thus, while The L Word smashes open stereotypes about lesbianism, we argue that its few images of female masculinity come across as visually sanitised for the viewing audience, and all too often reproduce and maintain negative stereotypes of masculinity as somehow naturally oppressive, dominating and sexually predatory. This limited view of female masculinity neglects the ways in which alternative masculinities can reshape and transform hegemonic gender norms, or the radical potentials that lie in genderqueer identities that challenge the binary understanding of gender (Halberstam 1998).

The second season of The L Word brings gains as well as misfires. Shane seems to deepen from her two-dimensional 'player' veneer. And as her character is fleshed out, she is simultaneously portrayed as more authentically androgynous – her gender bending becomes more organic to her character's makeup, rather than a tentative, visually safe representation seemingly scripted to straddle both butch and femme without potentially alienating a straight crossover audience. On the other hand, Ivan, who is excitingly portrayed as genderqueer in season one, has inexplicably become more fixed with regards to his masculine identity and, in season two, is depicted as ashamed, rather than comfortable, with how his gender matches up (or doesn't) with what's between his legs – an unfortunate, and politically sloppy turn that furthermore lacks character and plot continuity. While the producers may have been too wary of its new audience's reaction to present an FTM character in the first season, the second season confounded what could have been a revolutionary depiction, by first presenting a comfortably genderqueer character, and then manipulating the character to suddenly become essentialist about his/her gender in the season that followed. While transitioning is a process and people may change their perspective on their genders rapidly, the show handled a very complicated issue cursorily and surrounded Ivan's exposure of genitalia and his ensuing shame with a certain amount of childish shock value. Thus, while the first season's characterisation may have been imperfect, and even silly at times by attempting to conceptually represent drag king, butch and transgender within the same character, making Ivan a disgraced pre-op FTM disrespected both genderqueer identities and transsexual identities by acting as if there is no difference between them. It further locates Ivan into a discourse of shame and deceit, a narrative trope often used to represent transsexual characters (Gamson 1998).

There is no reason that The L Word should be made to bear the onus of being as groundbreaking for butch, transgender, or genderqueer identities as it has been for lesbian identity. Keeping in mind the way television works, with series renewed on a year-to-year basis, the second season was commissioned before there was any kind of press or public reaction to the first. It is understandable from a marketing standpoint that The L Word would, in its fledgling season, offer feminine main characters attractive to the widest audience, depict butch through scripting (i.e. Shane), and broaden representations once it had a fan base and through secondary or auxiliary characters, which it has proven to do in its second season – excepting, of course, the poor handling of the Ivan character. While our critiques are meant to elucidate how gender crossings are being approached, with perhaps some eye to the ratings, they are meant as part of an ongoing analysis and in-depth consideration of a quality show that does deserve kudos for being *good* as well as for breaking new ground, has a large burden to bear, being the first of its kind, and hopefully has a rich life to come.

Despite the problematic nature of some of The L Word's depictions, the show does render queer women's experiences as complex, and attempts to continually push the envelope, by increasingly introducing alternative sexualities and identities. Shane had a dynamic story arc in the second season. As a lesbian being with a certain degree of masculinity, she is evolving. We can only hope that Shane will continue to grow, and eventually present a kind of masculinity that is self-honest and also pro-woman. Additionally, pre-season-three gossip suggests that a transitioning FTM character is just around the turnpike and we have high hopes that this new character might provide an introduction to the dilemmas associated with transition for lesbian-identified partners of transfolk. However, the addition of a self-identified FTM character alone does not necessarily mean a more complex discussion of masculinity will take place. As Halberstam reminds us:

> cross-dressing, passing, and gender transitivity work in
> and through other forms of mobility ... I suggest we think
> carefully, butches and FTMs alike, about the kinds of men or
> masculine beings that we become and lay claim to: alternative
> masculinities, ultimately, will fail to change existing gender
> hierarchies to the extent to which they fail to be feminist,
> antiracist, and queer.
>
> (1998: 173)

With the new masculine characters (whatever their biological gender) to come on The L Word, we hope to see a wider representation of the enactment of alternative masculinities. And, we hope that these new characters will be man enough to present a challenge to hegemonic norms of masculinity, particularly in regard to their relations, sexual and otherwise, with women.

L 15
Interview with Katherine Moennig[1]

Sarah Warn

Katherine Moennig plays Shane on *The L Word*, the lesbian who hooks up with a different woman each night because she 'doesn't do relationships'. Moennig, who grew up in Philadelphia and moved to New York when she was eighteen, has previously been best known for playing a girl pretending to be a boy in the WB's series *Young Americans*, a fitting precursor to the gender-bending Shane.

Months before the first episode of *The L Word* aired, Moennig shared with us her perspective on her role, and the series overall.

AfterEllen.com: How would you describe the story and tone of The L Word?
Katherine Moennig: Part of the beauty with the show is that there is so much going on. Every character is so different than the other that it gives a whole spectrum of personality, and as the story progresses it will only add to that. Also, what I love is that it doesn't put these women in boxes. The story line is a very honest and realistic view on life, and how they deal with it.

How would you describe Shane, the character you play? How does she fit in with the rest of the characters?
I'm still trying to describe Shane for myself but on the outside Shane is someone who is a very sexual being and extremely comfortable with that. People's opinions about her don't faze her and she lives the way

she wants to and basically can get whoever she wants, and at the same time she also is very alone in the search for what she wants.

How are you similar or dissimilar to Shane?
I certainly think there are similarities between myself and Shane. There has to be. In every role you play you have to start with you, since you're the root. I can relate to a lot of what she is going through in the inside. And in the ways that I differ from her, I find that I learn more about myself.

How do you think The L Word *is different from* Queer as Folk?
The only relation our show has to *Queer as Folk* is that they are both gay-oriented stories on Showtime. It's easy to relate the two, but I think once people see our show the differences will be evident. One is about men and the other is about women. That sets the tone already.

As you probably know, The L Word *is the first television series about lesbians; do you think this development reflects a lasting and positive change in Hollywood, or just an attempt to capitalise on the latest trend?*
I would hope it would be a positive change in Hollywood, and I think it will. Slowly but surely women are having a stronger and more substantial voice in film and TV, and I think the show will only help propel that. The credit goes to Ilene Chaiken for creating such a wonderful truthful story with such rich, three-dimensional characters. And to be honest we're given a chance to help speak for a community that hasn't had much of a voice in the past. Why not capitalise on it?

Hollywood and life in general are all about timing. This is a prime moment to air a show on this subject, so I think... why not? Strike while the iron is hot.

Do you think The L Word *is likely to be a success (financially and critically)?*
I envision the show to be financially and critically acclaimed. By continuing to open people's minds through alternate voices there will hopefully be more compassion and openness to another way of thinking, and with that comes financial and critical acclaim. We do this in the hope that it will be successful in every way.

Are you at all concerned that playing a lesbian character will negatively impact your career?

I don't look at it as having a positive or negative impact. I see it as a chance to explore another part of myself and to learn something that's beyond positive. Everything is a stepping stone and that's how I see this. And if it is a risk and a little scary, then that's all the more reason to do it. Right now I'm focusing on giving this character a voice, and if I do that, I can't see that as being a negative thing. And just because I'm playing this role doesn't mean I can't do something else. That's the beauty of being an actor.

Note

1.   Originally published on AfterEllen.com, March 2003.

The other L word

16

Representing a Latina identity

Shauna Swartz

The second season of The L Word saw the addition of yet another character who is conventionally feminine, unusually good-looking and capable of passing as straight – departing from the mould only in that she is a woman of colour, one of just three in the large ensemble cast. The character of Carmen is portrayed by Sarah Shahi, a former Dallas Cowboys cheerleader and Texas beauty queen who is of Spanish and Iranian heritage. Since her debut, the show has garnered some criticism for awarding a Latina role to a non-Latina. This casting decision is particularly controversial given how few specifically Latino roles exist on television, and that Latino actors, along with other non-white actors, are so frequently overlooked for parts where ethnicity goes unspecified. Hollywood is infamous for presenting a whitewashed version of reality, so adding Carmen to the roster inches the show – set in predominately Latino Los Angeles – closer to representing local demographics. But, more importantly, does her arrival mark a step toward a more accurate portrayal of the diversity of lesbian identities – particularly in terms of race and ethnicity?

Carmen's character is initially so mild-mannered, it's as if The L Word's creators wince at portraying her as anything shy of a perfect role model. Her characterisation certainly taps into existing notions of Latinas as family-oriented. Although no relatives appear on camera, there is a hint that Carmen remains close to home ('Life, Loss, Leaving', 2:1). After tracking her down on the set of a music video, Shane says she hopes it's OK that Carmen's mother told Shane where to find her. When they make plans to see each other later that evening, Carmen suddenly remembers she is supposed to visit her grandmother and can't let her down. Filial duty supersedes certain sex with Shane. If a woman on the show turns down a chance to hop into bed with Shane it's worth noting her reason. We're meant to see that family is very important to Carmen – perhaps to bolster the notion of the character's Latina identity.

But Carmen's good-daughter demeanour doesn't preclude her from being sex-positive. After all, she and Shane had already made a go of it the first time they met, with both women AWOL while on the clock for their respective jobs. Carmen is simultaneously naughty and nice, sexy and sweet, confident and sincere, traditional and hip. Her flawlessness almost makes her bland compared to the other women on the show. She is more likely to incite moaning than the groaning her cohorts all manage to invite at one time or another – even Bette, who teems with embarrassingly bitter one-liners throughout her brief exile from coupledom. But in being level-headed and straightforward, Carmen embodies a much-needed check on the overbearing quirkiness that prevails among the cast of characters. And, as the season progresses, her dramatic presence becomes less tentative, and she reveals an emotional complexity and wardrobe of flaws much like everyone else. But by the time the show finally risks revealing her faults, it has already revealed more than a few of its own along the way.

While The L Word may at first tiptoe around portraying any imperfection in Carmen's character, there is nothing tentative in how it celebrates her Latina heritage. Rather, it is specified redundantly and ungracefully from the get-go. When the second season began, the show's official website went beyond simply proffering Carmen's decidedly Latino last name – de la Pica (with Morales appended to it only later in the season). Lest readers miss the nudge and wink, the site at that time also billed her as a 'Latina beauty'. No other character's ethnicity was broadcast in their bio. Right from her first appearance on the show, Carmen's Latina ethnicity is given centre stage. The opening episode makes explicit reference to her father's heritage: When Shane asks about her tattoos the first time the pair hook up, Carmen reveals that she's the daughter of 'some kind of Mayan medicine man' who died in a motorcycle crash before her birth. Later episodes refer to Carmen's Latina heritage less directly but in ways more overtly problematic: In 'Lágrimas de Oro' (2:6), the wardrobe department gives her a T-shirt that reads 'Everyone loves a Latin girl', while the sound department doctors the show's theme song with Spanish lyrics and Latinised percussion to serve as backdrop for the scene where she and Jenny return from their first date.

Representing Carmen's heritage without trivialising or exoticising it is a serious responsibility, and the T-shirt and modified theme song tread on very thin ice in this regard. One can only hope that if the show's creators finally write in an Asian-American character – currently a conspicuous absence considering the Southern California setting – they don't stoop to spicing up the theme song with a gong. Carmen's ethnicity is relegated to a fashion statement, tacked onto her like a costume. She volunteers this coming-out monologue in 'Late, Later, Latent' (2:9) for Mark's 'documentary':

> My name is Carmen de la Pica Morales. I was sixteen back then, and I fell madly in love with Lucia Torres. She was Pablo Fuentes' girlfriend. You just – you didn't fuck with Pablo's girl. [Pauses and smiles] But I did.

Her long and unmistakably Latina surname is trotted out, along with those of her childhood friends. And she's outfitted with a tough-girl personality streak that gives her barrio credibility, accessorised with a stereotyped Latino male possessiveness of women. Representation is reduced to decorative flourish, markers that audience members, particularly non-Latinas, will identify as signalling authenticity. Perhaps revealing a particularly American preoccupation with perceived racial and ethnic difference, the line between celebrating and reifying that difference is blurred.

The L Word has demonstrated it is capable of handling a character's ethnic identity less problematically than it does Carmen's. As with Carmen, family plays an important role in Jenny's life even though the viewer never sees her interact directly with any relatives. But, as the second season progresses, Jenny's family members become off-screen participants in an increasingly disturbed dialogue that she leads. Moreover, the more neurotic Jenny gets, the more her Jewishness is pushed to the forefront. There is certainly something of the stereotype in making the show's insufferably tortured soul Jewish. And Jenny's heritage doesn't escape cursory treatment altogether: In one of her scenes, viewers are treated to a klezmerized version of the theme song, thereby subjected to what has become the show's favourite tactic for telegraphing ethnic identity. But there is also a more serious approach to exploring her cultural identity, as in the references to her grandparents' experience of the Holocaust and her own struggle to come to terms with that history. Jenny's ethnicity is treated with more depth even as it is less visible than Carmen's.

While Jenny is unlikely to face bigotry on first sight, Carmen would probably encounter racism, from the subtle to the blatant, on a regular basis. The show needn't necessarily chronicle that – it portrays idealised lives, after all. But it isn't a matter of simply being unrealistic if it manages to highlight the historical oppression of Jews even as it denies the persistence of insidious racism.

In press interviews Shahi has hinted that her character's family roots and heritage will be explored in greater depth in the third season, so perhaps viewers can look forward to more meaningful treatment of Carmen's identity as a Latina lesbian. And in any event, it would be unreasonable to expect Carmen to represent all Latina lesbians, even if she bears that unfair burden in many viewers' minds as the show's only Latina character. Nevertheless, The L Word specifically sets out to give queer viewers images of themselves that are more than just ancillary. So viewers, Latina and non-Latina alike, have a right to expect the diversity of our community to be adequately portrayed – and every reason to expect the actual portrayal to fall far short. There are both positive and negative aspects to how Carmen's character is depicted, and a corresponding diversity of viewer responses, even amongst those who are aware of the negative facets. A Latina viewer may genuinely embrace the portrayal and enjoy the show all the more for it; she may get angry at yet another injustice; and/or she may simply roll her eyes and chalk up one more disappointment with Hollywood. But in every case, she does so from a different vantage point than a non-Latina viewer. The danger in the show's portrayal is that it risks white viewers, in particular, assuming that same privilege.

17 The glamour factor and the Fiji effect

Jennifer Vanasco

I love *The L Word*.

Saying that in the company of other lesbian feminists feels about as comfortable as saying, 'I love oppression,' or 'Give me some more patriarchy, please,' but I remain undaunted.

Sure, there are issues with the show. Every television show has issues. You can't name one groundbreaking show that doesn't. But I think that *The L Word* is the best publicist that the lesbian community can have. It spins us into something more glamorous, more gorgeous, more intriguing, more chic, than most of us really are.

Of course, some of us *are* that chic. Cynthia Nixon, former *Sex and the City* star – chic. Melissa Etheridge – chic. The new Ellen DeGeneres – surprisingly, pretty darn chic. But most of us really aren't. We might not wear flannel button-down shirts and hiking boots, but then again we don't wear Prada and Jimmy Choos either.

The L Word women do. And I love them for it. In America, glamour equals power, and the more perceived power television lesbians have, the more actual power actual lesbians have. Or at least, the better chance we have to gain that power.

There's also a secondary benefit to *The L Word*. It makes lesbians less frightening. Straight people who think they don't know anyone who's gay often have piles of questions about lesbians. What do they do in bed? Are they really in love, or is it just friendship? Why do they hate men so much? Why do they want children and how do they have them?

In this sense, *The L Word* is almost documentary-like. It patiently explains lesbian culture to the uninitiated, making it seem cool, chic – and fun. Who wouldn't want to sit around all afternoon and discuss one's sex life while drinking lattés? Who wouldn't want to have hot sex in one's own backyard pool? Who wouldn't want to road trip to a cool party with all one's best buddies? It also makes lesbian culture seem very, very normal. The women of *The L Word* get their hearts broken. They make good choices and bad ones. They revel in friendships and struggle not to betray themselves. They adore their pets and their children. They are compassionate. They get grouchy. In other words, they are just like everyone else.

Perhaps best of all, *The L Word* reveals homophobes for what they are: the bad guys. Or, at least, as dinosaurs who are holding onto an era of discrimination that is passing.

I do have my own concerns about the show. Some of them are these – too often, the sex scenes in the first season seemed geared toward heterosexuals, the central cast is predominantly white, and the characters are decidedly anti-political except, it seems, when it comes to art (Jennifer Beals's character Bette directs a contemporary art museum).

But my more lasting concern is what kind of effect *The L Word* will have within the lesbian community.

One of the most incredible, freeing aspects of being part of the lesbian community is the absence of the beauty culture. Gay men often complain about being judged by their looks alone; they deride the bar scene as shallow; they note that men age out of the community as they are no longer considered attractive.

Straight women often have the same issue. Much of their confidence comes from how thin they are, how well-dressed, how facially wrinkle-free. Feminists have worried about this for a long time but, even for straight feminists, it's very, very hard to crawl out from under an avalanche of beauty magazines, waif-like movie stars and a culture dominated by the beauty-queen school of values.

Lesbians, on the other hand, have been very, very lucky. For years,

our outsider status ensured that we used markers to identify ourselves
that had nothing to do with traditional female beauty – short hair, for
example, and strong, sports-buffed bodies. Women whom lesbians are
attracted to often have a certain swagger in their walk, a defiant tilt of
their chin, a smart and sassy mouth.

Lesbian culture is built on a bedrock of loyalty and inclusion, and so
we tend to be open to women of all sorts of body types and ethnicities,
rarely discounting a date on looks alone. We care more about who you
are than what you look like.

The Michigan Womyn's Music Festival is a great example of that. Every
year, three to seven thousand women of all shapes, sizes and cultural and
ethnic backgrounds gather half-naked to celebrate their fabulousness.
Fat, thin, buff or soft, women at Michigan prance happily around the
Land, most of them topless, many of them sparkling with glitter or
shiny with body paint. At Michigan, you don't have to be traditionally
feminine or chic to be beautiful – you just have to be confident.

This turning away from traditional beauty has of course led to
stereotypes about lesbians – that we are unattractive, or 'mannish' or
angry. For the most part, though, we've shrugged our shoulders at that
and continued to live the way we wanted to.

The L Word is dangerous because it might sabotage this culture from
the inside out. If you think that's overstating, then consider Fiji.

The people of Fiji traditionally valued more full-figured, robust
women. Women with curves on their hips and meat on their bones.
Thin women were considered weak.

Then came television.

Thirty-eight months after television arrived in 1995 showcasing
thin, western-sized women, seventy-four per cent of Fiji's teenage girls
surveyed by a Harvard anthropologist said that they were 'too big or
fat'. Along with a change in attitudes came a change in action. Girls and
women started dieting. And eating disorders – bulimia and anorexia
– started making their first ghastly appearance.

The study showed that a higher proportion of women are now
dieting in Fiji than in Massachusetts.

I worry that The L Word might have a Fiji effect on lesbians. For a long
time, we had few open role models – now we have glamorous lesbians

being broadcast into our living rooms. Whereas before, young lesbians were introduced to lesbian culture through books, magazines, sports teams and peer groups, now there is going to be a generation of lesbians whose first experience of lesbian culture may be the sophisticated, shallow, sexually oriented banter of The L Word women.

That would be too bad because, although The L Word gets a lot of our cultural nuances right – a strong affection for the Indigo Girls, the tendency to move in as soon as you're attracted to someone, the propensity of lesbians to date every other lesbian in their circle – it gets the overall vibe wrong. It doesn't quite hit the core values of the lesbian community – loyalty and inclusion, as I've mentioned, as well as community activism.

This is of course not to say that all lesbians value loyalty and inclusion. Indeed, many, if not most, lesbians aren't part of a lesbian community at all. And lesbian communities vary by region. It could very well be that some women never come out because they *are* typically feminine and they feel that the flannel-wearing, boyish stereotype just doesn't apply to them. But the overall ethos of what might better be called 'the lesbian movement' remains the same across the country.

So maybe The L Word is bad news for the inner workings of the lesbian community. But in terms of how straight America relates to lesbians, the news is very good indeed.

Lesbians have long been considered the dull, unfashionable, bitter, but funny younger sisters of stylish, witty charming gay men. Gay men, we all know, are handsome and talented. They are musicians, artists, florists, interior decorators, Broadway stars, closeted Hollywood leading men. Like the men on Queer Eye for the Straight Guy, gay men make the world a more beautiful place. Straight women want them to be their boyfriends; straight men, at least metrosexuals, want to ape their style.

No one wants to be a lesbian. Sometimes even lesbians don't want to be lesbians. Many women prefer using 'gay'. Others stay as far away from the lesbian community as they can, so that they don't come off as angry or man-hating.

The truth is, though, lesbians are fiercely stylish, even if it's not always in a traditional-beauty kind of way. As Guy Trebay pointed out in the *New York Times*, in an article called 'The Secret Power of Lesbian Style' (2004: 1, 6), many of America's street-fashion mavens are lesbians. Fred Segal, a Los Angeles retailer, responsible for a lot of that city's (and thus the country's) gender-bending fashion mix has lesbians who choose what will be on the floor each season. Award-winning knitwear designer, Liz Collins, is a lesbian. Successful fashion model, Amanda Moore, is a lesbian. Patricia Fields, who costumed the chic women on *Sex and the City* – yep, she's a lesbian, too. And many of America's hot streetwear looks for women, from the shaggy, spiky haircut to cargo pants to chain wallets to trucker caps, originated with lesbians. Basically, if the clothes seem to be ambiguously gendered, a lesbian probably started wearing it first.

Before *The L Word*, these influences were quiet, perhaps because being a lesbian didn't have the same cachet that being a gay man did. But thanks to *The L Word*, it looks like that is slowly changing.

This is the glamour factor, and it's important. Presidential candidates don't hang out on television with policy wonks. They hang out with celebrities. Americans care more about the size of JLo's engagement ring than they do about the deficit. Americans are glamour hungry, and they will follow whichever group promises to provide it to them.

Glamour in America equals power partly because all Americans think it is possible to achieve it, just like all Americans think that it is possible to achieve great wealth. It's one of the great founding American myths. Walk the right way, get your nose done, wear the right clothes bought in the right stores, have a gay guy design your living room, and there you go – instant glamour. Americans then seem to have a corollary: if someone is glamorous, then they must have done things the right way. Therefore, if someone is glamorous, they deserve our attention.

Not respect, mind you. No one thinks Americans respect celebrities. Heck, Americans don't really respect anyone: political figures, journalists, lawyers, doctors and bankers all fall pretty low on the trust-o-meter of the American public. But Americans give attention to the glamorous, and attention is what lesbians need.

Too often, lesbians have been dismissed. We're a fairly small minority – just one to two per cent of Americans, though if you believe Adrienne Rich that there's a lesbian continuum (1980: 631–60), there's likely to be a lot more – and we tend to get overlooked and shouted down. Dyke Marches aren't as well-attended as Gay Pride Parades. Lesbian health issues are all but ignored by the mainstream press, while attention to HIV and AIDS remains high. Few businesses cater to lesbians' needs or wants. Politicians almost never talk to us directly, unless they're lesbians themselves. Usually, we're lumped in with the way-more-powerful men. And our needs and their needs aren't always the same.

But shows like The L Word have the potential to start to change that. The L Word makes it clear that lesbians have our own vibrant culture, our own distinct needs and expectations. And because the women of The L Word are so glamorous, those needs and expectations are automatically given value and empathy by viewers.

Will The L Word bring about same-sex marriage or workplace equality or full family and adoption rights? Of course not. But it is another way of propelling America forward, of prodding the public to realise that we are here, we're queer, and heck – we're cooler than they think we are.

Radical acts

Biracial visibility and the L word

Sarah Warn

Much has been written about Showtime's ensemble drama The L Word's contribution to lesbian visibility, but little about its contribution to the visibility of biracial women through the character of Bette Porter, a lesbian museum director played by Jennifer Beals. Although it is an ensemble drama, Bette is one of the more prominent and popular characters on the show, and Beals (who rose to fame in the early 1980s for her starring role in Flashdance (1983) then played a number of smaller film roles prior to taking on The L Word) has been touted by Showtime from the beginning as the show's biggest star.

While some of the other characters may seem dispensable at various points in the series, most viewers would be hard-pressed to imagine The L Word without Bette. So central is she to the narrative and rhythm of the series, in fact, that her emotional state tends to drive the overall tone of the show. When she and Tina Kennard are happily planning to have a baby, the show's episodes tend towards the light and happy; in the second season, when Bette is in agony over losing Tina or when her father is dying, the episodes are darker overall. This cannot be said of all the other characters – Jenny Schecter, for example, is usually in a state of depression, and Alice Pieszecki is usually quirky and upbeat, regardless of the overall tone of the episode. Though both of these characters have their up-and-down moments, the episodes don't tend to rise and fall with their moods the way they do with Bette's.

In many ways, as Bette goes, so goes *The L Word*.

Given the scarcity of images of explicitly biracial and multiracial people in American entertainment, the character of Bette would be worth examining regardless of the size of her role, but the fact that she is arguably *The L Word*'s lead character gives her even more significance. Although the actual amount of time Bette spends dealing with race issues on-screen is minimal, and not always satisfactorily handled by the writers, her biracial identity is an indelible part of her, as defining as her gender and her sexual orientation. Bette's negotiation of race in her life, even in a limited fashion, not only brings visibility to an issue that is seldom addressed by television, but also makes the character, and the series overall, more complex, three-dimensional and challenging to the American status quo.

Bette was not originally slated to be biracial. After her initial meeting with series creator Ilene Chaiken about the role, 'I suggested that [she] be made biracial,' said Beals, 'so I could serve all those people who were like me and had never seen themselves represented, except for maybe in a Benetton ad. Ilene embraced the idea because she is that kind of spirit' (Beals 2004). Beals, who is not a lesbian in real life (she is currently married to Canadian Ken Dixon), finds it easier to play one on TV because she's biracial, and has 'always lived sort-of on the outside… The idea of being the "other" in society is not foreign to me' (Schenden 2002). She expanded on this theme in subsequent speeches and interviews, talking about how invisible she felt as a child, scouring magazines and television 'for images of girls that looked like me. As a biracial girl growing up in Chicago there wasn't a lot there, positive or otherwise. I mean, I had Spock. That was kind of it. My theme song was Cher's "Half-Breed"' (Beals 2004).

With an African-American father and an Irish mother, Beals belongs to the growing group of Americans – at least seven million, according to the 2000 census data – who have a racially mixed heritage. But this growing segment of America is not yet adequately represented in the entertainment our culture produces; although biracial or multiracial women are increasingly visible in American pop culture, they are still few and far between. Prior to taking this role on *The L Word* in 2003, for example, only two or three of the dozens of characters Beals has played over the years have been biracial; the rest have been white women or women whose race was unspecified but generally assumed to be white.

There are a growing number of biracial actresses like Beals in roles on the big and small screen, but few are playing explicitly biracial or multiracial characters. There have even been several lesbian characters on television in the last few years played by biracial or multiracial actresses – like Sonja Sohn on *The Wire*, Iyari Limon on *Buffy the Vampire Slayer* and Karina Lombard on *The L Word* – but none of their characters have been identified as biracial or multiracial. There have been few TV characters of any sexual orientation, in fact, who identify as biracial – and in the rare instances when their mixed racial heritage is noted on-screen in some way, its impact on their lives and their broader identity is almost never mentioned or explored.

But Bette's biracial identity has been embraced by the writers and Beals from the very beginning. In early interviews about *The L Word* before it debuted, Beals described Bette as 'a total type-A, multi-tasking, slightly bossy women, who is moved the most by art ... and she's bira-cial. So there's all kinds of things you get to play with. You get to play with the mystery of sexuality and you get to play with race and you get to play with class and all kinds of things' (quoted in Spaner 2003).

Bette's struggle with issues of race and sexuality are highlighted in the very first episode of the series, when she and Tina argue over whether to have a biracial child after Tina discovers the sperm donor Bette prefers is black:

> Tina: How could you not tell me that Marcus Allenwood
>   [Mark Gibson] is black?
> Bette: God, I... I don't know. I guess I should have. I just
>   didn't think it would be a problem for you to use a
>   black donor.
> Tina: I didn't say I didn't want a black donor. I just think we
>   should have discussed it.
> Bette: We absolutely discussed it, Tina. Right at the very
>   beginning. We said that if you were going to be the

birth mother, that we should consider finding an
African-American donor. That way the child would be
more like our child.

Tina: But I wasn't prepared.

Bette: I don't understand. Other than being committed to
spending the rest of your life with me, what more do
you need to do to prepare?

Tina: Look at me, Bette. I don't feel qualified to be the
mother of a child who's half African-American. I don't
know what it means to be black.

Bette (tearing up): I think I can make a contribution in that
department.

Tina: And don't you think, on top of everything else, to also
have two moms, that is a lot of otherness to put on one
child?

This prompts an unsettling conversation in the same episode between
Bette and her older, black half-sister, Kit, about how Tina sees, or
doesn't see, Bette's racial identity, and Bette's own complicity in this:

Kit: When she looks at you, she's not looking at a black
woman or a white woman, she's looking at the woman
she loves.

Bette: She sees what she wants to see.

Kit: Maybe she sees what you *let* her see. I mean, maybe
this wasn't important before, maybe what's worked
best for you all these years, you know, getting all your
pretty things and, you know, putting together your
pretty life, is that you let people see what they want to
see.

Bette: What are you trying to say?

Kit: Nothin'! Just... maybe it's been easier for you that way.

Tina comes around in the next episode ('Let's Do It', 1:2), telling Bette
that 'there's no reason on earth that I wouldn't want to make a baby
with you using a donor who's black,' and Tina eventually gets pregnant

using Allenwood's sperm. But although the immediate question of whether they're willing to have a biracial child is answered, the underlying issues – Tina's fears that she won't be able to adequately raise a black child, or that they are putting too much 'otherness' on the child – aren't addressed any further.

Issues around Bette's racial identity are raised again in a later episode ('Listen Up', 1:8), when Yolanda, an African-American member of Bette and Tina's group therapy session, accuses Bette of trying to pass as white:

> Yolanda (to Bette): You talk so proud and ... forthright about being a lesbian. But you never once refer to yourself as an African-American woman. All I hear you saying is that white people should only take care of white babies.
>
> Bette: I said nothing of the kind. In fact, I was just about to say that Tina and I chose an African-American donor because it was important to us to have a family that reflects who we are.
>
> Yolanda: Before you can reflect who you are, you have to be who you are. I mean, look, they're wondering what the hell we're talking about because they didn't even know you were a black woman. I think before you have a child, you need to reflect on what it is you're saying to the world while hiding so behind the lightness of your skin.
>
> Bette (calm): You know... you know nothing about me. You don't know how I grew up. You don't know how I live my life.

This dialogue raises issues and concerns that are almost never discussed on television, or in any form of American entertainment intended for a mass audience. This is partly a reflection of the fact that American entertainment continues to be predominantly produced by and created for people who don't identify as multiracial, or people of colour, or anything other than 'white'; it's also because multiracial identity and passing are complicated issues with no easy answers. And if there's anything American entertainment doesn't like and doesn't accommodate well, it is complicated issues with no easy answers.

Unfortunately, this exchange between Bette and Yolanda, and the issues raised by it, are never really addressed again on the series. This is typical of the show's hit-and-run approach to messy topics (like Alice's bisexuality, and transgender character Ivan), which are often raised, briefly touched upon, and then dropped with no explanation. Of course, there are no 'solutions' to these kinds of issues – in real life or on TV – but implicitly promising an exploration of meaty subjects like these, then never truly delivering on that promise, can leave viewers feeling dissatisfied and frustrated.

But perhaps the writers believed that, having established Bette's identity as biracial in the first season, they could move on. After all, it's not like this is a new issue for the character – Bette has been biracial all her life, and would have dealt with people like Yolanda for years. In fact, Bette seems to have made her peace with those who think she should behave in a certain way, appearing more irritated than upset at having to explain or defend herself again. And, beginning halfway through the first season and into the second, she was caught up in dealing with the ramifications of her affair, problems at work, and the worsening health of her father, so it's easy to argue that there was little room for dealing with race issues as well.

It could, though, be argued that Bette's racial identity issue didn't disappear at the end of the first season, it simply assumed a more subtle role. When Bette had an affair with Candace towards the end of the first season, the fact that they were both women of colour didn't go unnoticed by viewers (Candace's race is unspecified on the series, but appears to be black/Latina). Many were overjoyed to see a lesbian relationship between two women of colour, regardless of the circumstances. Others were less charitable, disappointed that the show's sole lesbian relationship between two women of colour was an illicit one, and the source of so much strife; the series added a Latina lesbian character, Carmen de la Pica Morales, to the second-season cast but, to date, there have been no other relationships on The L Word between lesbians of colour.

In the context of Bette's character, however, the more important question is: what does it say about Bette that, after seven years of faithfulness to her partner, she has an affair with someone who is not only the complete opposite of Tina, but much closer to her other (racial) half? Having grown up being accused by women like Yolanda and her sister of passing as white because of her light skin tone, is Bette attracted, at least in part, to Candace's very inability to pass? Through her relationship with Candace, Bette literally and figuratively crosses over to the dark side; her actions, if not her words, indicate that those comments about passing as white bothered Bette a little more than she let on. In rejecting Tina for Candace, Bette may be on some level rejecting her white heritage and embracing her black heritage, at least for the moment.

But then the affair ends, Candace exits stage right early in the second season, and Bette spends the better part of the second season trying to win Tina back. In the process, Bette undergoes a lengthy and arduous mental transformation, as she comes to terms with her controlling behaviour, takes accountability for her actions and re-examines what's really important in her life – none of which involves her (bi)racial identity. Bette and Tina finally reunite, and their biracial daughter, Angelica, is born in the final episode of the second season, giving the writers the perfect platform to further explore racial identity issues in the third season. But they probably won't. If issues of race surface at all in season three, it will most likely be through the character of Carmen, who finally brings her (white) girlfriend Shane home to meet her Latina family.

Would more explicit attention to and exploration of Bette's racial identity interest viewers? From viewer feedback and discussion on L *Word* fan sites and forums, it would seem so. When asked in a recent AfterEllen.com reader poll whether the character of Bette and her biracial identity had made them more aware of the issues biracial people face in real life, a full forty-eight per cent of over 2,000 respondents answered 'yes' (nine per cent answered 'not sure' and forty-three per cent answered 'no'; poll result, August 2005). This is just an online poll, not a scientific study, but it underscores the power television has to effect change, and the necessity for more images of biracial and multiracial women in entertainment. 'I had a slight idea but now

I see that they are constantly pressured to "pick a side",' said one respondent, while another commented, 'It has made me more aware of issues facing biracial people. I think it is another very important social issue they tackle really well on the show!' Still another wrote simply, 'Yes, I have tons of biracial friends and I don't think that they are represented enough, especially my gay/bi/trans biracial friends.' Some of the biracial poll respondents indicated they were influenced by Bette's storyline to think differently about their own identity. 'Even though I'm half-Mexican,' commented one respondent, 'I never really thought about biracial issues before the first season. The counselling episodes made me think about how often I hide behind the lightness of my skin.' Another added, 'After watching the series and Bette's struggles, it got me to wondering how much black I had in me.' Many biracial respondents were grateful to see images of themselves on-screen, even as they criticised the show's handling of the topic. 'I'm biracial, and know there is a lot more out there then what she's going through, but I love that they have a biracial character on the show,' said one respondent. 'I am biracial (same "mix" as Bette),' said another, 'and I think the "black racism" towards Bette has been more explored than the "white racism", which in my opinion is harder to deal with. But on the whole it's just nice to see a mixed face on TV who isn't playing some unfortunate slave girl in a crap TV movie.' A third answered, 'I think addressing her identity issues in season one was a start, but I'd definitely like to see some more soul searching and confront her very unresolved issues again in season three.'

Although the show's silence on the topic of Bette's biracial identity, aside from the handful of scenes mentioned, does blunt its impact on biracial visibility, it doesn't negate it. Bette's ongoing presence on the series as an openly identified biracial character chips away at America's practice of casting race in black-or-white terms, regardless of whether the topic is ever explicitly addressed again. This fact wasn't lost on the Mixed Media Watch (2005), an online coalition tracking media representations of multiracial people and issues, who commended The L Word in its 2004 Image Awards for 'tackling difficult racial issues and portraying this mixed race family with depth and complexity' and gave an individual award to Jennifer Beals for convincing Chaiken to make

Bette biracial, and for her 'unwavering commitment to promoting the visibility of mixed race people in a thought-provoking manner' throughout her acting career.

'They talk about the fact that history is written by the victors,' Beals has said, 'but if you can make yourself victorious by writing your own history and supplying your own images, then you've done yourself and the world a great service' (quoted in Shapiro 2003). Through the character of Bette, *The L Word* supplies those images not only to lesbian and bisexual women, but to biracial women as well, and provides those viewers who are not biracial or multiracial a window into the issues these women face in American society. 'When society fails to tell your story, it sends the unspoken message that your story is not worth telling,' Beals summarised in accepting an award for outstanding contribution in combating homophobia from the Gay and Lesbian Alliance Against Defamation (GLAAD) in June of 2005. 'Being part of *The L Word* allows me to offer up some sort of mirror, however imperfect, to people who may have never before seen themselves represented, and that is very fulfilling. And in a country and culture so dominated by media, by the manipulation of words and stories, sharing the stories of people whose narratives have been historically ignored is a radical act – an act that can change the world and help rewrite history' (Beals 2005).

Hot stuff

19

Music as a language of lesbian culture

Zoë Gemelli

Bette Porter's bare back fills the screen as she rolls over in a bed just as an orchestra begins a familiar lush and melancholic ballad. In the first three bars we see the sun's rays peaking through a window, Bette's eyes motion her ecstasy. Dusty Springfield's tender tenor chimes in, 'Just a little lovin'/early in the morning...'[1] Bette sways, wiggles and twists in the light blue sheets. 'Beats a little coffee/for starting off the day...' With a pleased smile, Bette peeks under the sheet. Candace Jewell, Bette's no longer secret fling, finds her way up to meet Bette's face. '... Just a little lovin'/when the world is yawnin' ...' Candace stares into Bette's eyes, she kisses her chin, then their lips meet. '... Makes you wake up feeling/good things are coming your way...' Candace says, 'I'm so happy to have you here,' as Bette stares blankly at her. Candace probes Bette's lost look. '... This old world/wouldn't be half as bad/it wouldn't be half as sad/if each and everybody in it had, yeah/Just a little lovin' ...' Bette is clearly somewhere else. Her eyes are wet; she breathes deeply; she sighs. She's not happy to be there anymore. The next scene not-so-coincidentally jumps to Alice Pieszecki and Shane McCutcheon drinking coffee at the Planet.

The scene plays out like a well-choreographed music video. Springfield's inflections juxtapose the elation of the romp with the reality of the real world waiting beyond the bed. The gloomy drawl of the song fits Bette's blues, her sombre mood and the sobering moment when she realises that she had been dreaming of another woman between her legs. In just over sixty seconds we see the stuff that made the second season of *The L Word* even hotter: sexy women having sexy sex with sexy music as the backdrop.

Using a Dusty Springfield song on a show about lesbians could be construed as far too obvious for those who knew that she was a publicly closeted lesbian. Many of us music lovers already adored Springfield's heroic southern soul masterpiece *Dusty in Memphis* long before we learned of her private love of women. But placing Springfield's brilliant blue-eyed soul number early in the series establishes the show's distinctive command of music as a language of lesbian culture. Who knew that lesbians listened to cool music? We did.

In a post-politically correct era, the idea that lesbians listen to anything outside of stereotypical lesbian music (e.g. Melissa Etheridge, Indigo Girls, Ani DiFranco) seems as far fetched as a TV series about a segment of lesbian life. It's still cool to give props to our musical foremothers – Cris Williamson, Holly Near, June Millington and the womyn's music lot – but that doesn't mean we have to only listen to their music any more. The average *L Word*-watching lesbian probably doesn't even know the names of those founders of the lesbian music matriarchate. That doesn't mean we are not grateful; we are aware that there were those who came before us in the fight for lesbian visibility. It's just that thirty years on we have eclipsed the need to only listen to music written by lesbians, for lesbians, about lesbians, all the lesbian time.

The art of song placement

Supervising the music for a TV show is tricky work. There's more to it that just playing a song as background music. The magic of a music supervisor's job is finding the right bit of music that will emotionally connect the scene, the character and the viewer for that specific moment. The music found on *The L Word* was a collaborative effort by creator, Ilene Chaiken, the show's music supervisor, Natasha Duprey, executive soundtrack producer, Rosie Lopez, season two newbie, Elizabeth Ziff of the band Betty, and cast and crew input. Where season one was full of folk-pop, Latin and quirky jazz songs, season two had Ziff's drama-inducing score and hipper electronic sounds. And let's not forget the new (and questionable) theme song by Betty.

To make the musical part of a TV show about lesbians accessible also requires some tapping into the music-listening quotient of the prospective audience. What kind of music do viewers want to hear? What is lesbian music? What will make them pre-order the soundtrack when it arrives on CD? Although the soundtrack CD that hit the stores for the first season is equal parts male and female, it leaned very heavily on singer-songwriterly odes: Lucinda Williams – 'Right In Time'; Shelley Campbell – 'Drivin' You'; Rufus Wainwright – 'Hallelujah'; Joseph Arthur – 'In The Sun', and others. Folk-pop tunes do perpetuate lesbian stereotypes, but the collection was all top-notch easy listening, even if it only represented a small segment of the show's overall edginess and unconventional plotlines.

In the first season, the team ambitiously added clever jazzy songs like Connie Francis' version of 'Everybody's Somebody's Fool', and Frances Faye's 'Frances and Her Friends' to flex a little witty lyrical muscle. The Marina Ferrer character facilitated the use of more Latin-based music like the Portuguese fado track by Fantcha, 'Sol Ja Camba'. Who wasn't moved by the genius double entendre scene with transgender-identified character Ivan lip-synching to Leonard Cohen's 'I'm Your Man' to woo Kit Porter? As the show aired each week there were songs that made me read the credit roll and run to Google to find out more about performers like Mr. Airplane Man's 'Up in the Room', the Be Good Tanyas' 'In Spite of the Damage' and Kinnie Starr's 'Alright'.

The season two soundtrack is full of cool cuts like Ladytron's 'Playgirl', Le Tigre's 'On The Verge' and Martina Topley-Bird's 'Iiya'. We were treated to Canadian singer/songwriter Jane Siberry's beautiful rendition of 'Love Is Everything', a song she wrote that k.d. lang covered on *Hymns of the 49th Parallel*. As with the first CD, there were many songs used that they couldn't get the rights to release on the soundtrack, not to mention that it would have been a multi-disc venture had they been able to. Tracy Chapman's poignant 'Say Hallelujah' that was used during the memorial service for Bette and Kit's father, Melvin Porter (Ossie Davis), is missing. And so is the stunning gospel-esque version of Ferron's 'Testimony' recorded by Sweet Honey and the Rock that was brilliantly placed as the end credits of the season two finale. There were a few songs that touched on a stereotypical lesbian playlist but weren't heavy on the lesbian themes, like tracks by Joan Armatrading, Le Tigre and the Murmurs (out singer and L Word star Leisha Hailey's band). For completists, Natasha Duprey sent website thelwordonline.com a complete list of all of the songs played the Monday after an episode aired on Showtime for the site to post. Several fans began making their own multi-disc compilations of all of the music used on the show; some even showed up on eBay.

If you Google all of the artists used on the show you'll find that many of them, including the musicians Ziff used for the score, are from Canada. Since the show is produced in Canada, it makes sense that Duprey is based in Vancouver, British Columbia. She is a Canadian musician herself, so she was able to tap into Canada's thriving music scene. (Disclosure: I'm Canadian too, so I was able to easily spot the Canucks.) Kinnie Starr, the Organ, Be Good Tanyas, Jane Siberry, Rufus Wainwright, Leonard Cohen – all Canadian. This is just one of the many ways it is cheaper to make American television shows and movies in Canada. Canadian music may only cost Canadian dollars, but it has added texture in terms of quality and quantity. (Again, this is my Canadian opinion.)

The music of season one didn't overtly emphasise character development as much as it seemed to try to brand a 'lesbian' sound. Most episodes ended with a strongly placed pop song that usually fell into a dated and more general idea of what lesbians listen to, as if we only ever listen to Lilith Fair spin offs. The first season did have many funky eclectic sounds used mainly as a backdrop, but most of those didn't make it to the soundtrack. Although most of the songs were choice folk-pop cuts, they didn't totally reflect the diversity of the lesbian community, and they certainly didn't fit the perception of what chic LA model-esque lesbians listen to.

The L Word also successfully migrated from musical guest stars playing characters, like Snoop Dogg as Slim Daddy for one episode ('Liberally', 1:10), to creating community-building events like a Shawn Colvin concert ('Land Ahoy', 2:10) or a Peaches show ('L-Chaim', 2:12).

Even though Kit was written as a former R&B crooner, we rarely got to hear her sing. During the opening night of the Planet, Kit gets on stage with Betty to cover 'Some Kinda Wonderful' ('Loneliest Number', 2:3). Pam Grier has the chops enough to carry it and the song comes off marvellously. Betty's performance on that episode was one that was marvelled at by many, not for their musical performance but for Elizabeth Ziff's hot on-stage kiss with Shane.

Turning the Planet into a music venue in season two allowed the writers more space to develop characters: Carmen de la Pica Morales was written as a DJ who spins at the Planet; guitarist Sharon Isbin comes to play ('Luminous', 2:7), Shane and Alice explain to Kit that lesbians like hip music, so they try to get Pink to perform there. The Organ made a splash when they played the subject of a music video shoot that Carmen was working on ('Lap Dance', 2:2). The season two finale had rockers Heart (a group many women came out to) performing at a benefit show where Gloria Steinem (cast as herself) speaks. Adding this element of musical life to the show successfully mirrored real lesbian social life. In my experience, lesbians often create and build community around live music.

The search for songs for the first season was much harder than for the second, because Duprey had to explain an unknown entity to prospective artists. It wasn't on the air yet, therefore it wasn't a known commodity either. The process of securing the rights to a song goes like this: after the song is picked for a scene, the music supervisor (Duprey) calls the music publishing house that owns or manages the rights to the song. Duprey pitches them the show and, more specifically, the scene the song may be used for. This is where it can get tricky, especially on a sexually charged show like The L Word, because she has to give all of the details of the scene. So, if she wanted a certain song as the backdrop to Marina going down on Jenny Schecter, Duprey had to describe the scene in detail. In the second season this part of the job got easier because the show had already made a name for itself.

There are many reasons a song that L Word staffers really wanted for a scene might not actually make it to the screen. A few artists declined participating because they were religious and didn't feel comfortable with their music on a show that promoted lesbianism. Most times the artist didn't get wind of the show's request at all. Some music publishers turned Duprey down but when she dug deeper and approached the artists themselves they agreed to have their song used. In some cases the artists were unhappy to find out that the publisher had said no.

Character development 101

The success of the first season of *The* L *Word* probably helped increase the music budget for the second season. Several things then changed: they hired Elizabeth Ziff as a composer to score the show; they turned the Planet coffeehouse into a night-time music venue; they added a new theme song by Betty. With these changes came a whole new way of experiencing *The* L *Word*. They realised that lesbians don't only listen to girls with guitars, they listen to the popular stuff that everyone else is grooving to.

The most notable innovation in season two was how Ziff created sounds for each character: a 'Shane' sound, a 'Bette' sound, a 'Jenny' sound. Her lush atmospheric orchestrations upgraded the show's dramatic value by adding dimensions to each character. The one character that benefited the most from this added emotive layer was Jenny. I witnessed a large group of women watching the second season première in Provincetown, Massachusetts where the reactions to Jenny were unbelievably vocally venomous. They called her 'manipulative bitch' and other one-dimensional expletives. As season two played out, Ziff effectively revealed Jenny's deeply tormented (and at times histrionic) soul by letting viewers experience the soundtrack to her nightmares. It was as if Ziff had read Jenny's angst-ridden mind and was relaying its narrative through music.

Ziff picked up where the storylines took us and dug deeper – way deeper – giving the scenes ambience far beyond what was on the screen. When Jenny recalls being molested at a circus, Ziff uses eerie menacing sounds to emphasise her haunting and sometimes terrifying memories. As Jenny begins to dig into her family history, Ziff weaves in multi-layered traditional Jewish music sounds. Ziff used her talents to get into the heads of the characters and connected the music to their stories.

Through a kind of character mapping, Ziff found a way to tell the musical story behind each of them. Shane's hard edges are matched with rockier sounds. Bette's inner brooding is marked by pensive moody instrumental bits. Alice and Dana Fairbank's blissful elation is pronounced with quirky pop sounds. Carmen is often portrayed with funky beats. Ziff may not have a traditional scoring background, but her dramatic experience with Betty's off-Broadway show 'Betty Rules' and her eclectic flair was an incredible triumph for the show's feel and sale-ability. Ziff's musical accoutrements gave the show texture and depth. She ingeniously mixed the voices of the characters into songs, like Bette smirking while Tina Kennard attempted to masturbate. Her thumping dance beats aptly enhanced Shane and Carmen's first fucking scene.

Just as Ziff's score added depth to the characters, the songs chosen in the second year gave them all enhanced dimensions. Ladytron's track emblazoned Shane's sexual prowess to the point where that song heard on its own means sex. The folky train-like motions of Iron & Wine's 'Naked As We Came' coupled with title's lyrical significance perfectly matched Jenny's bittersweet rite of passage scene when Shane cuts off her long hair making way for a much dykier look and, alas, life ('Lynch Pin', 2:4). The second season felt much more like a batch of hand-picked songs that added lyrical or emotional context to certain scenes or characters. It was a welcome upgrade from the mixed-bag approach of the first season, which felt more like something a record company executive wanted the show to sound like.

Win some, lose some

Although Ziff's scoring was a huge hit, the new theme song by her band Betty was an enormous disappointment. Sounding a lot like a dated pop song that never charted, it's the lesbian sister of the American Enjoli TV commercial of the 1970s: 'I can bring home the bacon / fry it up in a pan'. This time it's: 'Talking / Laughing / Loving / Breathing / Fighting / Fucking / Crying / Drinking ... It's the way that we live / and love.' Chaiken called the song 'exuberant, audacious, explicit, memorable.'[2] It has oomph; I find myself tapping my leg when it's on. And it is memorable, because I do manage to still hear it in my head even after hitting the mute button. But the song's audacity is where it falls short in my opinion. It sounds like an elevator pitch to the executive who's never heard of lesbians before.

The last I checked, the main audience is lesbian, which makes the theme song preachy and wrought with cliché. Perhaps that's what it takes for a lesbian show on mainstream television to be watched by a straight person. The *Queer As Folk* theme song is also very stereotypical, but so is the show. Dan Gagnon's little electronic bleeps and blurbs on the original theme made me think we'd finally been upgraded to the dance music lovers that we are in real life. It may not have been an in-your-face rant about lesbian life, but it subversively outed us as hipsters. I miss those bubbly ten-second bits.

Ziff wrote several variations of the theme song that she slipped in with little detection or fanfare. Like the raucous 'Punk Version (The Hell Word)', 'French Version (The Elle Word)', 'Muzak Version (The Elevator Word)' and 'Klezmer Version (The El Al Word)'. These smart bits deviated from the theme's overwrought tediousness.

No more wimpy folk songs

On listserves, in living rooms and in weekly reviews of the show, many voices gushed and jeered at the music of *The L Word*. I'm not alone in my need to hit the mute button rather than hearing Betty's new theme song with every episode: AfterEllen.com's poetic pundit, Scribe Grrrl, continually panned the thing in her spirited weekly play-by-plays of the show. 'What? No boop-de-boop? Instead we get some group that probably can't even get an audience at the Michigan fest. Okay, that was too harsh,'[3] she wrote of Betty after her first listen to the song. But, at a special viewing of the second-season finale, I witnessed one woman sing enthusiastically along to every note of the song. I guess if one person (outside of Ilene Chaiken) sings along, it has some merit. Viewers seem to like what they are hearing overall because they are also supporting the lesser-known acts like the Organ, who now apparently have a huge following after their appearance on *The L Word*. The music's diversity allows for many segments (not all – it's impossible to reach everyone) of the lesbian community to relate to the show.

If you made a mixtape of the second-season soundtrack without a label and gave it to an unknowing music lover, they wouldn't dub it 'lesbian music'. If the show has broken new ground anywhere, it was in the music chosen to represent the new lesbian culture. Sure, they threw in a Joan Armatrading song for good measure, but they also gave us Ladytron, Granddadbob and Dusty Springfield to groove to.

The stereotypical pop culture view of lesbians has always skewed them as folky Birkenstock-wearing granola types with mullets and flannel shirts: the female lumberjack look. Sure, there are many out there who fit that description, but there are many other lesbians who refuse to give in to stereotypes, like the punker rockers, the lipstick disco lesbians, the Broadway musical lovers and the Coldplay-loving crowd.

Bottom line is that lesbians listen to music like rest of the world does: whatever is hot, being played on the radio or at dance clubs right now. And they listen to the conventional evergreen lesbian favourites too. What The L Word has managed to do in just two seasons is to portray lesbians as lovers of music period, not just of lesbian music. That integral distinction socially upgraded us to a new level of cool, even down to the beats.

Notes

1. 'Just a Little Lovin'' by Dusty Springfield from *Dusty in Memphis*, Atlantic Records, 1969. Words and music by Barry Mann and Cynthia Weil: Screen Gems-Columbia, BMI.

2. Quoted in *The L Word: The Second Season, Sessions – Original Score*, 2005, CD liner notes.

3. Scribe Grrrl, *The L Word*: recaps: Episode 2:01 'Life, Loss, Leaving', *AfterEllen.com* (http://www.afterellen.com/TV/theword/recaps2/201/1.html).

L20 Interview with Erin Daniels[1]

Sarah Warn

When talking to The L Word's Erin Daniels, one thing becomes clear almost immediately: she's really smart, as comfortable discussing French existentialism (she took a course devoted to the subject in college), furniture design (what she might do if she wasn't acting), or her favourite books (anything by Milan Kundera, and all the Harry Potter books, which she calls 'candy for the brain') as she is talking about what drives the insecurities of the closeted tennis player she currently plays on Showtime's new lesbian ensemble drama.

Daniels first got into acting when her mom (a clinical social worker) and dad (an architect) enrolled her in acting classes as a child in St Louis, Missouri, and she began to pursue acting professionally while an undergrad at Vassar, where she received a degree in architecture and art history.

Daniels had a small but powerful role in last year's big-screen thriller One Hour Photo (2002) starring Robin Williams, but it is her role as Dana on The L Word that's really getting people's attention, as she discusses in the following interview.

AfterEllen.com: Did you immediately go for the part of Dana?
Erin Daniels: No, actually, it was funny – I first read for the part of Bette, then I read for the part of Alice, and then one of the producers asked me to read for the part of Dana, and it just sort of went from there.

What do you like about Dana? What do you find most challenging?
It's such a joy to play Dana because she's so complicated and she's still figuring out who she is; she's struggling with so many real issues and she doesn't claim to have it all figured out. She might pretend to, which is what a lot of people do, but she's still trying to figure out where she fits in. That's my favourite part about her, that she sticks her foot in her mouth, she makes mistakes, she trips over her own words, she's not even close to perfect.

The only thing I find challenging about Dana is when she has to deal with really emotional situations, because I think you have to find a certain amount of your own personality in the character you play. So when she has really emotional events happen in her life, I go through them with her, and it's emotionally taxing. But it feels great at the same time, because I want to do her as much justice as I can.

Overall, I'm really proud of my work on this show – I think Dana's a really honest character. She's just lost, you know? It was a challenge to blend the comedy and the drama, and that was one of my goals.

How much of the character is in the writing and how much is your spin on it?
It's funny, when I first read the script, there wasn't a whole lot of definition to Dana. But the beautiful part was that we were able to sit down with Ilene and Rose and Guin [Turner] and talk to them about ideas we had; it was very collaborative, and a lot of times those ideas would end up on the show.

It was obvious to me from the beginning that Dana is defensive in a very sarcastic way because she has something to hide. I think it's very honest when you see people's flaws because everyone has them. And for a woman who's struggling so hard to fit in and figure out who she is, who just wants so badly to be loved... I decided to spin her that way, and in sort of a goofy way, because I think most people are goofy... She tries so hard to be cool and it just backfires, which (laughing) God knows I've done, so many times.

Dana is really graceful and confident on the court, but awkward and insecure off the court. How did you capture that so well?
I approached it more from a psychological standpoint: here's a girl

who grew up playing tennis, and she's really, really good at that. She's capable of being herself on the court because she knows she's good at it but, off the court, she has to suppress who she is.

When she's on the court, she can gauge where she is in the sports strata: Am I good? Am I acceptable? The more successful she is on the court, the better she feels about herself, but the minute she steps off the court, she has to struggle again. That's a really difficult way to live because it forces you to question your identity.

Did your gay friends give you any particular advice for playing Dana?
Their advice was more emotional, around what it's like to be out to friends and not to family. I gave Dana a back-story, which you may see bits and pieces of later on in the series. Dana's always been a lesbian, since the day she was born...

"SO gay" is how her friends describe her on the show...
She is! She tried to fight it and she couldn't, she fell in love with the wrong person and when her parents found out, it was messy. They're in denial about the whole thing, think it's a phase and all that, very similar to the stories I've heard.

There will be episodes in the future that involve Dana's family, especially if we go to a second season. The Pandora's box will definitely be opened.

How do you think Dana fits into the group?
Dana's entertaining, that's for sure. On the subconscious level, she's the sort of *schadenfreude* character of the group, she makes the others feel good about themselves because she has so many problems. But at the same time she's a really good person, a really good friend. She's very open about questions she has with her friends, especially Alice and Shane. I give Alice a hard time because she's bisexual and I want her to pick a side, so I know where to put her, and I give Shane a hard time because she has everything that I don't, everything that I think I want.

Also, Shane being so out is a direct threat to Dana...
Exactly, but at the same time I think there's a lot to be learned from

Shane because she's so comfortable being out, and Alice is so comfortable being bi, she knows who she is, too. I think they're a really good influence on Dana. But I also think Dana's a really good influence on them, because she asks them questions and forces them to question who they are. Dana's one of those friends you just love because she is who she is, she can't pretend to be anyone else when she's around you.

Do you have a favourite scene?
Definitely. I'd hate to spoil anything, but there's a scene with Dana and Mia's character Jenny that is one of the funniest scenes I've ever done.

What was it like working with such a strong group of writers, actors and directors?
It was amazing, the creativity and energy on the set was incredible. It was really inspiring. The cast is a group of smart, sophisticated, but very laid-back women, who can just hang out and watch a movie, order pizza, whatever, and just step outside the whole Hollywood bubble.

Kate [Moennig], Leisha [Hailey] and I work together all the time because our three characters are together all the time, and the three of us are super close and support one another.

Are you concerned at all that playing a lesbian on The L Word *will negatively impact your ability to get future roles?*
No, not even remotely.

Because you think people don't care?
Because I don't care. Anybody who did care about that I probably wouldn't want to work with. I don't pick roles based on how famous they're going to make me, I pick roles based on how they're going to inspire me intellectually.

I've played a lesbian before, on [the Fox TV series] Action – well, she was really more bi-opportunistic (laughing). We all know people like that. It was so much fun – I played Ileana Douglas' girlfriend. It was a great show, but I don't think the network really knew what to do with it, so it got cancelled.

Do you think The L Word *is going to be successful?*

I do. I think the beautiful thing about this show is how well it blends humour and drama. You really do see humanness going on. I think the show is amazing. I've heard some people say we don't represent enough of a cross-section of women, but if I look at my group of friends, for example, they don't represent a cross-section. You gravitate towards people you have things in common with, so that's one thing I'll certainly argue for. Of course I'm biased, but I think I can honestly say it's a really good show. It's really well written, very smart and very honest.

That's another reason I wanted to do this show: it's very rare in this business that you get to do something that's socially important. I'm really proud of us.

Note

1.   Originally published on AfterEllen.com, January 2004.

The essential L word episode guide

Prepared by Scribe Grrrl

Season one[1]

US première: Sunday 18 January 2004, Showtime
1:1 'Pilot'
writer: Ilene Chaiken
(story by Chaiken, Kathy Greenberg and Michele Abbott)
director: Rose Troche

The day begins with an ovulating earth-mother-type named Tina Kennard and a caffeine-seeking lothario-type named Shane McCutcheon. Doesn't every day? Jenny Schecter, a budding writer, arrives in LA to start a new life (or at least have un-pretty sex) with her boyfriend, Tim Haspel. Tina and her partner, Bette Porter (a type-A museum director) have an awkward therapy session, followed by a disappointing doctor's appointment, and, still later, a sperm donor party. At the party, Jenny flirts with the sexy, mysterious Marina Ferrer, who owns the Planet, a cafe popular with lesbians.

Bette and Tina reject a French sperm donor and consider an African-American one, prompting discussions about otherness. Bette's sister, Kit Porter, knows that love can conquer all. Alice Pieszecki, Dana Fairbanks, and Shane talk about their dating pool. Shane swims in it regularly, while Alice and Dana often miss the boat. These three like to talk about weighty matters like 'bush and nipple confidence'. And Alice, who writes for *L.A. Magazine*, has a chart of lesbian connections on her wall. She tries to share her wisdom with Dana, the clueless tennis player. Jenny and Marina finally have sex, while Bette and Tina try to seduce a possible sperm donor. The would-be donor figures out their scheme and dashes out the door.

We end with two visions of partnership: Tim proposes to Jenny, but her response is less than gleeful. But glee is in the air next door at Bette and Tina's, where a hot sex scene leads to a contented morning after. Even Shane approves.

1:2 'Let's Do It'
w: Susan Miller
d: Rose Troche

Tina and Bette decide they're ready to make a baby, 'here at home, sexy and in love' – and complete with syringe and jar. Alice hooks up with Gabby Deveaux (Guinevere Turner), a former girlfriend (but Dana and Shane are not impressed). Shane is also less than thrilled about her stalker, Lacey (Tammy Lynn Michaels). Shane and Lacey once had a fling, but for Lacey it was much more than that, so she sets out to expose Shane's lechery. The sous-chef, Lara Perkins (Lauren Lee Smith), at Dana's country club sends her a plate of goodies. Dana is flattered, and cluelessly (and adorably) refers to Lara as the 'soup chef'.

Marina leaves a message for Jenny, to say she's thinking about her. Meanwhile, the others are talking about her: Dana says she thought Jenny was straight, but Alice points out that 'most girls are straight until they're not', and Shane ruminates about the fluidity of sexuality. Dana obsesses about Lara, so the others 'deploy a mission to ascertain the disposition' of the soup chef. One of the tests consists of Shane flirting with Lara, but Lara doesn't respond, so Dana despairs. But then Dana gets an endorsement deal with Subaru, and something even better: a kiss from Lara in the locker room.

Tim and Jenny have a dinner party. Marina, Bette and Tina are among the guests. The sexual tension between Marina and Jenny, accompanied by the announcement of Tim and Jenny's engagement, gives Bette a headache and a superiority complex.

1:3 'Longing'
w: Angela Robinson
d: Lynne Stopkewich

Bette works on bringing a show called *Provocations* to her art museum, the California Arts Center. The board is more interested in safe things like Monet. Jenny confronts Marina, telling her (and telling herself) that she wants to be with Tim. Marina pretends to believe that. Gabby and Alice get closer, causing Shane to scowl while still maintaining her generally blank expression. The other new couple, Dana and Lara, make plans to go on a date. Tim and Marina play pool, which causes Jenny to freak out and faint.

Kit's hobbies seem to be DJ-ing and drinking – the latter of which earns her a few glares from Bette and Tina. Bette seeks out billionaire Peggy Peabody (Holland Taylor), hoping she will help Bette convince the museum board to mount the *Provocations* show. Peggy and Bette bond over strong drinks and Stendhal's Syndrome, which is an overwhelming reaction to art. (Viewers experience a Stendhal moment in reaction to Jennifer Beals's acting.) Peggy also reveals that she was a lesbian once in college – Bette says that's called a 'has-bian'. Gabby treats Alice like dirt so, with encouragement from the rest of the gang, Alice tells Gabby to 'step off, bitch'. Shane takes the opposite approach with her stalker, Lacey: they make out on the sidewalk and then head to bed.

Jenny tells Marina that she feels 'completely dismantled' every time she looks at her. 'Dismantle' is another word for 'disrobe', so that's what Jenny does.

1:4 'Lies, Lies, Lies'
w: Josh Senter
d: Clement Virgo

Dana and Lara have just had sex, but Dana isn't happy. She confides in Alice and Shane. They assure her that female ejaculation is not only perfectly natural; it's something to be proud of and proof that Lara is good in bed. Tim and Jenny go to the Planet; Jenny promptly goes off to have sex with Marina in the bathroom. Tim eventually wonders what's up and almost catches them. While Tina pees on a stick to see if the baby-making is working, Alice decides to go back to 'uncomplicated, boring boy-girl sex'. The test comes up positive. Alice and Kit are there to share the moment with Tina, but where's the other mommy?

Shane introduces Alice to 'Lisa' (Devon Gummersall), who is a 'lesbian-identified man'. Alice just thinks he's cute. She also thinks her mother, Leonore Pieszecki (Anne Archer), who interrupts the flirting, is insane and annoying. Bette arrives home to find a pregnancy test stick on her dinner plate. A thousand emotions play across her face and her smile lights up the entire city. Just as Dana is ready to conclude that Lara doesn't want her, Lara shows up with a rose. Meanwhile, Peggy Peabody sings Bette's praises and secures the *Provocations* show. Jenny and Marina have sex in Marina's office, and (again) Tim almost catches them.

Bette and Tina have a party to celebrate their good news. Dana and Lara cuddle while Shane and Alice's mom flirt. Next door, Jenny writes and tries to make Tim think she still cares.

1:5 'Lawfully'
w: Rose Troche
d: Heike Brandstatter

Alice is nauseated by her mother's interest in Shane. Elsewhere, Tina is truly ill with morning sickness. At the tennis club, Dana and Lara kiss and flirt. Dana's agent, Conrad Voynow (Ari Cohen), disapproves, and later tells Dana she can't take Lara to an event that Subaru is hosting. At the Planet, Alice and Shane talk about Alice's mom, whom Alice labels a 'slutty, slutty, chicken-chasing pervert'. Tim, who's a swimming coach, is about to leave for a meet, but has forgotten his lucky stopwatch. He goes home to get it and gets more than he bargained for: he finally catches Jenny and Marina having sex.

Bette and Tina go to dinner with Bette's dad, Melvin (Ossie Davis), who cannot seem to understand why he would ever think of Tina's baby as his grandchild. Jenny tells Tim that the thing with Marina was a mistake, so Tim drives her right over to the Planet and makes her tell Marina that too. Lara arrives at Dana's house, expecting to go with her to the Subaru event. But Dana has decided to play it straight. Tim and Jenny go to Tahoe and get married. It's a very solemn occasion. Dana asks Lara to give her one more chance. Lara does, but says Dana has to start to come out, because she's 'so gay.' Bette tells Kit about the disastrous dinner with their dad. Kit is not surprised and later goes to Melvin's hotel room to scold him.

In another hotel room, Jenny wakes up, but Tim is gone.

1:6 'Losing It'
w: Guinevere Turner
d: Clement Virgo

Shane is at a bar with a bunch of guys who knew her when she turned tricks as a twink on the streets. One of them offers up a client for her current trade: hairstyling. She also gets another favour: some OxyContin. Tina is craving a Slurpee. Bette chooses to accept the mission. Outside Tahoe, Jenny writes Tim an anguished letter – even the sentence structure is suffering. Bette and Tina get ready to go to NYC for the opening of the *Provocations* show, but Tina's not feeling up to it. Jenny hitches a ride with some kids who offer her sympathy and 'shrooms. Meanwhile, Tim calls Jenny's mom, and finds out Jenny is OK.

Tina sees a Chinese herbalist about her morning sickness. Marcus Allenwood (Mark Gibson), aka the sperm donor, is there, and his girlfriend freaks out about his generosity. Tina leaves a frantic message for Bette. The gang gathers at Tina's house to play poker and offer support. Alice's date is Lisa the lesbian-identified man. They all crash there for the night. Dana and Lara try to have a quickie, thinking everyone's asleep, but Kit clears her throat to alert them to their audience. A worried Bette arrives home early to a sleepy group of friends, rather than an emergency, and is both relieved and irritated.

Tim goes to the Planet, looking for Jenny but finding Marina. He pushes her around, but she stands her ground. Jenny, in the middle of nowhere, mails the letter to Tim.

1:7 'L'Ennui'
w: Ilene Chaiken
d: Tony Goldwin

Jenny arrives home. Tim asks her when she first slept with Marina, having found out the truth from Bette. Jenny hands him a lie, so he throws her stuff all over the lawn. Tina and Bette share too many details about the pregnancy. Shane, Alice and Dana later perform an intervention, complete with clipboards. They gently inform the happy couple that baby-making has made them boring. Dana's agent says she can't come out – there's a 'lifestyle clause' in the Subaru contract. Dana later breaks up with Lara because Lara wants to get kissy in public.

Shane hosts a party on a yacht she has borrowed. It's a wild affair, where Dana gets drunk, Alice gets naked with Lisa, the lesbian-identified man, Shane gets naked with everyone, Marina and Jenny get down on the dance floor, and Bette and Tina get tired of trying not to be boring. The next day, Kit asks Bette to go with her to meet David (Colin Lawrence), her estranged son. But David sees Kit at the bar and assumes she's fallen off the wagon. He leaves before they see him. Jenny wants to move in with Marina, but Marina already lives with someone: Francesca Wolff (Lolita Davidovich), her girlfriend who travels a lot. The Subaru Rep (Peter Shinkoda) reveals that the company wants Dana to be out and proud in their ad campaign. Dana fires her agent on the spot.

With nowhere else to go, Jenny asks Tim if she can stay in the studio/garage. He gives her one night.

1:8 'Listen Up'
w: Mark Zakarin
d: Kari Skoglan

Bette and Tina try group therapy for parents-to-be. Bette is not exactly receptive, especially when a woman named Yolanda Watkins (Kim Hawthorne) accuses Bette of hiding the fact that she's black. Bette points out that she and Tina chose an African-American sperm donor for a reason. Jenny's college roommate, Annette Bishop (Sarah Strange), visits her and is fascinated by the Marina story. She decides to help Jenny stalk Francesca to see what kind of woman has captured Marina's heart. Everyone's excited about Dana's Subaru ad, which says, 'Get out and stay out.' Dana's worried about how her parents will react.

At the art museum, Bette fields calls from a fundamentalist who's not happy about the 'blasphemous filth' called the *Provocations* exhibit. Dana's mom, Sharon Fairbanks (Susan Hogan), is being honoured by the Orange County Republican Women; Dana and Alice are in attendance. Dana starts to try to come out to her parents, but ends up saying that 'Get out and stay out' refers to 'outdoorsy' girls. Later, she finally tells them the truth. They run away. At group therapy, Bette and Yolanda continue to talk about who's hiding what – it seems Yolanda has been letting people think she's straight. At a theme night called 'Twat', Shane and Alice help Dana drown her coming-out sorrows. Annette and Jenny pretend to be a couple in order to make Marina jealous. Francesca invites them to come over for dinner sometime.

At group therapy, Bette begins to wonder whether she really is keeping a secret: the secret of falling out of love.

1:9 'Luck, Next Time'
w: Rose Troche
d: Rose Troche

Lisa and Alice wake up together: he's content, but she mutters, 'What a lez.' Slim Daddy (Snoop Dogg), a hip-hop artist, is sampling a song Kit wrote back in the 1980s. Kit introduces Slim to her half-sister; he figures Bette is 'the beautiful half', but Bette says, 'More like the gay half.' Dana comes out to her cat, Mr. Piddles, and is rewarded with much purring. Dana's mom, meanwhile, sets her daughter up on a blind date with a guy. Shane gets a new hot-shot client, Cherie Jaffe (Rosanna Arquette), who sees more in Shane than styling skills. She leaves a huge tip and later sends her assistant to arrange a hairstyling house call.

At the art museum, Bette deals with more right-wingers. She meets their evil leader, Fae Buckley (Helen Shaver). Jenny goes to Marina and Francesca's house for dinner, and ends up kissing Marina again. Francesca tries to play diva, so Jenny just leaves. She goes home to find Tim watching a movie, and they end up having sex. Shane goes to Cherie's house to offer her services. Cherie's husband, Steve (James Purcell), almost catches them having sex, but ends up thanking Shane for making his wife so happy. Dana lets the blind date guy down gently, so Alice moves right in and flirts with him, right in front of Lisa.

Bette is late for a doctor's appointment with Tina. But Tina has already gone home: she has lost the baby. Bette goes home too, to find a sobbing Tina on the floor and crazed fundamentalist protesters on the lawn.

1:10 'Liberally'
w: Ilene Chaiken
d: Mary Harron

Marina seems to be a kept woman: Francesca is helping her keep the Planet afloat. But Marina can't take it any more, so she dumps wine in Francesca's suitcase and bids her adieu. Alice worries that she is pregnant, while Tina and Bette mourn the loss of their baby. Alice thinks about giving them hers, if she has one to give. Fae Buckley has spliced her earlier conversation with Bette into a PR disaster, but Bette refuses to back down and challenges Fae to a debate. Cherie takes Shane to an empty building, where they make plans for Shane's own shop and then make whoopee. At group therapy, Tina is shattered, but Bette doesn't need to cry. Yet.

Bette goes to a club to hear Kit sing; she bumps into Yolanda, the woman from therapy, and Yolanda's ex, Candace Jewell. Sparks fly between Bette and Candace. Tina volunteers at the Headquarters for Social Justice, where she learns that Fae Buckley's daughter, China (Michaela Mann), once starred in a porn film. Shane hangs with Cherie's daughter, Clea Jaffe (Samantha McCloud) – who immediately develops a crush. Dana goes to a lesbian bar, feeling sorry for herself. She sees Jenny there, so they have a drink. They end up going back to Jenny's studio and demonstrating just how hilarious and awkward foreplay can be between two people who have no chemistry.

Fae and Bette have their debate, and it gets very ugly: Fae says that God took Bette's baby so that he wouldn't have a 'depraved life.' Bette finally cries.

1:11 'Looking Back'
w: Guinevere Turner
d: Rose Troche

Alice gets her period. Bette and Tina wonder why that's exciting. Dana, Shane, Tina, Alice, and Jenny go to the Dinah Shore weekend, which is a gathering of drunk, horny women. On the way, they tell their coming out stories and sing (or howl) 'Closer to Fine'. Bette asks Candace, who is a carpenter, to bid on the *Provocations* job. Candace is happy to comply. She soon has an estimate ready, along with some take-out so they can 'talk'. At the Dinah Shore weekend, Dana is a celebrity. She has her own 'guest liaison' named Tonya (Meredith McGeachie). Alice, Tina and Jenny talk about how to spot lesbians – some are obvious from a hundred feet away, while others, like Jenny, need a companion to 'tip' them one way or the other.

They find a white party; Jenny wanders off and finds an audience. It includes Robin (Anne Ramsay), who rescues Jenny from a misguided phone call to Marina. Elsewhere, Dana meets her fans, but Tonya keeps them from getting too close. And then she gets too close: back in the hotel room, Tonya slams Dana against the door. Tina tells the others the sweet story of how she and Bette first met. Meanwhile, Bette and Candace share their own first: a searing, complicated kiss. Tonya ends up going back to LA with the gang, even though Dana's the only one who wants her there.

Tina surprises Bette at the museum. At first, Bette thinks the arms wrapping around her waist belong to Candace.

1:12 'Locked Up'
w: Ilene Chaiken
d: Lynne Stopkewich

Tim and Jenny share a civil dinner, but Tim almost laughs at Jenny's latest writing idea: a story about a girl who can speak the language of manatees. At the Planet, a drag king named Ivan A. Cock (Kelly Lynch) notices Kit and likes what he sees. Robin – Jenny's new fan – is there too, and Marina decides to see whether she can seduce her away from Jenny. The fundamentalists stage a protest at the art museum. Candace makes her way through the throng, eager to get as close to Bette as she possibly can. Bette resists, but barely. Bette and Candace go outside to fend off the protestors. They are soon joined by Alice and Shane, and later Dana, Kit and Ivan – whom Kit almost didn't recognise out of drag.

Dana, Bette, Candace, Alice and Shane end up getting arrested. Alice flirts with one of the right-wingers while Candace and Bette flirt with each other. Jenny meets a guy named Gene Feinberg (Tygh Runyan) at an aquarium. Later, she has her date with Robin. Their goodnight kiss promises more. At the police station, Candace and Bette get their own cell. With nothing much to do, they let their minds and hands wander. Bette is against the wall and Candace is on the bunk, but their sounds and shudders are perfectly synchronised.

Bette's boss posts bail for her; Tina's co-worker helps out with the rest. Bette and Tina reunite awkwardly, while Shane looks around for Cherie. Four hours later, she's still looking.

1:13 'Limb from Limb'
w: Ilene Chaiken
d: Tony Goldwyn

Bette and Candace start their day by finding a bed-and-breakfast, and can't get to the room quickly enough. Meanwhile, Jenny and Robin have their own breakfast in bed. Cherie thinks Shane has slept with her daughter, Clea. Shane tries to make Cherie understand. Dana's cat, Mr. Piddles, has died. Tonya is unsympathetic, but Alice is there ready to let Dana cry. Bette warns Kit that Ivan is madly in love with her. Kit is still not sure what to think. Everyone attends Mr. Piddles' funeral, where Tonya and Dana decide it's the perfect time to announce their engagement. At home, Tina tells Bette that Candace will be doing some work at the Headquarters for Social Justice. Bette panics and ends up sleeping on the couch.

The next day, Candace and Bette have hungry, desperate sex in Bette's office. Everyone goes to the *Provocations* opening. Tonya and Dana play happy couple while Robin realises something strange is going on between Marina and Jenny. Elsewhere, Cherie dumps a sobbing Shane. Candace tells Tina she looks beautiful, but that's not how Tina looks when she sees Bette and Candace chatting outside the museum. When Bette arrives home, Tina is in a very dark place. She tells Bette she knows about Candace; they attack each other, with words and with slaps – and with sex.

Alice goes to Dana's house and tells her she can't marry Tonya. When Dana asks why not, Alice leans in for a kiss and then runs away.

Season two[2]
US première: Tuesday 15 February 2005, Showtime
2:1 'Life, Loss, Leaving'
w: Ilene Chaiken
d: Daniel Minahan

Bette and Candace are still together, but Candace can see that something's wrong. Tina is at the doctor's office, very pregnant and on her own. At the Planet, Alice and Shane banter about knitting and how cruel God is for letting Tina and Bette come apart. Alice also notes that the coffee tastes like 'poopy shit'. Tonya shows up to tell them that Marina has attempted suicide. Dana arrives, and they all talk about the Bette/Candace thing, unaware that Tina is behind them. Gene (that guy from the aquarium) and Jenny go to the farmers' market. Gene buys a clue and figures out that Jenny is a 'full-on lesbian'.

Back at the Planet, Dana and Alice chat in the bathroom, wondering if they should kiss again. Then they do. Bette shows up to tell Tina she can't live without her and has left Candace. Tina's reply is an overturned table. Ivan, the mechanic to the stars, has restored Kit's car. They almost kiss, but Ivan wants Kit to be sure. Tim moves out, and tells Jenny to stay in the house. Shane does Arianna Huffington's hair on the set of something-or-other, and meets Carmen, a sexy PA and DJ, who immediately has plans for Shane. Kit catches Ivan in a moment of undress and finds his strap-on. Ivan throws her out.

Alice and Dana flirt and remind each other they mustn't flirt any more. Bette and Jenny face life alone, and stare across the way at each other's solitude.

2:2 'Lap Dance'
w: Ilene Chaiken
d: Lynne Stopkewich

Tina hires a brash lawyer, Joyce Wischnea (Jane Lynch), to help her find her autonomy. Joyce seems to want to help Tina in other ways. At a substitute coffee shop (because the Planet is closed), Tonya orders something for Dana, because Dana likes what she likes. Jenny enrols in a writing class; it's taught by Charlotte Birch (Sandra Bernhard), who sees right through Jenny. Shane finds Carmen on the set of a music video, and the word 'relationship' gets tossed around. Kit finds Ivan at his cabin and tries to apologise. Ivan doesn't want much more to do with her, but eventually agrees to be a silent partner so she can buy the Planet now that Marina is out of the picture.

Tonya meets Dana's parents, and somehow wins them over. Later, Dana and Alice have coffee and win each other over. Bette confronts Alice, who recommended that Tina get a lawyer. Alice is just worried about Tina – and in her own way, so is Bette. Jenny meets Robin's friends, who are coupled and parenting and expect Jenny and Robin to join the club. Shane, Dana, Tonya, Alice and Tina go to a strip club, where Tina enjoys a lap dance from a stripper who looks a bit like Bette. Bette and Kit meet Marina's father, Manfredi Ferrer (Derek de Lint), to finalise the sale of the Planet. Turns out he's really Marina's husband.

Shane, Bette and Jenny share a moment on Bette's back step, and Shane and Jenny realize they're both in need of a roommate.

2:3 'Loneliest Number'
w: Lara Spotts
d: Rose Troche

Bette and Tina and their lawyers meet to talk about the separation. Bette is not ready to finalise anything. After the meeting, Bette's emotions affect her driving. She slams into an SUV and then slams her attitude into the whiny driver's face. Charlotte Birch challenges Jenny to really write fiction instead of 'journaling'. It seems to work; she gives Charlotte something new, and it earns her a spot in the class. Tina moves into her lawyer's guesthouse. Alice visits her there and says Tina is 'eating her pain,' so Tina reveals the real reason for her weight gain. At Shane and Jenny's place, Carmen looks for a beer and a way to make Shane beg. She finds both. But Shane still doesn't like pillow talk.

Tonya gathers together a bunch of reps for what she calls the first ever 'corporate-sponsored celebrity lesbian wedding'. Dana's amazed, and not in a good way. At the museum, Bette's boss thinks Bette can schmooze Helena Peabody for grant money, because Helena is 'one of Bette's people'. Dana visits Alice at her apartment, and they somehow manage to avoid falling into bed together. A forlorn Bette crashes Shane's party and makes everyone uncomfortable. Alice and Shane take her home and tuck her in.

At the grand re-opening of the Planet (now owned by Kit), Bette and Jenny bond, Dana and Alice flirt, and Kit sings. Meanwhile, Tina gets some of her clothes at Bette's place, and finds an email from Candace.

2:4 'Lynch Pin'
w: Ilene Chaiken
d: Lisa Cholodenko

Bette is in New York, trying to secure a grant from Helena Peabody – but Helena thinks social justice is more important than art. Jenny and Shane interview potential roommates and settle on a guy named Mark Wayland, who has a video camera and a questionable sort of charm. Kit attends a seminar called 'Theory of Everything', where she learns how to be a bold businesswoman and finds herself attracted to the bald seminar leader, Benjamin Bradshaw (Charles S. Dutton). Tina's lawyer finally makes her move, much to Tina's disgust. While Jenny writes, she imagines creepy, ominous scenes at a carnival. Shane rescues her (and the viewers) by interrupting.

Shane has a new hairstyling gig on a movie set, where she meets blustery hot-shot Veronica Bloom (Camryn Manheim). Shane soothes the petulant starlet and earns Veronica's respect, or at least her attention. At the Santa Monica pier, Tonya introduces Alice to a guy. Alice and Dana escape at the first opportunity, and reintroduce each other to the joy of kissing. In New York, Bette meets with Peggy Peabody, hoping she'll be more supportive than Helena was. But Peggy's busy with a boy toy. So Bette goes to a bar and finds her own plaything, who is definitely not a boy. They have hot, sad sex in Bette's hotel room.

At Jenny and Shane's house, Carmen flirts with both of them, but leaves when Shane starts to make out with someone else. After the party, Jenny says she needs a change, and asks Shane to cut her hair.

2:5 'Labyrinth'
w: Rose Troche
d: Burr Steer

Tina knocks on Bette's door, hoping to stay in the spare bedroom until she finds an apartment. Dana, Tonya and Alice go to a sex-toy shop in search of bachelorette party favours. Tonya finds a 'penis pop' and a 'nipple pop' and asks Alice which she prefers. Alice nips the nipple pop. Bette and Tina have dinner, but it isn't quite the right time for Tina to give Bette the news. The next morning, they go to the Planet, and Alice assumes they're 'really' together. In Kit's office, Bette meets Benjamin Bradshaw, the seminar leader. Bette is not impressed, but Kit is smitten. Helena Peabody visits the Headquarters for Social Justice to award them a grant, and to hit on Tina. Bette shows up to witness the flirtation, and to learn that Tina is pregnant – something Helena realised right away.

Dana and Alice finally give in and have funny, hot sex over and over again. They rearrange themselves just in time to greet Tonya and her parents. Bette tells Jenny about Tina's pregnancy; Jenny is supportive and kind. They are both unaware that Mark is watching the whole thing via hidden cameras. At Dana and Tonya's bachelorette party, Shane figures out that Dana and Alice have 'done it'. She also encourages Jenny to flirt with Carmen. Tina shows up with Helena on her arm to everyone's surprise.

Bette finishes off the evening by toasting Tonya and Dana, but her words are really meant for Tina.

2:6 'Lágrimas de Oro'
w: Guinevere Turner
d: Jeremy Podeswa

Alice helps Tina move into her new apartment. They goof around and play air guitar. Helena stops by to smirk at their antics. At the Planet, Alice refuses to be Dana's 'back-door woman' and tells her she has to leave Tonya. Bette visits Tina, trying to give her the space and time she needs, but desperate to talk. Shane and Jenny have a party; Mark films the whole thing and asks inappropriate questions.

Bette has a bad day and calls Tina for support. She also tries to warn Tina away from Helena, but Tina's not ready to have that conversation. Mark arranges to have flowers delivered to Shane and Jenny's house – the perfect set-up for his hidden cameras. But he's not prepared for how much the delivery girl actually likes Shane, after being paid to sleep with her on film. Charlotte Birch gives Jenny an assignment: she tells her not to speak for the rest of the day. The result is a very quiet date with Carmen, which ends with a quiet kiss. Benjamin gives Bette some advice about Tina; he tells her to give up some of that control she likes so much.

Alice and Shane go to La Jolla to support Dana, who's playing in a tournament and trying to break up with Tonya. But Tonya leaves her first for Melissa Rivers (playing herself). Shane finds the whole thing hilarious. Helena and Tina have sex in a pool, while Tina's cell phone buzzes. Bette's calling, but nobody's answering.

2:7 'Luminous'
w: Ilene Chaiken
d: Ernest Dickerson

Alice and Dana wake up to each other's smiling faces, but then worry about how they will tell their friends. Tina and Helena have their own good morning, until Helena's kids barge into the room and make Tina feel self-conscious. Veronica forces Shane to hang out with her, and wonders whether she ought to become a lesbian. Shane says women are a lot of work. Veronica herself turns out to be more work than Shane can handle; she's not ready to be at anyone's beck and call. Tina and Helena have sex on the roof of Helena's hotel, or at least begin to; Helena's ex shows up and interrupts.

During a concert at the Planet, Bette learns she's been 'meat-tagged' – marked as a hot item. Several women step right up to demonstrate their interest. Tina shows up and sits next to Bette, uncertain but friendly. Elsewhere, Jenny and Carmen flirt and kiss, until Carmen sees Shane watching them. Carmen introduces Dana and Alice as the 'happy new couple in the house' – it seems everyone already knew. Jenny and Carmen go to Jenny's house to make out, but Shane interrupts, having brought home some twins. Mark watches on the hidden cameras as Shane ignores the twins and snorts Oxy instead.

The next morning, Jenny and Carmen decide their neuroses are made for each other. Shane wanders around in a dodgy part of town and gets beaten up; she calls Mark, who comes to the rescue.

2:8 'Loyal'
w: A. M. Homes
d: Alison Maclean

Dana and Alice have been in bed for days. They decide it's time to get on with the rest of life. At the Planet, Tina and Bette have tea, and Bette reveals that she's getting some therapy. Bette tells Tina she's happy for her – 'for us'. They agree to be co-parents, no matter what else happens. Helena interrupts, whisking Tina off to go house-hunting. At the museum, Bette's boss informs her that Helena will be joining the steering committee. Carmen confronts Shane about the black eye she got in the dodgy part of town. Shane continues to shut Carmen out.

Everyone gathers at the Planet to chat about Alice and Dana's five-day romp – including Helena, who hints that she and Tina have been having their own fun. Alice bumps into Gabby, her ex, who is now dating Lara, Dana's ex – the classic lesbian swap. It seems Lara is the new chef at the Planet. Jenny's writing teacher has given Jenny's name to an actor friend, Burr Connor (Tony

Goldwyn), who needs a ghost-writer. When he realises she's gay, he sends her home. Alice has an interview at KCRW. They like her best when she thinks they're not recording, and give her a show called 'The Chart', so she can spin her tales of lesbian connections.

Rather than going to Helena's housewarming, the gang (except Tina and Helena) descends on Bette's house. Bette revels in the feeling of the family she thought she'd lost.

2:9 'Late, Later, Latent'
w: David Stenn
d: Tony Goldwyn

Carmen and Jenny experiment with golden showers, while Dana and Alice consider experimenting with sex toys. Charlotte meets with Jenny and the homophobic actor, Burr Connor. She insists that Jenny is the perfect ghost-writer for him, because Jenny knows how to excavate emotional navel lint. Dana and Alice shop for sex toys, but Dana gets a little freaked out when she recognises some of the other customers. After an ultrasound appointment, Bette helps Tina put away the groceries, and then helps her into bed. No, not to sleep – to have sweet, slow, quiet sex. Carmen confronts Shane about the 'thing' between them. Shane thought Jenny and Carmen were the real deal, but Carmen says Jenny is lost in her own darkness. Again, Mark gets the whole thing on tape.

Bette and Tina say goodbye for now, not ruling anything out, but not making any promises. Helena shows up a few minutes later, and finds herself at the mercy of Tina's raging hormones. Even Helena isn't that desperate, so she leaves. Bette tells her therapist about the 'amazing' sex she and Tina had, and admits that Tina seems to be a different person now. Dana goes back to the sex-toy shop alone, determined to find just the right surprise for Alice. Jenny goes into Mark's studio to retrieve some DVDs she loaned him, and discovers the hidden camera tapes.

Bette and Helena both decorate rooms for Tina's baby. Meanwhile, Dana decorates herself with a strap-on, for Alice.

2:10 'Land Ahoy'
w: Ilene Chaiken
d: Tricia Brock

Jenny poses for the hidden camera, effectively letting Mark know she's uncovered his little secret. He tries to explain, but she's hurt and furious. Carmen finds Jenny, wondering whether her 'girlfriend' is ready to go on the cruise they have planned. Jenny knows Carmen would rather be going with Shane, so she only agrees to go if Shane goes too. Bette's father, Melvin, is in town looking frail. But he is thrilled to meet Kit's new man, Benjamin. Dana, Alice, Carmen, Jenny and Shane go to the airport, where Dana's bag gets searched. The screener finds a strap-on and some nipple clamps. Jenny and Carmen grin while Alice and Dana try to stay cool.

On the cruise ship, Carmen, Shane and Jenny are shocked to discover only one bed in their room. Jenny tries to keep the threesome vibe going on the dance floor. Bette confronts her father, demanding that he acknowledge her relationship with Tina. Jenny gets crazy on the cruise, while Dana and Alice play Captain Stubing and Julie the Cruise Director. During a particularly hot moment, Dana gets seasick. Bette goes to a Peabody Foundation awards dinner, where Tina is being recognised. Tina tells Bette she'd like to start spending more time with her. During dinner with Kit and Benjamin at the Planet, Melvin collapses.

Jenny, Carmen and Shane arrive home to see Mark taking down the cameras. Carmen insists that she wasn't trying to hurt Jenny, but Jenny knows Carmen wants to be with Shane.

2:11 'Loud and Proud'
w: Elizabeth Hunter
d: Rose Troche

Tina finds Melvin and Bette at the hospital. Melvin has advanced prostate cancer and is refusing treatment. Kit supports that, but Bette is frantic. Shane watches the hidden camera tapes of herself while Jenny explores her history and her nightmares. Shane tells Jenny she feels at home with her. Alice and Dana play maid and master. Alice breaks character long enough to tell Dana she loves her. Dana is stunned and saved by the doorbell: it's her little brother, Howie Fairbanks (Andrew Francis). Tina tells Helena she wants to see other people. Helena knows that's really about Bette. Mark tries again to explain himself, and Shane is willing to listen but Jenny is not.

At the Pride parade, Dana has a spot on the Gay and Lesbian Center float, but Alice is not allowed to join her. Alice and Shane ride with the Dykes on Bikes instead. Dana and Alice try to be brave and check out the dungeon at Pride, but they leave about five seconds after they go in. At the Pride bash at the Planet, Alice and Dana see Howie dancing with a hot guy. Turns out he's got something to be proud of too. As they dance, Dana finally tells Alice she loves her too. Jenny finds the dungeon, and straps herself in. Almost immediately, she flashes back to a memory of boys attacking her.

Shane finally gives in to what she feels for Carmen, while Bette and Kit give in to the hopelessness of their father's poor health.

2:12 'L'Chaim'
w: Ilene Chaiken
d: John Curran

Jenny tries to exorcise her demons by stripping at a seedy bar. She continues to flash back to her past, trying to put the pieces together. Meanwhile, Mark tries to pick up the pieces of his friendship with Jenny and Shane. Bette has brought her father to her house, over Kit's objections. At the Planet, Tina sees Helena, who is getting cosy with an artist named Leigh Ostin (Cobie Smulders). Tina says she's fine with that, which is more than Alice can say when Lara shows up to ask Dana if she'd like to have dinner sometime. Tina and Bette sit at Melvin's bedside and cuddle. He wakes up and seems to be happy to see Tina, but he's delirious and thinks she is Maxine, Bette's mother. After he drifts off, Bette and Tina flop into bed, needing to hold each other and just sleep.

The next morning, Melvin gives Tina a friendly hello, shocking everyone. Kit and Bette help him to the bathroom, but he crashes to the floor. Shane and Mark reach a comfortable truce. They go to Bette's house, where they gather on the back porch with Alice and Dana. Bette isn't really up for company. Dana goes to dinner with Lara; she later meets Shane and Carmen at the strip club. Jenny has invited them all to see her performance. Alice was there at first too, but she's gone off in search of Dana, convinced she's lost her.

Melvin dies, and his daughters mourn.

2:13 'Lacuna'
w: Ilene Chaiken
d: Ilene Chaiken

Jenny tells Shane that stripping makes her feel in control. Shane thinks there are better ways. At Bette's house, Bette and Tina try to assemble the birthing tank. Tina quietly says that she wants to move back in and have her baby in 'our home'. At Melvin's memorial service, Dana flirts with Lara just a little. Alice, seething with jealousy, asks Dana to move in with her. Bette's boss decides that a memorial service is as good a time as any to fire an employee. Bette calls him a 'class act'.

Everyone goes to a benefit for the Ms. Foundation, where Gloria Steinem gives a rousing speech, and Heart and Betty entertain the crowd. Shane thinks of it as her first official date with Carmen. Bette confronts Helena, who insists she had nothing to do with Bette losing her job. Peggy shows up and puts Helena in her place, while putting Bette on a pedestal. Tina's water breaks, so she and Bette rush home. Dana and Alice talk about the awkwardness they've been feeling. They agree that it's gotten 'super intense super fast'. Shane takes Carmen home and takes her to bed. Shane says, 'I love you.' Tina's labour is not going well; the midwife suggests they head for the hospital. Shane looks for Jenny, to see if she wants to go to the hospital to see the baby. She finds Jenny on the bathroom floor, slicing her thighs.

At the hospital, they all gather around the baby, Angelica. Kit tells the little one she's going to have a very, very interesting life.

Notes

1. For full recaps on season one visit: Scribe Grrl @ http://www. afterellen.com/TV/thelword/recaps.html.
2. For full recaps on season two visit: Scribe Grrl @ http://www. afterellen.com/TV/thelword/recaps2.html.

Film and TV guide

Films

Alfie (Lewis Gilbert, 1966)

Alfie (Charles Shyer, 2004)

Ballad of Little Jo, The (Maggie Greenwald, 1993)

Boys Don't Cry (Kimberly Peirce, 1999)

Chant d'amour, Un (Jean Genet, 1950)

Coffy (Jack Hill, 1973)

Desert Hearts (Donna Dietch, 1985)

Edward II (Derek Jarman, 1991)

Flashdance (Adrian Lyne, 1983)

Foxy Brown (Jack Hill, 1974)

Fried Green Tomatoes (Jon Avnet, 1991)

Hours and Times, The (Christopher Münch, 1991)

Incredibly True Adventures of Two Girls in Love (Maria Maggenti, 1995)

Khush (Pratibha Parmar, 1991)

Morocco (Josef von Sternberg, 1930)

Mulan (Tony Bancroft and Barry Cooke, 1988)

One Hour Photo (Mark Romanek, 2002)

Orlando (Sally Potter, 1992)

Paris is Burning (Jennie Livingston, 1990)

Poison (Todd Haynes, 1991)

Prick Up Your Ears (Stephen Frears, 1987)

Querelle (Rainer Werner Fassbinder, 1982)

R.S.V.P. (Laurie Lynd, 1991)

Swoon (Tom Kalin, 1992)

Sylvia Scarlett (George Cukor, 1935)

Tongues Untied (Marlon Riggs, 1990)

Virgin Machine (Monica Treut, 1988)

Young Soul Rebels (Isaac Julien, 1991)

TV

Action (Christopher Thompson Productions/Columbia TriStar/Fox
    Network, 1999)

All in the Family (Norman Lear/Tandem Productions/CBS, 1971–1979)

All My Children (ABC, 1970–)

Angels in America (Mike Nichols/HBO, 2003)

Brideshead Revisited (Granada Television, 1981)

Buffy the Vampire Slayer (Mutant Enemy Inc./20th Century Fox Television,
    1997–2003)

Dallas (Lorimar Television/CBS, 1978–1991)

Dark Angel (20th Century Fox Television/Fox Network, 2000–2002)

Desperate Housewives (Cherry Productions/ABC, 2004–)

Doctor Who (BBC Wales/BBC, 2005–)

ER (Constant Productions/Amblin Entertainment/WB Television Network/
    NBC, 1994–)

Ellen (Touchstone Television/ABC, 1994–1998)

Ellen Show, The (Artists Television Group/CBS, 2001–2002)

Friends (Warner Bros. Television/NBC, 1994–2004)

Hill Street Blues (MTM Productions Inc, 1981–1987)

Howard Stern Show, The (WOR-TV, 1990)

!Huff (Allenford Productions/Sony Pictures Television, 2004–)

Jeffersons, The (CBS Television/CBS, 1975–1985)

K Street (Section Eight Ltd/HBO, 2003)

L.A. Law (20th Century Fox Television/NBC, 1986–1994)

Law and Order (Wolf Films/NBC, 1990–)

Law and Order: Special Victims Unit (Wolf Films/NBC, 1999–)

Love Boat, The (Aaron Spelling Productions/ABC, 1977–1986)

M*A*S*H (20th Century Fox Television/CBS, 1972–1983)

Melrose Place (Darren Star Productions/Fox Network, 1992–1999)

Once and Again (Bedford Falls Productions/ABC, 1999–2002)

One Tree Hill (Warner Bros. Television/The WB Television Network, 2003–)

Oranges Are Not the Only Fruit (Beeban Kidron/BBC, 1990)

Out of Order (Coast Mountain Films/Showtime Network Inc., 2003)

Picket Fences (20th Century Fox Television/CBS, 1992–1996)

Popular (Murphy/Matthews Productions/The WB Television Network,
    1999–2001)

Queer as Folk (Channel 4 Entertainment, 1999)

Queer as Folk (Cowslip Productions/Showtime Networks Inc, 2001–2005)

Queer Eye for the Straight Guy (Scout Production/Bravo, 2003–)

Relativity (Bedford Falls Productions/ABC, 1996–1997)

Roseanne (Carsey-Werner Company/ABC, 1988–1997)

Scrubs (20th Century Fox/NBC, 2001–)

Sex and the City (Sex and the City Productions/HBO, 1998–2004)

Six Feet Under (The Greenblatt Janollari Studio/HBO, 2001–2005)

Sopranos, The (Chase Films/HBO, 1999–)

Star Trek (Desilu Productions/NBC, 1966–1969)

thirtysomething (Bedford Falls Productions/ABC, 1987–1991)

This Life (BBC, 1996–1997)

Tipping The Velvet (Sally Head Productions/BBC, 2002)

Will & Grace (KoMut Entertainment/NBC, 1998–)

Wire, The (Blown Deadline Productions/HBO, 2002–)

Xena: Warrior Princess (MCA Television Entertainment Inc./Universal TV, 1995–2001)

Young Americans (Columbia TriStar Television/WB Television Network, 2000)

Bibliography

Aaron, Michele. 'Introduction'. Aaron, ed. *New Queer Cinema: A Critical Reader*. Edinburgh: Edinburgh University Press, 2004: 3–14

Anapol, Deborah M. *Polyamory, the New Love without Limits: Secrets of Sustainable Intimate Relationships*. San Rafael, CA: IntiNet Resource Center, 1997

Andrews, Betsy. 'Glamour and Lots of Sex'. *Gay City News*. 30 October 2003: 30

Arroyo, José. 'Death, Desire and Identity: The Political Unconscious of "New Queer Cinema"'. Joseph Bristow and Angelia Wilson, eds. *Activating Theory: Lesbian, Gay, Bisexual Politics*. London: Lawrence and Wishart, 1993: 70–96

Ashton, Charlotte. 'Getting Hold of the Phallus: "Post-Lesbian" Power Negotiations'. Nicola Godwin, Belinda Hollows and Sheridan Nye, eds. *Assaults on Convention: Essays on Lesbian Transgressors*. London: Cassel, 1996: 157–74

Barthes, Roland. *A Lover's Discourse: Fragments*. Richard Howard, trans. New York: Hill and Wang, 1978

Bauer Maglin, Nan, and Donna Perry. 'Introduction'. Nan Bauer Maglin and Donna Perry, eds. *Bad Girls/Good Girls: Women, Sex and Power in the Nineties*. New Brunswick, NJ: Rutgers University Press, 1996: xiii–xxvi

Bersani, Leo. *Homos*. Cambridge and London: Harvard University Press, 1995

Butler, Judith. *Gender Trouble: Feminism and the Subversion of Identity*. London and New York: Routledge, 1990; reprinted 2nd Edition, 1999

Butler, Judith. *Undoing Gender*. New York and London: Routledge, 2004

Califia, Pat. *Public Sex: The Culture of Radical Sex*. 2nd Edition. San Francisco: Cleis Press, 2000

Capsuto, Steven. *Alternate Channels: The Uncensored Story of Gay and Lesbian Images on Radio and Television*. New York: Balantinel, 2000

Carson, Anne. *Eros the Bittersweet*. Normal, IL: Dalkey Archive Press, 1998

Castiglia, Christopher, and Christopher Reed. '"Ah, Yes, I Remember It Well" Memory and Queer Culture in *Will and Grace*'. *Cultural Critique*. 56. 2003: 158–88

Chambers, Samuel A. 'Telepistemology of the Closet; Or, the Queer Politics of *Six Feet Under*'. *Journal of American Culture*. 26. 2003: 24–41

Chambers, Samuel A. 'Revisiting the Closet: Reading Sexuality in *Six Feet Under*'. Kim Akass and Janet McCabe, eds. *Reading Six Feet Under: TV To Die For*. London: I.B.Tauris, 2005: 174–88

Chambers, Samuel A. 'Desperately Straight: The Subversive Sexual Politics of *Desperate Housewives*'. Janet McCabe and Kim Akass, eds. *Reading Desperate Housewives*. London: I.B.Tauris, forthcoming 2006

Clark, Danae. 'Commodity Lesbianism'. *Camera Obscura*. 25–6. 1991: 180–201

Damsky, Lee. 'Introduction'. *Sex and the Single Girl: Straight and Queer Women on Sexuality*. Ed. Damsky. Seattle: Seal Press, 2000: xi–xx

Davidson, Gustav. *A Dictionary of Angels: Including the Fallen Angels*. New York: The Free Press, 1967

D'Erasmo, Stacey. 'Lesbians on Television: It's Not Easy Being Seen'. *New York Times* (Sunday). Section 2. 11 January 2004: 1, 26

Diva. The L Word Special. 10. July 2005

Ducornet, Rikki. 'Voyage to Ultima Azul, Chapter 79'. *The Complete Butcher's Tales*. Normal, IL: Dalkey Archive Press, 1994: 160–2

Ducornet, Rikki. *The Monstrous and the Marvelous*. San Francisco: City Lights, 1999

Dworkin, Andrea. *Intercourse*. New York: The Free Press, 1987

Easton, Dossie, and Catherine A. Liszt. *The Ethical Slut: A Guide of Infinite Sexual Possibilities*. San Francisco: Greenery, 1997

Ferguson, Kathy. 'This Species Which Is Not One: Identity Practices in *Star Trek: Deep Space Nine*'. *Strategies* 15. 2. 2002: 181–95

Fonseca, Nicholas. 'Return of the Pink Ladies'. *Entertainment Weekly*. 18
    February 2005: 38
Foucault, Michel. 'Sexual Choice, Sexual Act: Foucault and
    Homosexuality', Lawrence D. Kritzman, ed. *Michel Foucault:
    Politics, Philosophy, Culture: Interviews and Other Writings, 1977–
    1984*. London and New York: Routledge, 1988: 286–303
Foucault, Michel. *The Will to Knowledge. The History of Sexuality Volume 1*.
    Trans. Robert Hurley. London: Penguin, 1998
Gamson, Joshua. *Freaks Talk Back: Tabloid Talk Shows and Sexual
    Nonconformity*. Chicago: University of Chicago Press, 1998
Garber, Marjorie. *Vested Interests: Cross-Dressing and Cultural Anxiety*. London:
    Penguin, 1993
Geller, Jaclyn. *Here Comes the Bride: Women, Weddings, and the Marriage
    Mystique*. New York: Four Walls Eight Windows, 2001
Griggers, Cathy. 'Lesbian Bodies in the Age of (Post)mechanical
    Reproduction'. Michael Warner, ed. *Fear Of A Queer Planet: Queer
    Politics and Social Theory*. Minneapolis, Minnesota: University of
    Minnesota Press, 1993: 178–92
Grossberg, Lawrence. *We Gotta Get Out of this Place: Popular Conservatism and
    Postmodern Culture*. London and New York: Routledge, 1992
Hall, Stuart. 'Encoding/Decoding'. Stuart Hall, Dorothy Hobson, Andrew
    Lowe and Paul Willis, eds. *Culture, Media, Language*. London:
    Hutchinson, 1980: 128–38
Halberstam, Judith. *Female Masculinity*. Durham, North Carolina: Duke
    University Press, 1998
Halperin, David M. *Saint Foucault: Towards a Gay Hagiography*. Oxford:
    Oxford University Press, 1995
Heasley, Robert. 'Queer Masculinities of Straight Men'. *Men and
    Masculinities*. 7. 3. 2005: 310–20
Henry, Astrid. *Not My Mother's Sister: Generational Conflict and Third-wave
    Feminism*. Bloomington: Indiana University Press, 2004
Heywood, Leslie, and Jennifer Drake, eds. *Third Wave Agenda: Being
    Feminist, Doing Feminism*. Minneapolis: University of Minnesota
    Press, 2003
Hoberman, J. 'Out and Inner Mongolia'. *Premiere*. October 1992: 31
Hollibaugh, Amber, and Cherie Moraga. 'What We're Rollin' Around
    in Bed With'. Ann Snitow, Christine Stansell and Sharon

Thompson, eds. *Powers of Desire: The Politics of Sexuality*. New York: Monthly Review Press, 1983: 394–405

hooks, bell. *Outlaw Culture: Resisting Representations*. London and New York: Routledge, 1994

Huff, Richard. 'The Final Frontier: Lesbians'. *Daily News*. 24 October 2003: 143

Jermyn, Deborah. 'In Love With Sarah Jessica Parker: Celebrating Female Fandom and Friendship in *Sex and the City*'. Kim Akass and Janet McCabe, eds. *Reading Sex and the City: Critical Approaches*. London: I.B.Tauris, 2004: 201–18

Kennedy, Margaret, and Elizabeth Davis. 'I Could Hardly Wait to Get Back to That Bar'. Brett Beemyn, ed. *Creating a Place for Ourselves: Lesbian, Gay, Bisexual Community Histories*. London and New York: Routledge, 1997: 27–72

Ingraham, Chrys, ed. *Thinking Straight: The Power, the Promise, and the Paradox of Heterosexuality*. New York: Routledge, 2005

Inness, Sherrie A. *The Lesbian Menace*. Amherst: University of Massachusetts Press, 1997

Irigaray, Luce. *This Sex Which Is Not One*. Trans. Catherine Porter. Ithaca, New York: Cornell University Press, 1985

Jagose, Annamarie. *Queer Theory: An Introduction*. New York: New York University Press, 1996

Johnson, Merri Lisa, ed. *Jane Sexes it Up: True Confessions of Feminist Desire*. New York, Four Walls Eight Windows, 2002

Johnson, Merri Lisa. 'Pearl Necklace'. Johnson, ed. *Jane Sexes It Up: True Confessions of Female Desire*. New York: Four Walls Eight Windows, 2002: 311–26

Kipnis, Laura. *Against Love: A Polemic*. New York: Pantheon, 2003

Lavery, David. '"It's Not Television, It's Magic Realism": The Mundane, the Grotesque and the Fantastic in *Six Feet Under*'. Kim Akass and Janet McCabe, eds. *Reading Six Feet Under: TV To Die For*. London: I.B.Tauris, 2005: 19–33

Lawson, Mark. 'Reading *Six Feet Under*'. Kim Akass and Janet McCabe, eds. *Reading Six Feet Under: TV To Die For*. London: I.B.Tauris, 2005: xvii–xxii

Lowry, Brian. 'Showtime Skeds Sex in the Company of Women'. *Variety*. 12 January 2004: 52

MacKenzie, Gordene Olga. *Transgender Nation*. Bowling Green, Ohio: Bowling Green University Press, 1994

Marcuse, Herbert. *Eros and Civilization: A Philosophical Inquiry into Freud*. Boston: Beacon, 1974

Marech, Rona. 'Nuances of Gay Identities Reflected in New Language'. *San Francisco Chronicle*. 8 February 2004: A1

Maso, Carole. *Aureole*. Hopewell: The Ecco Press, 1996

Maso, Carole. *Break Every Rule: Essays on Language, Longing, & Moments of Desire*. Washington, DC: Counterpoint, 2000

McCarthy, Anna. 'Ellen: Making Queer Television History'. *GLQ: A Journal of Lesbian and Gay Studies*. 7. 4. 2001: 593–620

McCroy, Winnie. '"L" is for Invisible'. *Washington Blade*. 7 November 2003: 42

McCroy, Winnie. 'Panel Discusses Success of Lesbian TV News'. *Gay City News*. 1 April 2004: 20, 26

Morgan, Tracy. 'Butch-Femme and the Politics of Identity'. Arlene Stein, ed. *Sisters, Sexperts, Queers: Beyond the Lesbian Nation*. New York: Plume Books, 1993: 35–46

Mulvey, Laura. 'Visual Pleasure and Narrative Cinema'. Bill Nichols, ed. *Movies and Methods II*. Berkeley and Los Angeles: University of California Press, 1985: 305–15

Munson, Marcia, and Judith P. Stelboum, eds. *The Lesbian Polyamory Reader: Open Relationships, Non-Monogamy, and Casual Sex*. Binghamton, New York: Haworth, 1999

Newton, Esther, and Shirley Walton. 'The Misunderstanding: Toward a More Precise Sexual Vocabulary'. Carole S. Vance. ed. *Pleasure and Danger: Exploring Female Sexuality*. Boston: Routledge and Kegan Paul, 1985

Pacteau, Francette. 'The Impossible Referent: Representations of the Androgyne'. Victor Burgin, Donald James and Cora Kaplan, eds. *Formations of Fantasy*. London and New York: Methuen, 1986: 62–84

Pearl, Monica B. 'AIDS and the New Queer Cinema'. Michele Aaron, ed. *New Queer Cinema: A Critical Reader*. Edinburgh: Edinburgh University Press, 2004: 23–35

Plath, Sylvia. 'Poem for a Birthday', sub-section of 'Witch Burning'. Ted Hughes, ed. *The Collected Poems*. New York: Harper & Row, 1981: 131–7

Polly, John. 'Girls Who Like Girls'. *Next*. 9 January 2004: 20

Rich, Adrienne. 'Compulsory Heterosexuality and Lesbian Existence'. *Signs*. 5. 1980: 631–60

Rich, B. Ruby. 'New Queer Cinema'. *Sight and Sound*. 2.5. September 1992: 32

Roethke, Theodore. 'The Rose'. *The Collected Poems of Theodore Roethke*. New York: Anchor, 1975: 196–8

Rubin, Gayle. 'Of Catamites and Kings: Reflections of Butch, Gender, and Boundaries'. Joan Nestle, ed. *The Persistent Desire: A Femme-Butch Reader*. Boston: Alyson Publications: 1992: 466–82

Rubin, Henry. *Self-Made Men*. Nashville, Tennessee: Vanderbilt University Press, 2003

Sawicki, Jana. 'Desexualizing Queer Politics'. Dianne Taylor and Karen Vintges, eds. *Feminism and the Final Foucault*. Chicago: University of Illinois Press, 2004: 163–82

Schwartz, Ruth L. 'New Alliances, Strange Bedfellows: Lesbians, Gay Men and AIDS'. Arlene Stein, ed. *Sisters, Sexperts, Queers: Beyond the Lesbian Nation*. New York: Plume, 1993: 230–44

Sedgwick, Eve Kosofsky. *Epistemology of the Closet*. Berkeley and Los Angeles: University of California Press, 1990

Sedgwick, Eve Kosofsky. 'The L Word: Novelty in Normalcy'. *Chronicle of Higher Education*. 16 January 2004: B10–B11

Singleton, Brian. 'Queering The Church; Sexual and Spiritual Neo-Orthodoxies in Six Feet Under'. Kim Akass and Janet McCabe, eds. *Reading Six Feet Under: TV To Die For*. London: I.B.Tauris, 2005: 161–73

Smith, Sarah. 'A Cock of One's Own: Getting a Firm Grip on Feminist Sexual Power'. Merri Lisa Johnson, ed. *Jane Sexes It Up: True Confessions of Feminist Desire*. New York: Four Walls Eight Windows, 2002: 293–309

Stanley, Alessandra. 'Women Having Sex, Hoping Men Tune In'. *New York Times*. 16 January 2004: E1, E30

Stein, Arlene. 'From Old Gay to New: Symbolic Struggles and the Politics of Lesbian Identity'. Arlene Stein, ed. *Sex and Sensibility: Stories of a Lesbian Generation*. Berkeley: University of California Press, 1997: 23–46

Stoller, Robert. *Sex and Gender: On the Development of Masculinity and*

Femininity. London: Hogarth Press and the Institute of
    Psychoanalysis, 1968

Straayer, Chris. *Deviant Eyes, Deviant Bodies*. New York: Columbia University
    Press, 1996

Sullivan, Andrew. *Virtually Normal: An Argument About Homosexuality*. New
    York: Knopf, 1995; reprinted, New York: Vintage, 1996

Tanner, Tony. *Adultery in the Novel: Contract and Transgression*. Baltimore:
    Johns Hopkins University Press, 1981

Taubin, Amy. 'Beyond the Sons of Scorsese'. *Sight and Sound*. 2.5.
    September 1992: 33

Taylor, Verta, and Leila Rupp. *Drag Queens at the 801 Cabaret*. Chicago:
    University of Chicago Press, 2003

Trebay, Guy. 'The Subtle Power of Lesbian Style'. *New York Times*. Sunday
    Style Section. 27 June 2004: 1, 6

Walker, Rebecca, ed. *To Be Real: Telling the Truth and Changing the Face of
    Feminism*. New York: Doubleday, 1995

Walters, Suzanna Danuta. *All the Rage: The Story of Gay Visibility in America*.
    Chicago: University of Chicago Press, 2003

Warner, Michael. *The Trouble With Normal: Sex, Politics, and the Ethics of Queer
    Life*. New York: Free Press, 1999

West, Celeste. *Lesbian Polyfidelity: A Pleasure Guide for the Woman Whose Heart
    Is Open to Multiple, Concurrent Sexualoves, or How to Keep Monogamy
    Safe, Sane, Honest and Laughing, You Rogue!* San Francisco:
    Booklegger Publishing, 1996

Winterson, Jeanette. *The Passion*. New York: Grove Press, 1987

Wittgenstein, Ludwig (1967). *Zettel*. G. E. M. Anscomb, trans. G. E. M.
    Anscomb and G. H. von Wright, eds. Berkeley: University of
    California Press

Websites

Anon. 'Showtime Bids Farewell to *Queer as Folk*, Welcomes New Season of
    The L Word'. *The Advocate*. 14 January 2005: http://www.advocate.
    com/news_detail_ektid02740.asp

Beals, Jennifer, POWER UP Gala, 7 November 2004: http://www.power-
    up.net/pages/news_events2.html

Beals, Jennifer. GLAAD MEdia Awards. 11 June 2005: http://www.glaad.
    org/mEdia/release_detail.php?id=3821

Bell, Emily. 'Tragedy of Lost Sales: A Paper Mourns'. *The Guardian.*
    Wednesday 3 April 2002: http://www.guardian.co.uk/
    queenmother/article/0,2763,677891,00.html

Black, Shona. 'The L Word: Paragon Paradox'. *LesbiaNation.com.*
    28 January 2005: http://www.lesbianation.com/article.
    cfm?section=9&id=5309

Chaiken, Ilene. Showtime Live Chat. 11 April 2004: http://www.
    thelwordonline.com/sho_chat_Ilene.shtml

Cutler, Jacqueline. 'The L Word Breaks New Ground'. *Zap2it.* 14
    January 2004: http://tv.zap2it.com/tvEditorial/tve_main/
    1,1002,274%7C85546%7C1%7C,00.html

D'Erasmo, Stacey. 'Lesbians on Television: It's Not Easy Being Seen'. *New
    York Times.* 11 January 2004: http://www.nytimes.com/2004/01/11/
    arts/television/11DERA.html?ex=1121832000&en=27af9563910f
    f07e&ei=5070

Freedland, Jonathan. 'Summoning the L-Word'. *The Guardian.* 20
    December 2000: http://www.guardian.co.uk/Columnists/
    Column/0,5673,413745,00.html

Gudz, Cheryl. 'As Critical Eye for the "Queer" Guy – Gay TV not to be
    confused with Queer TV'. *The Uniter.* Issue 13. 17 November
    2003, 11: http://uniter.uwinnipeg.ca/issue13/pg11.html

Havrilesky, Heather. 'Land of the Lipstick Lesbians'. *Salon.* February 2004:
    http://www.salon.com/ent/tv/review/2004/02/11/l_word/index_
    np.html?x

Johns, Elizabeth. 'Big Party, Big Ratings for Ellen'. *eOnline.* 1 May 1997:
    http://www.eonline.com/News/Items/0,1,1053,00.html

Jowitt, Deborah. *Village Voice.* 28 February 1995: http://www.pipeline.
    com/~jordinyc/torr/clippings.htm

L Word site, The. *AfterEllen.com:* http://www.afterellen.com/TV/thelword.
    html

Lo, Malinda. 'Does The L Word Represent? Viewer Reactions Vary on the
    Premiere Episode'. *AfterEllen.com.* January 2004 (2004a): http://
    www.afterellen.com/TV/thelword/reaction.html

Lo, Malinda. 'It's All About the Hair: Butch Identity and Drag on The L
    Word'. *AfterEllen.com.* April 2004 (2004b): http://www.afterellen.
    com/TV/thelword/butch.html

McCroy, Winnie. 'L is for Invisible'. *New York Blade Online.* 31 October 2003:

http://www.nyblade.com/2003/10–31/viewpoint/Editorials/
  invisible.cfm

Merriam-Webster Online Dictionary: http://www.m-w.com/

Mixed Media Watch. 9 February 2005: http://www.mixEdmEdiawatch.
  com/2004imageawards.htm

Moore, Candace. 'Through Mark's Lenses'. *AfterEllen.com*. 6 April 2005:
  http://www.afterellen.com/TV/2005/4/mark.html

New York Magazine. 12 January 2004: http://newyorkmetro.com/nymag/
  toc/20040112/

Poll Result: 'Does The L Word Misrepresent Lesbians?' *AfterEllen.com*. May
  2005: http://afterellen.freepolls.com/cgi-bin/pollresults/251

Poll Result: 'Has Bette's biracial identity made you more aware of issues
  facing biracial people in real life?' *AfterEllen.com*. 9 August 2005:
  http://afterellen.freepolls.com/cgi-bin/pollresults/259

Rainbow Network. 'Fact'File: *The L Word*. 24 September 2004: http://www.
  rainbownetwork.com/Features/detail.asp?iData=21706&iCat=3
  0&iChannel=25&nChannel=Features

Schenden, Laurie K. 'Folks Like Us'. *Curve Magazine*. December 2002:
  http://www.katemoennig.net/thelword_curve_dec02.html

Schenden, Laurie K. 'Something for the Girls'. *Curve Magazine*. 14 January
  2004: http://www.curvemag.com/Detailed/536.html

Shapiro, Gregg. 'The L Word's Jennifer Beals Flashdance Star in
  Town for HRC Gala'. *Windy City Times*. 21 May 2003:
  http://outlineschicago.com/gay/lesbian/news/ARTICLE.
  php?AID=2342

Spaner, David. 'Big Buzz Around The L Word'. *The Vancouver Province*. 30 June
  2003: http://www.katemoennig.net/thelword_vancouverjuly03.
  html

Stewart, Jenny. 'An Interview with Jennifer Beals'. *PlanetOut*. Accessed 10
  September 2005: http://www.planetout.com/entertainment/
  interview.html?sernum=700&navpath=/entertainment/lword

Teeman, Tim. 'Cult Corner: *The L Word* Needs To Be More Soap Than
  Sermon'. *TimesOnline*. 11 June 2005: http://entertainment.
  timesonline.co.uk/article/0,,14934–1647218,00.html

Theobald, Stephanie. 'From Icon to Dykon'. *Guardian*. 24 September
  2004: http://www.guardian.co.uk/theguide/features/
  story/0,,1295769,00.html

Warn, Sarah, 'Will *Earthlings* Be the Lesbian *Queer as Folk?*' *AfterEllen.com*.
    September 2002: http://www.afterellen.com/TV/lesbianqaf.html

Warn, Sarah. 'Sex and *The L Word*'. *AfterEllen.com*. April 2003: http://www.
    afterellen.com/TV/thelword-sex.html

Warn, Sarah. 'Too Much Otherness: Femininity on *The L Word*'. *AfterEllen.
    com*. April 2004 (2004a): http://www.afterellen.com/TV/
    thelword/femininity.html

Warn, Sarah. 'Review of *The L Word*'. *AfterEllen.com*. January 2004 (2004b):
    http://www.afterellen.com/TV/thelword/review.html

Warn, Sarah. 'The L Word Season 2 Review'. *AfterEllen.com*. 15 February
    2005: http://www.afterellen.com/TV/2005/2/thelword.html

Media Interviews
Fresh Air. Interview with Jennifer Beals and Ilene Chaiken, hosted by Terry
    Gross. NPR. WHRV, Norfolk, VA. 6 April 2004

Index

AIDS 37, n39, 100, 152, 188
Aycock, Ivan 56, 134, 143, 146, 147,
    148, 149, 150, 151, 152, 153,
    154, 155, 156, 160, 164–8,
    169, 170, 201

Beals, Jennifer 55, 106, 140, 184,
    189, 190, 191, 196, 197
Betty 34, 200, 204, 205, 206
Bradshaw, Benjamin (Charles S
    Dutton) 144, 154, 156
Buckley, Fae (Helen Shaver) 59, 60,
    61, 62
Buffy the Vampire Slayer 12, 15, 17, 19
Bush, George W 24, 25, 38
Butler, Judith 84, 85, 92, 100, 168

Chaiken, Ilene 12, 27, 71, 115, 134,
    174, 190, 196, 200, 205, 206,
    210
Chart, The 111–14, 162

Daniels, Erin 13, 209–13
D'Erasmo, Stacey 44, 54, 55, 67,
    145
DeGeneres, Ellen 81, 183
Desperate Housewives 24, 85
Duprey, Natasha 202, 203, 204

Dworkin, Andrea 105, 108, 153

Ellen 15, n39, 81
Episodes:
    'Labyrinth' 66
    'Lacuna' 25, 145
    'Land Ahoy' 53, 107
    'Lap Dance' 50, 203
    'Late, Later, Latent' 26, 52,
    67, 108, 134, 145, 167, 179
    'Lawfully' 64, 65, 76, 91, 119
    'L-Chaim' 202
    'L'Ennui' 107, 148
    'Let's Do It' 91, 94, 95, 103,
    141, 192
    'Liberally' 37, 59, 60, 64, 202
    'Limb From Limb' 95, 104,
    129
    'Lies, Lies, Lies' 50, 73, 75,
    93, 95, 102, 141
    'Life, Loss, Leaving' 167, 177
    'Listen Up' 62, 126
    'Locked Up' 25, 123, 146
    'Loneliest Number' 203
    'Longing' 56–7, 58, 63, 92,
    130, 141
    'Looking Back' 161
    'Losing It' 65, 91, 160

'Loud and Proud' 53, 67, 108
'Loyal' 102
'Luck Next Time' 122
'Luminous' 109, 203
'Lynch Pin' 37, 52, 65, 205
'Pilot, The' 77, 97, 111, 118

Fairbanks, Dana 36, 38, 70, 77, 83,
    95, 96, 97, 102, 107, 108, 112,
    117, 127, 128, 141, 205, 209,
    210, 211
Fashion 71, 186–7
Ferrera, Marina 35, 50, 59, 63, 64,
    65, 70, 73, 75, 76, 77, 91, 92,
    93, 102, 103, 104, 107, 117,
    118, 119, 120, 121, 123, 124,
    125, 128, 129, 141, 201, 203
Foucault, Michel 156, 159
Friends 11, 29, 145

Garber, Marjorie 151, 152
Grier, Pam 145, 146, 203

Hailey, Leisha 13, 29, 30, 202, 211
Halberstam, Judith 45–6, 88, 159–
    60, 169, 171
Haspel, Tim 35, 49, 50, 58, 63, 64,
    65, 76, 90, 91, 92, 93, 104,
    118, 119, 120, 121, 122, 128,
    129, n135, 169
HBO 16, 17, 20, 24
Henry, Astrid 46, 106, 108, 150, 155
Holloman, Laurel 11, 12, 13, 37
hooks, bell 144, 145

Jaffe, Cherie (Roseanna Arquette)
    77, 131

Jewell, Candace 99, 102, 123, 124,
    125, 126, 127, 129, 141, 142,
    154, 194, 195, 199
Johnson, Merri Lisa 150, 155

Kennard, Tina 28, 30, 35, 36, 37,
    49, 50, 51, 59, 61, 62, 70, 77,
    83, 91, 92, 94, 95, 96, 99,
    104, 105, 106, 116, 117, 118,
    123, 125, 126, 128, 129, 130,
    132, 134, 140, 165, 166, 191,
    192, 193, 195
Kipnis, Laura 118, 119, 128

Lisa (Devon Gummersall) 28, 29,
    30, 56, 77, 107, 108, 148
Living TV 15, 17, 23
Lo, Malinda 44, 87, 88
Lynch, Kelly 28–9, 56

McCutcheon, Shane 36, 37, 38,
    49, 51, 52, 53, 58, 65, 66, 67,
    70, 76, 77, 83, 99, 101, 109,
    112, 114, 129, 130, 131, 132,
    n137, 140, 160, 161–4, 165,
    168, 169, 170, 171, 173, 174,
    178, 195, 199, 203, 204, 205,
    211, 212
Moenning, Katherine 173–5, 211
Music 199–207

New Queer Cinema 33–9

Peabody, Helena 36, 99, 106
Peabody, Peggy 36, 57, 58, 59, 63
Perkins, Lara 95, 96, 141
Pica Morales, Carmen de la 66,

108, 129, 163, 177–81, 194, 195, 203, 205

Pieszecki, Alice 26, 29, 30, 37, 50, 70, 83, 107, 108, 111, 112, 113, 117, 119, 127, 128, 141, 148, 162, 189, 199, 203, 205, 209, 211

Planet, The 34, 63, 92, 102, 117, 146, 199, 203, 204

Porter, Bette 25, 26, 28, 30, 35, 36, 37, 49, 50, 51, 57, 59, 60, 61, 62, 63, 67, 70, 71, 77, 83, 91, 92, 94, 95, 99, 102, 103, 104, 105, 106, 116, 117, 118, 123, 124, 125, 126, 127, 129, 130, 132, 134, 140, 141, 142, 152, 154, 164, 165, 166, 184, 189, 190, 191, 192, 193, 194, 195, 196, 197, 199, 201, 209

Porter, Kit 19, 36, 37, 38, 125, 134, 143–4, 145, 146, 148, 149, 150, 151, 152, 153, 154, 155, 156, 164, 165, 166, 192, 201, 203

Queer as Folk 21, 22, 23, 39, 90, 91, 95, 96, 101, 133, n137, 174, 206

Queer Eye for the Straight Guy 100, 186

Race 62, 83, 144, 145, 177–81, 189–97

Rich, Adrienne n136, 187

Schechter, Jenny 30, 31, 35, 36, 37, 38, 49, 51, 53, 58, 62, 63, 64, 65, 66, 67, 73, 75, 76, 77, 90,

91, 92, 93, 96, 97, 102, 103, 104, 107, 108, 117, 118, 119, 120, 121, 122, 123, 124, 125, 126, 128, n135, 140, 141, 163, 179, 180, 189, 203, 204, 212

Second-wave feminism 99, 106

Sedgwick, Eve Kofosky 43, 56, 97

Sex and the City 12, 15, 20, 24, 56, 74, 144, 183, 187

Shahi, Sarah 177, 180

Showtime 12, 13, 23, 24, 33, 43, 56, 67, 70, 134, n136, 159, 174, 189

Six Feet Under 15, 20, 24, 25, 39

Sopranos, The 15, 24, 54

Stendhal's Syndrome 56–9, 61, 63, 64, 67

Steinem, Gloria 25, 38, 163, 203

Straayer, Chris 154, 155

Third-wave feminism 46, 106, 143

Tonya 95, 102, 127, 128

Troche, Rose 12, 13, 27, 37, 71, 210

Turner, Guinevere 27–31, 37, 210

Warn, Sarah 83, 86, 87, 88

Warner, Michael 84, 95, 132, 133, 134

Wayland, Mark 51, 52, 53, 65, 66, 67, 119, 163, 179

Will & Grace 15, 24, 25, n39, 86, 100

Xena: Warrior Princess 15, 17, 19, 25

Ziff, Elizabeth 200, 201, 202, 203, 204, 205, 206